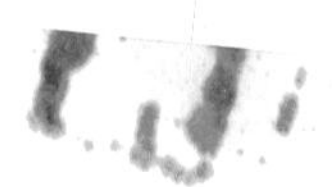

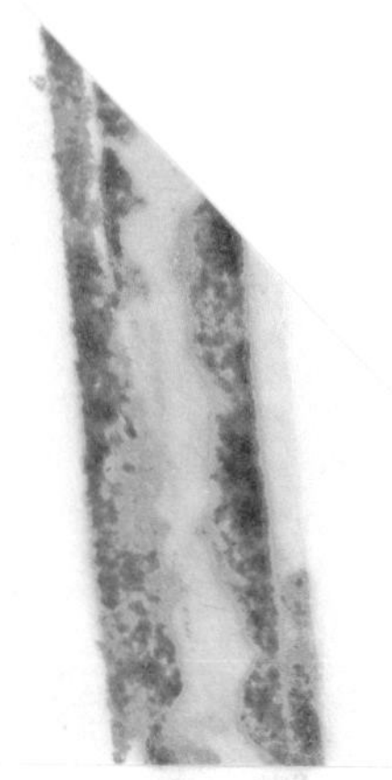

SHAKESPEARE'S POETICS

Edited by Russell A. Fraser

THE COURT OF VENUS (1955)
THE COURT OF VIRTUE (1961)

SHAKESPEARE'S POETICS

In Relation to *King Lear*

by

RUSSELL A. FRASER

Nashville, Tennessee
VANDERBILT UNIVERSITY PRESS

First published in 1962
by Routledge & Kegan Paul Limited
Broadway House, 68-74 *Carter Lane*
*London, E.C.*4

Published in the United States of America
by Vanderbuilt University Press
Nashville, Tennessee, U.S.A.
1966

Second Printing 1967

Library of Congress catalogue card number : 62-51781

Printed in Great Britain.

Totus mundus agit histrionem

CONTENTS

PLATES

Between pages 68 and 69

PLATES

PLATES

XXXIII. THE SACRIFICE OF THE PELICAN
(*New Testament*, London, 1552, by R. Jugge.)

XXXIV. THE WOODWOSE
(J. Berjeau, *Early Dutch, German, & English Printers' Marks*, London, 1869, no. 2.)

XXXV. TWO WILDMEN
(*Ad Serenissimum . . . Iacobum Quintum . . . strena*, Edinburgh, *c.* 1530?)

XXXVI. BESTIAL TERMINI
(Sir A. Fitzherbert, *La Graunde Abridgement*, London, 1565, t.p.)

XXXVII. IGNORANCE AS A MONSTER
(*Emblemes d'Alciat*, Sig. P4v, p. 232.)

XXXVIII. ART CORRECTS NATURE
(Cesare Ripa, *Iconologia*, Padua, 1611, Sig. D4r, p. 31.)

XXXIX. THE BEAR LICKS ITS CUB
(Boissard, *Emblemata*, Frankfurt, 1596, Sig. M2r.)

XL. NAKED TRUTH
(William Burton, *The Description of Leicester Shire*, London, 1622, t.p.)

XLI. THE WOLF CONFUSES SHADOW AND SUBSTANCE
(*Fables D'Esope*, Paris, 1689, Sig. A3r, p.5.)

XLII. TRUST AND CIRCUMSPECTION: THE HEART AND THE SEEING HAND
(Rollenhagio, *Nucleus Emblematum*, emblem 72.)

XLIII. THE GRASSHOPPER AND THE ANTS
(Phillipe Desprez, *Le Theatre des Animaux*, Paris, 1620, Sig. G3r, p. 53.)

XLIV. 'SIC TRANSIT GLORIA MUNDI'
(Rollenhagio, *Nucleus Emblematum*, emblem 86.)

XLV. DEATH THE LEVELLER
(Rollenhagio, *Nucleus Emblematum*, emblem 48.)

XLVI. 'VITA AULICA SPLENDIDA MISERIA'
(Boissard, *Emblematum liber*, Sig. Olr, p. 89.)

XLVII. THE FLY AND THE CANDLE
(Rollenhagio, *Nucleus Emblematum*, emblem 40.)

XLVIII. JUSTICE WEIGHS POVERTY AND POWER
(M. Silesio, *The Arcadian Princesse*, London, 1635, t.p.)

XLIX. THE FOOL BEARS HIS ASS ON HIS BACK
(Sebastian Brant, *La nef des folz du monde*, Paris, 1497, Sig. e4r, fol. XXIIII).

L. THE NAKED SURVIVE
(Ioannes Sambucus, *Emblemata*, Antwerp, 1564, Sig. Olv, p. 210.)

LI. THE GREAT TREE SHATTERS
(*Fables D'Esope*, p. 241.)

LII. THE DRY BONES ARE MADE FRUITFUL
(Rollenhagio, *Nucleus Emblematum*, emblem 21.)

LIII. CHRIST RESTORES THE LOST SHEEP
(John Calvin, *Sermons . . . on . . . Timothy and Titus*, London, 1579.)

PREFACE

I have written of Shakespeare because I believe that his plays are more than splendid verse and exciting theatre and the evocation of memorable characters: I think a total experiencing of them, and of the basic principles or poetics on which they depend, involves a reading of the world and man's place in the world that remains essentially true. I have sought, in exploring that opinion, to give as complete an account as I can of the Shakespearean experience, particularly in terms of one play but in general against the context of all of Shakespeare's work and that of the age in which it was created.

I wish to thank for their help Professor Erwin Panofsky of The Institute for Advanced Study, Princeton; my colleague, Professor Alan S. Downer; and the staff of the British Museum; the Bodleian Library; the Firestone Library, Princeton University; and the Houghton Library, Harvard University. My work has been generously supported by the American Council of Learned Societies, the American Philosophical Society, and Princeton University, which designated me a Junior Fellow of the Council of Humanities.

This book is for George Frost who, though he deplored so much writing on Shakespeare, would perhaps have accepted one book more, as from a friend.

RUSSELL A. FRASER

London, 1961

I

KING LEAR IN THE RENAISSANCE

IF I enumerate in a work of art those pure forms which carry primary meanings, I subject that work of art to pre-iconographical description. Thus, in describing *King Lear*, one might list the configurations or forms he finds in that particular play: pelicans, vipers, blind men, mad men.

To go beyond such elementary listing, and treat those configurations as carriers of secondary meanings, to treat, that is to say, not simply the thing itself but what that thing stands for beyond the primary level of mere denotation, is to enter on iconography. A pelican is a kind of bird. But conventionally it has been used as an emblem of Christ, who feeds or repasts his flock—the phrase belongs to Laertes, in *Hamlet*—with his own life's blood. A winged man, a lion, an ox, an eagle, these, in conjunction, in Christian literature and art, figure by convention the Four Evangelists. The image of a fish betokens Jesus Christ. In vaticinal poetry, men and women are symbolized in the character of animals and birds. The magpie may stand for an odious priest, and the dragon for any Welsh prince; or, if the time is propitious, for Owen Glendower; or later, Robert Aske, the Lincolnshire rebel; or, it may be, for Anti-Christ, the Dragon of Babylon.

The form, then, is charged with a secondary meaning. It has become an image. *King Lear*, of course, is compounded of images. It is the business of the iconographer to describe them.[1]

[1] Thus the work of Robert B. Heilman, *This Great Stage*, Baton Rouge, La., 1948; and Caroline Spurgeon, *Shakespeare's Imagery and What It Tells Us*, New York, 1935.

But to see in those images the manifestation of underlying principles, symbolic of the basic attitude of a nation, or class, or era; to get at the psychology, the state of mind, which may be implicit or even unconscious, that led Shakespeare and his fellows to see and use the pelican, say, as a symbol pat to their purpose, this is the business of iconology. Ideally, the iconologist will muster many documents—poems, sermons, proverbs, ballads, pictures—concurrent in time with the work he has chosen to discuss, and revealing, in their use of like symbols, pretty much the same notion of the way the world goes.

The documents at issue, if one is treating of the Renaissance, are likely, all of them, and whatever their formal nature, to be illustrative or graphic in manner, if not expressly pictorial. What they would communicate, they are likely to couch in the form of a similitude or image, and this on the principle, as Bacon puts it, that 'that which is sensible more forcibly strikes the memory and is more easily imprinted on it than that which is intellectual'. To stigmatize pride: '*si grand orgueil*', is nothing. To embody pride in the Tower of Babel, as Holbein does in his *Icones Historiarum*,[1] is to yoke the abstraction to earth. The bizarre notion of a virgin who conceives and remains a virgin still is only a piece of mystification until it is represented as the garden enclosed, the sealed fountain, the shut gate, the immaculate mirror. That man is sometimes feeble or vicious is only a commonplace, not really apprehensible, in a sense not really true, until analogy demonstrates and so approves it:

> How from the finny subject of the sea
> These fishers tell the infirmities of men.
>
> (*Pericles*, 2.1.52f.)

Figures are useful, indispensable even, in that they 'reduce intellectual conceptions to sensible images'.[2] What is more, resort to them is a matter of innate predilection.

> Euen litle children as soone as they can vse their hands at libertie, goe with a Cole to the wall, indeuoring to drawe the forme of this thing or that,

and for the reason, according to Samuel Daniel, that 'to

[1] Lyons, 1547, Sig. B2v.
[2] Bacon, *De Augmentis Scientiarum*, Bk. 5, ch. 5.

represent vnto the sence of sight . . . is more natural in act, and more common to al creatures then is hearing.'[1]

We have of course our images also, although, with a kind of heroic fatuity, we have sought since the late seventeenth century more and more to dispense with figurative language, have denied, at least implicitly, that we lean on it at all. But even if you concede that Avogadro's Hypothesis is really a kind of figure, you will agree, I suppose, that the terms in which it is couched are nothing like so analogical as those which the Renaissance astronomer Robert Recorde employed to describe the constellation Andromeda, whose head 'lyeth on the navel of Pegasus'.[2] Recorde did not seek to be poetic, in the facile and faintly pejorative sense of the word. He might have said simply, with Ben Jonson in *Discoveries*, that 'Whosoever loves not Picture is injurious to Truth'. Himself a partisan of the truth, he attended and necessarily to the metaphorical way.

The mind of Recorde, like that of Shakespeare—I would add, the mind of the Renaissance—is enamoured of what is literal and concrete. *Rien ne vit qu'en détail.* The extraordinary popularity of the emblem—defined by Francis Quarles as 'a silent Parable'[3]—is one manifestation of the zeal for particulars. When, in 1531, the Italian jurist Andrea Alciati published his premier collection, he offered only a slender volume of less than one hundred emblems. Forty years later, Alciati's *Emblematum Libellus* had grown in bulk to ten times its initial size. Its great vogue was by no means peculiar to itself: more than seven hundred volumes of emblem literature were in print in Shakespeare's lifetime. In England, in the sixteenth and seventeenth centuries, virtually every writer of standing drew in his published work on the new form, inaugurated in Italy only a few years before.[4]

[1] Sig. Alv, Epistle to the Reader, in Daniel's translation of Paolo Giovio, London, 1585.

[2] *The Castle of Knowledge*, London, 1556, p. 265.

[3] 'Epistle to the Reader', *Emblemes*, 1635.

[4] A partial list of those whose debt to emblem literature has been documented includes Lyly, Nashe, Sidney, Spenser, Daniel, Joshua Sylvester, Marlowe, Marston, Chapman, Shakespeare, Jonson, Middleton, Webster, Heywood, Burton, Sir Thomas Browne, George Herbert, Crashaw, Milton, Marvell, Bunyan, Quarles, Henry Peacham, Wither, William Drummond, Henry Vaughan. See Praz, *Studies*, I, 193–206; E. N. S. Thompson, *Bypaths*, ch. II, 'Emblem Books', pp. 29–67.

Not only the emblem flourished, but exemplary literature in general. The reasons in each case are essentially the same. If you would instruct, you must dramatize, give your precept some palpable, at best some historical, antecedent:

> For the remembrance of matters past, furnisheth men with examples sufficient to guide and direct them in their consultations of future things.[1]

Hence the vogue of *florilegia*, and the *De Casibus* theme:

> Stately and proud, in riches and in traine,
> Whilom I was powerfull and full of pompe,
> But what is he, whome rule and emperie
> Have not in life or death made miserable?
> (*Edward II*, ll. 1879–82)

If you would clarify, you must levy on metaphor: 'Poesie is a speaking picture, and picture dumb Poesie.'[2] Hence the currency of illustration, in sacred books and profane books: Amman's *Icones Novi Testamenti*, published at Frankfurt in 1571, offers in colour scenes from the New Testament; Thomas Cranmer's *Catechismvs* defines the Ten Commandments, not abstractly but by depicting them. Philippe Desprez, early in the following century, ekes out his Biblical tags with pictures of animals, documenting, making manifest, the thesis.[3] Editions of Aesop are the grand exemplar of the method: the mere moral, a thing of bare bones, is not felt to suffice.[4] When Pericles, in Shakespeare's play, would express his love for Thaisa, he is not content simply to declare it. He must exemplify it, rather, as his knightly competitors do, by means of a device or *impresa*:

> A withered branch, that's only green at top;
> The motto, '*In hac spe vivo.*' (2.2.43f.)

When Francis Bacon, assisting at the trial of Essex, would make clear the nature of that nobleman's ill-fated rebellion, he does not argue in terms of a disembodied principle: words, words,

[1] Plutarch, *Morals*, tr. Philemon Holland, 1603, p. 11; quoted Lily B. Campbell, *Shakespeare's Tragic Heroes*, Cambridge, 1930, pp. 26f.

[2] Holland's Plutarch, p. 34, quoted Campbell, pp. 26f.

[3] Thus he gives a cut of the lion entoiled in the net, at which his friend the rat is nibbling, and comments: '*Chacun peut faire recompense . . . fais bien au iuste, & tu trouveras grande retribution.* Eccles. 12.1.2.' See Sig. A3v, p. 6.

[4] See, for example, *Fables D'Esope, avec les Figures de Sadeler*, Paris, 1689.

words, but calls to mind the Duke of Guise, thrusting himself into the streets of Paris, and seeking, like Essex, to cover his treason with 'an all-hail and a kiss to the City'; or, a more learned exemplum, summons up the case of Pisistratus, 'of whom it was so anciently written how he gashed and wounded himself, and in that sort ran crying into Athens that his life was sought and like to have been taken away; thinking to have moved the people to have pitied him and taken his part by such counterfeited harm and danger: whereas his aim and drift was to take the government of the city into his hands, and alter the form thereof.' When Sir John Eliot would bring home to the Commons the danger to liberty centring in Charles's counsellor Buckingham, he enforces a parallel with Sejanus, thereby making the danger a palpable, a particular thing. On Buckingham's fall, Eliot, still refusing to be placated, is analogical still: 'Though our Achan is cut off, the accursed thing remains.'[1]

The age of Shakespeare finds its way to truth by means of indirections, through analogies and images, those stricken metaphors which Sprat and the Fellows of the Royal Society sought to banish from wit's commonwealth. As you might expect, the images tend to recur. The contracted similitudes of Taverner or Whitney are those of the dramatist also. They are likely, moreover, to shadow the same understanding. Whitney, in *A Choice of Emblemes* (1586), will illustrate the twin resource of Scripture, to save, or 'serve only for springes and snares', by presenting a single flower, fruitful of honey and poison.[2] And after Whitney, Shakespeare or, more precisely, Friar Laurence, in *Romeo and Juliet*:

> Two such opposèd kings encamp them still
> In man as well as herbs, grace and rude will.
>
> (2.3.27f.)

Ben Jonson's Sir Politic Would-Be is alive also to the sense of Whitney's gloss, familiar also with the emblem which gives it a local habitation:

> The spider and the bee oft-times
> Suck from one flower.
>
> (*Volpone*, 2.1.30f.)

[1] Lytton Strachey, *Elizabeth and Essex*, London, 1928, pp. 252, 250; John Richard Green, *A Short History of the English People*, New York, 1900, II, 631, 637.

[2] Sig. G2r, p. 51.

Shakespeare's Escalus, in a celebrated crux, remarks of Claudio, in *Measure for Measure*, and, presumably, of the deputy who has sentenced him to death:

> Some rise by sin, and some by virtue fall.
> Some run from brakes of ice, and answer none,
> And some condemnèd for a fault alone.
> (2.1.38–40)

But if Escalus is cryptic, it is not by intention. His purpose is rather, by means of a speaking picture, to clarify; as Whitney, dilating on the sovereign power of chance, would clarify also, and in similar manner. Observing the fox on ice, as it did 'to . . . peeces brake', he finds in that misadventure the moral:

> No subtill crafte will serue,
> When Chaunce doth throwe the dice.[1]

The many collections of 'parables and semblables' drawn, most of them, at least purportedly, from the wisdom of the ancients—again, the penchant for analogy, or precedent—demonstrate also their connexion with the greater writing of the age, help even to form it. Thus the *Chiliades* of Erasmus moralizes, before the fact, the unhappy case of Macbeth: '*Quod factum est, infactum fieri non potest.* The thynge that is done can not be vndone.'[2] The *Chiliades* was recognized widely and as widely esteemed as a storehouse of classic and pseudo-classic wisdom. As such, it was redacted by moralists like William Baldwin, Richard Taverner, Thomas Palfreyman, and John Hall, whose versions were rifled in turn by Elizabethan dramatists and poets. In the same way, the commonplaces of Renaissance dictionaries, which resorted for their proverbial wisdom to classical authorities, found their way into the literature of the age.[3]

Comparisons, illustrations, the saws and sayings appended to them, are consequential, then, in this: they tend to fix, in the popular imagination, an image or grouping or attitude or

[1] *Emblemes*, Sig. C3v, p. 22.

[2] *Prouerbes or Adagies, gathered oute of the Chiliades of Erasmus by Rycharde Tauerner*, London, 1552, Sig. E3r, fol. xxxv.

[3] See Starnes and Talbert, *Classical Myth and Legend in Renaissance Dictionaries*, Chapel Hill, N.C., 1955; Baldwin, *A treatise of Morall Phylosophie*, London, 1547 and ?1550; Palfreyman, *A Treatice of Morall philosophye*, London, 1567; Hall, *The Court of Virtue*, London 1565.

bias which, canonized by use and wont, help to explain and to determine, in obvious ways or subtle, the dramatist's handling of his materials. Sometimes the image is familiar enough, of sufficient currency and antiquity, to strike with immediate effect, and so to constitute a kind of shorthand. If you want to present an indubitable villain, you will say with Hieronimo, in *The Spanish Tragedy* (4.4.135): 'And let their beards be of Judas his own colour'; or, less explicitly, with Shakespeare's Rosalind, in *As You Like It* (3.4.7): 'His very hair is of the dissembling colour.' Judas, in the medieval drama as in the Renaissance, is always red-haired.[1] If you want, in abbreviated fashion, to represent the intervention in human affairs of a destiny or fate beyond human contriving, you will, with King John, propitiate dreadful Occasion. (4.2.125) A distich is enough, for the image of the goddess, whose head is partially bald, whose hand holds a razor, whose winged feet stand on the whirling wheel is, by virtue of the emblem book, a popular cliché.[2] (Plate I) The various sins or vices are known also by their customary marks. Lust you may always recognize by the sharp whip she carries at her girdle. That is how Webster, in *The White Devil* (2.1), describes her. No less conventional is the image of a woman distracted:

> Enter Cassandra, raving, with her hair about her ears.[3]
> (*Troilus and Cressida*, 2.2)

The melancholy lover opens himself to you at once: his arms are folded like a rabbit on a spit athwart a thin-belly doublet—this to keep down his rising heart, his hose is ungartered, his

[1] See the representations of him in Amman, *Icones Novi Testamenti*, 1571, Sigs. E4r, Flr.

[2] See also *2HIV*, 4.1.70–73; *Lucrece*, ll. 869–82; and, for other representations of Occasion: Alciati, *Emblematum Libellus*, Paris, 1536, p. 20; *Emblemes d'Alciat*, Lyons, 1564, Sig. K3v, p. 150 (given also in Henry Green, *Shakespeare and the Emblem Writers*, London, 1870, p. 259); Rollenhagio, *Nucleus Emblematum Selectissimorum*, Cologne, 1611, emblem 4; Panofsky, *Studies in Iconology*, New York, 1939, fig. 35; Boissard, *Emblematum liber*, Metz, 1588, Sig. H3r, p. 61. Tourneur, in *The Revenger's Tragedy*, makes his hero, Vendice, say of 'that bald madam', Opportunity or Occasion: 'If I meet her,/I'll hold her by the foretop fast enough;/Or, like the French mole, heave up hair and all.' (1.1) Until confused with Fortune during the Middle Ages, Occasion or Opportunity was conceived of as a nude young man with winged shoulders and heels, and balancing a pair of scales on the edge of a shaving knife. His head displayed the proverbial forelock, which Shakespeare glances at, in *All's Well*: 'Let's take the instant by the forward top.' (5.3.39)

[3] And see *RIII*, 2.2, for the description of Queen Elizabeth.

bonnet unbanded, he pulls his hat penthouse-like over the shop of his eyes.[1]

Stage persons, by definition, are not truly dimensional. They assume the aspect of life to the degree that the dramatist establishes in them a connexion with what is given, outside the theatre. He achieves the connexion by appealing to the popular wisdom, embodied in stereotypes, in 'quaint Emblems and devices begg'd from the olde Pageantry of some Twelfe-nights entertainment at *Whitehall*', as Milton in *Eikonoklastes* described them. 'Having told you that her name was Justice,' says Thomas Dekker of an allegorical figure in a pageant prepared for King James, 'I hope that you will not put me to describe what properties she held in her hand, since every painted cloth can inform you.'[2] The representations woven on tapestry or arras—the sort of hoary fables which Iachimo peruses, hiding in Imogen's bedroom, that he may write down 'the contents o' the story' (*Cymbeline*, 2.2.26f.)—constitute for the dramatist a point of departure. 'Every painted cloth' has made familiar the sense of the Seven Deadly Sins, the Combat between the Virtues and the Vices, the Triumph of Truth, the empery of Fortune, the character of Pride and Luxury, Patience and Perseverance.[3] The dramatist is able, therefore, in a way to skimp his business, to evoke his protagonist by a series of notations, generally no more than just sufficient—if he is crude, some foible, or trick of speech,[4] or morality name, which is itself the only felt source of praise or blame attaching to the stock figure who bears it. Tendered its cue, the audience does the rest, collaborates insensibly in the creation of character. Hence the efficacy of convention: what seems impoverished in print need not, in the theatre, be absolutely poor. Enter Shame, Ambidexter, Meretrix, and Commons Cry. If you will: Enter, Sir Epicure Mammon.

Everyone will think of the Malevoles and Vendices, the Cataplasmas and Corvinos of the Jacobean stage; or, earlier

[1] *LLL*, 3.1.18–21, 4.3.135f.; *Two G.*, 2.1.19–22, 79; *AYLI*, 3.2.392–400; and see *TA*, 3.2.6f.

[2] *The Magnificent Entertainment given to King James*, 1604.

[3] S. C. Chew, *The Virtues Reconciled*, Toronto, 1947, pp. 23f., lists conventional representations on tapestries.

[4] So Dekker's Margery Eyre, in *The Shoemakers' Holiday*, and her recurrent, 'But let that pass.'

and even more explicit, of Marlowe's show of the Seven Deadly Sins—traditional matter, given, and so ready to the dramatist's hand. 'I am one that loues an inch of raw Mutton better then an ell of fride stock-fish.' But what Faustus sees is allegory still, only the medieval abstraction, made more expressive but not, essentially, more dramatic. Shakespeare's use of convention, as it is less overt, is more interesting. Only rarely is he concerned, as in 2*Henry IV*, to present on stage an allegorical figure: Enter Rumour, painted full of tongues. But the impress on his work of what is traditional, of what is given, is evident, nonetheless, if oblique and, I daresay, unconscious. Lear is a proud man, and not the personification of Pride; and yet, as surely, he owes something in his creation and reception to the first of the capital sins, in the same way that Holofernes, who is also *sui generis*, is indebted to the Pedant of the *Commedia dell' Arte*. Shylock, in his origins, is cousin german to avarice; and Cleopatra and Antony to lust; and Hotspur to anger; and Falstaff to gluttony; Iago to envy. Sloth is harder; but it has, I think, to do with that man who, slow to stir about his business, is called duller than the weed that roots itself on Lethe wharf. The description, of course, is of Hamlet.

Shakespeare's stage, lacking the proscenium arch and front curtain depending from it, teases the dramatist with this problem, among others: how to get a man off, whom the plot in some drastic way has made incapable. If the man is dead, the problem is easily resolved: let some other lug his guts into the neighbour room.[1] If, on the other hand, he is only asleep and not yet to be wakened; or thrust in the stocks and not yet to be freed, then the dramatist must leave him, whatever the perplexity of the spectators, while the action continues on its way. The Soul of Mankind, in the fifteenth-century Morality, *The Castle of Perseverance*, must lie dormant on stage, beneath the bed of Mankind but exposed to the view of the audience, from the very beginning of the play. But in that awkward situation there is unexpected profit. The curiosity of the audience is

[1] The removal of the body needs only to be plausible, as when young Clifford bestows the corpse of his father, fallen in the battle of St. Albans. (*2HVI*, 5.2) More impressive, however, are those scenes in which necessary stage business is made also to delineate character and so to advance the plot, as when Crookback, having murdered the King, says whimsically to his victim, 'I'll throw thy body in another room.' (*3HVI*, 5.6.92)

piqued, its expectation aroused. Nor is that curiosity slaked until the crisis of the action, which is to say until the moment of the hero's regeneration when, as the MS. reads, the Soul of Mankind 'schal ryse and pleye'.[1]

Shakespeare also, like the author of the Morality, puts to positive use his silent actors. Thus Demetrius and Lysander, Helena and Hermia, sleep on the open stage, according to the Folio version of *A Midsummer Night's Dream*, all through the Act—that is, through the interval—between Acts III and IV. They are not in fact roused until Theseus bids the huntsmen wake them with their horns; and this despite the eruption on stage of Titania and Nick Bottom, a rout of fairies (making rural music with tongs) and, behind them, Oberon their king. 'All this', observes an editor, 'is improbable, not to say fantastic.' It is rather, I think, deliberate—at least a willing acquiescence in the limitations of the stage—and, given the play's business, at once probable and decorous. For what could more emphatically make the point of the play than the living tableau with which Act IV opens: the sleeping lovers, whose love is engendered in the eye and, over against them, the delicate queen, cozened also by appearance, kissing the large ears of a clown. The enforced presence of the two couples is turned to advantage, made to serve, by juxtaposition, as an emblem, dumb poesy, of all the play.

> Tell me where is fancy bred,
> Or in the heart or in the head?

Now, the practice of juxtaposing—mutely comparing, to elicit a comment—is not peculiar to the theatre nor original with it. In a pair of sixteenth-century tapestries, a man and woman are contrasted. The one, caught in a trap, is released by the hand of God. The other, trapped also but busy with mundane pleasures, is succoured by Blind Cupid, who involves her of course in destruction. The situation in each case is superficially the same, and crucially different in its issue. But the comment is in the juxtaposition.[2] (Shakespeare also, in

[1] The same use of the convention is illustrated, if not so dramatically, by the enfeebled state initially of Good Deeds in *The Summoning of Everyman*.

[2] Allegory of Profane and Sacred Love, Paris, Musée des Arts Decoratifs; figs. 116, 117 in *Studies in Iconology*. Below the trapped man are representations of a phoenix (*figura resurrectionis*) and pelican (*figura passionis*). See chs. VIII and VI.

The Tempest, and in precisely the same manner, reserves explicit comment, is content to rely on the perception of his audience. He presents to you Caliban, a proper slave improperly seizing his freedom—this, at the end of Act II; and Ferdinand, a prince and so in expectation a master, unexpectedly forfeiting his—this, without intermission, at the beginning of Act III. The one, abjuring labour, will bear no more sticks; the other, welcoming labour, enters bearing a log. The parallel is perfect in that it enforces, not sameness but distinction: the emancipation of the servile man is imprisonment, rightly read; the fettering of that man who is ostensibly free, as it serves to try him, to quicken in him the understanding that poor matters often point to rich ends, is in actual fact emancipation.)

The *Biblia Pauperum* and *Speculum Salvationis* are marked also by complementary representation. If a centre panel illustrates a scene from the New Testament, analogues or complements from the Old Testament will flank it. So Christ carrying the Cross is juxtaposed with Isaac carrying wood for his own immolation; and Jonah delivered, with Christ resurrected from the tomb. (Plate II) The Last Supper is prefigured (and clarified) by Melchizedek giving Abraham the bread and wine, and Moses and Aaron collecting the manna from Heaven.[1] An Elizabethan artist, portraying the death of Christ, will pose against the dead body the exuberant figures of children, oblivious of loss and grief and decay, and in themselves a pledge of renewal.[2] A Tudor portrait will flatter a young man in his pride; and place in his hand, or lay at his feet, a grinning skull.[3] From the living tree, a man will prune the dead branch, and recapitulate thereby the beheading of a felon, the cutting away of an infected member from the state. (Plate III) An illustrator of Bibles like Hans Sebald Beham (1500–50) will set Christ in his triumph, miraculously multiplying the loaves and fishes,

[1] Fig. 1 and pp. 7f. in Strachan, *Early Bible Illustrations*, Cambridge, 1957.

[2] Isaac Oliver, 'The Burial of Christ', *c.* 1556–1617, British Museum; and Woodward, *Tudor and Stuart Drawings*, London, 1951, pl. 11.

[3] So the portraits of Edward Grimston, 1590, by an unknown artist, Gorhambury, the Earl of Verulam; Sir Thomas Gresham, School of Holbein, London, Mercers' Hall; and Sir Thomas Aston, by John Souch, 1635, City Art Gallery, Manchester. See Collins-Baker and Constable, *English Painting of the Sixteenth and Seventeenth Centuries*, Florence and Paris, 1930, pls. 34, 8; and E. K. Waterhouse, *Painting in Britain 1530 to 1790*, London, 1953, pl. 36.

beside the austere Christ, ascending a barren hill, there presumably to begin his fasting in the wilderness alone. *Respice finem.* Both scenes, at once antithetical and complementary, are given in a single cut. And so the correspondence is suggested.[1] The emblem writer Boissard, depicting the creation of man, reveals, amid the idyllic scene in which Adam, awakening, is set, the serpent. In the moment of birth is death.[2] 'The audiences', as a recent critic has remarked, 'were trained by their whole dramatic tradition'—one might add, and by conversance with pictorial literature—'to feel an allegorical significance behind a formal or rhythmic grouping.'

But not only painting and engraving but also the conventions of the *tableaux vivants* suggest and inform dramatic pictures. The manner, a silent but an eloquent parallel, is kindred. Louis de Nevers, Count of Flanders, grants privileges to the city of Bruges (or so the citizens trust, in fashioning the pageant), while Moses from the mountain brings the Tables of the Law. Philip II, his father having abdicated, goes to Italy and the Low Countries to be installed as king, and admires in street theatres constructed for his progress the analogical figures of Solomon and David, Titus and Vespasian, and (ironically) Abraham and Isaac. The motifs and forms on which the pageant is founded are common coin, moreover, throughout Europe. When, a few years later, Philip enters London as the husband of Mary Tudor, he sees on his route the same allegorical groupings, wrested anew to speak to his present situation, as had been offered him at Antwerp in 1549. The *tableau vivant* was as familiar, then, in England as abroad.[3] Its conjunction with the drama is explicit in the final act of *The Tempest,* when Prospero pulls the curtain, discovering the young lovers at chess, and discourses on them, in his role as doctor or presenter, to Alonso. So the orator-expositor who presented the street shows revealed

[1] Sig. OOiiv in *Biblia Insignium Historiarum simulachris . . . Gryphius,* 1541.

[2] Sig. C4r, 'Creatio Hominis', in *Theatrum Vitae Humanae,* Metz, 1596. Bocksperger's emblem of the temptation defines the future in the present: in the foreground Adam and Eve hearken to the serpent; afar off they are driven from Paradise. See *Neuwe Biblische Figuren,* Frankfurt, 1564, Sig. Alv.

[3] From the beginning of the century, the erecting of street theatres was customary, first in London as part of the Lord Mayor's Pageant or to celebrate a royal entry (as in 1501, 1520, 1522, 1533, 1546, 1553, 1554, 1558), and later, in Elizabeth's reign, in the provinces, to honour the progresses of the Queen: G. R. Kernodle, *From Art to Theatre,* Chicago, 1944, p. 70. And see pp. 60, 68, and fig. 26.

to his audience a silent tableau and proceeded to expound it.[1]

Sometimes, on stage, the tableau is reminiscent merely, like that of

> Patience gazing on kings' graves and smiling
> Extremity out of act;
>
> (*Pericles*, 5.1.139f.)

or that of Love, as valorous as Hercules,

> Still climbing trees in the Hesperides.
>
> (*Love's Labour's Lost*, 4.3.340f.)

Behind the image is a tangible representation: Hercules, figuring this great man or that, in quest of the golden apples.[2] (Plate IV) The dramatist remembers a formal grouping and glances at it cursorily in his verses. It is the stuff of an image. It does not otherwise impinge on the play. Sometimes, however, the grouping, while essentially static, is recreated on stage to form the living picture of a memorable moment, as in the emblematic scene in which Philip of France drops the hand of King John:

> England, I will fall from thee;
>
> (*King John*, 3.1.320)

or, even more striking, as in the little tableau with which *Titus Andronicus* commences, when the bickering contenders for the imperial throne, vying with one another from opposite sides of the stage, are overtopped abruptly by the brother of the hero, the grand disposer of their fortunes:

> Enter Marcus Andronicus, aloft, with the crown.
>
> (1.1)

And sometimes the stage emblem ramifies, speaks to the entire business of the play. Like meets like when Sly, the drunken tinker, looks down from above and comments without comprehending on the story of a shrew in which every decorous convention is flouted. (*Taming of the Shrew*, 1.1.255) Heroism

[1] Kernodle, pp. 134–47, cites many examples of the collaboration of street shows with the Elizabethan theatre.

[2] Guigue, p. 42, comments on the tableau: 'Mais ce qui caractérise l'action que veut représenter cette composition bizarre, toute imprégnée de symbolisme compliqué, c'est un superbe pommier, couvert de pommes d'or, par rappel des Hespérides—le roi François étant Hercule.' A similar illustration appears in G. Mourey, *Le Livre des Fêtes Françaises*, Paris, 1930, p. 27, fig. 16.

and ranting come perilously close together when Henry V, the ideal king of the commentators, exhorts his men once more into the breach; and Pistol, Nym, and Bardolph, as it were the other face, are driven to it, protesting. (*Henry V*, 3.1,2) Lepidus, a triple pillar of the world, drunk in Italy, is made to enforce a parallel more acute and more cynical when he is carted off, cheek by jowl with Pacorus, a Parthian chief and an enemy to Rome, slain by Ventidius, a subordinate merely, but true to his business, in Syria, half-way across the world.[1] (*Antony and Cleopatra*, 2.7; 3.1) In the juxtaposing of the two events, like and unlike, the dramatist, in an emblem or mute figure, addresses the audience, obliges it to compare, and so, willy-nilly, to judge.

Shakespeare, in a similar manner, addresses the audience in *Lear*. Edgar, far off and in hiding, is made to occupy the stage simultaneously with Kent, set in the stocks before Gloucester's castle. (2.2,3) Simultaneous action of this kind is partly, I suppose, a legacy to the Renaissance of the medieval drama, which derives it, and necessarily, from the fixed or conventional representation that marks the performance of the earliest plays. Action in the church nave oscillates between *locus*, *sedes*, and *domus*, the given areas or positions which are always on stage, which indeed are all the stage. This means that the *domus*, say, will have to represent the manger in which Christ is born, and the *sedes* or seat the throne of Herod, in pretended fact far away, in actual fact a few paces away. So much for the illusion of reality. Shakespeare, however, accepting his inheritance, discovers novel uses for it, taking a hint perhaps from the static character of the *tableau vivant*, which manages to be eloquent for all that its action is merely ceremonious. He presents on stage, as he is constrained to do, Kent and Edgar, at once together and apart. But in the unrealistic defiance of the possible that has brought the two good men, unjustly made wretched, together, he voices an appeal to a higher reality, an unspoken comment close to the heart of the drama. The audience sees the better how the world wags. When Goneril and Regan, dead, are carried on stage to be posed with Edmund, dying; when Coriolanus falls, and Aufidius stands on the body; when—another tableau—Hal, the victor of Shrewsbury, surveys at his feet Hotspur and Falstaff, each of them prone, and each, in a sense, the embodiment of

[1] The modern and quite arbitrary division into acts largely obscures the effect.

courses he might have followed, of characters he might have assumed, it seems plausible to suggest a collaboration with the dramatist of the street pageant and pictorial literature, in the fashioning of stage glosses, of emblematical scenes.

The emblem or image is memorable to the degree that it is suggestive: it bodies forth, it crystallizes, the better to instruct. Those who climb on Fortune's wheel come full circle, at last. Pride, that spends its mouth to no purpose, is subversive at last of itself. Frivolity is dieted; ill-weaved ambition is shrunk. The gloss is not private to Shakespeare, but the common property of his age. Nor is the emblem or image, which is its stalking horse, likely to be idiosyncratic. I should think, therefore, to find the analogies of proverb lore, the continued and fixed representation of themes and allegorical conventions like the Dance of Death or the Seven Deadly Sins, the illustrations in catechisms, in tapestries, in the *Biblia Pauperum*, in emblem books and bestiaries, and on Elizabethan title pages, the traditional arrangement of the figures in street pageants, all involved, necessarily, with the imagery of Shakespeare's plays. It is my purpose to determine the degree and the nature and also the meaning of that involvement in terms of the imagery of one particular play.

I propose, then, to treat of the iconology of *King Lear*. In that play, I find the following central motifs: the idea of Providence; of Kind; of Fortune; of Anarchy and Order; and Reason and Will; and Show against Substance; and Redemption. Each of these motifs may be fixed or crystallized in an image. With those crystallizing images—call them emblems, or icons—I am concerned. It is my intention, moreover, to locate the central motifs of *King Lear* in the work of other men roughly contemporaneous with Shakespeare, and then at length to make plain, as best I can, what the currency of those motifs really means.

Though Shakespeare may have looked into Whitney and did certainly read Holinshed, I have no interest in establishing whether he ever saw one of the emblems I have represented, or read in any of the volumes I have cited. I have not sought to study the influence of this on that. Neither would I pretend that Shakespeare is simply the voice of his time, a lyre swept by tendencies, by what are called main currents: a Churchyard or a Tusser, writ large. If he is of his time, he is alien to it also.

On occasion, in making use of a conventional image—that, for example, of the kingfisher or halcyon—he will find in the image a legend antithetical to that perceived by the greatest number of his contemporaries. The same eccentricity will, I take it, be remarked in any other dramatist of stature. And so I do not think to discover in *Lear* a precise delineation of the Elizabethan World Picture nor, certainly, a panegyric thereon. And, if the writings of his age afford a clue to Shakespeare, I do not suppose that they suffice to explain him. The poet who puts to use the threadbare commonplaces of an indifferent philosophy does not so much redact as transmute them. Shelley is not Shaftesbury *redivivus*. It remains, however, true that Shakespeare's imagery is rooted in his time, that he levies on what is traditional and most common. Though the great play and the inconsiderable homily are, in the crucial sense, more different than the same, I think it fruitful to try to illuminate the one by resort to the other, not least when images occurring in them both suggest a divergent understanding; and by collation, by comparison and contrast, to divine the common spirit interpenetrating each, the spirit of man in a particular time—to quote Professor Wittkower's tribute to Fritz Saxl—'working in the images he made to express himself'.

The images of Shakespeare and his particular time are not, as it happens, valid coin any more. There is in real fact no goddess Fortuna, nor any wheel that she spins, on which the reckless ascend and descend. God's eye does not look down, from the summit of creation, on the demi-god man at the centre of creation. The strife of wit and will has been displaced by that of Id, Super-Ego, and Ego. And whoever would figure the king as the vessel and the master of his people[1] must be either disingenuous or simple. But the imagery of *Lear*, if you put away the vizard or correlative and look for the thing bodied forth, has pith in it still: it enjoins on man certain governing imperatives, eliciting these from a reading of his nature; it affirms the result when those imperatives are disputed or ignored. The affirmation remains tenable, at least admissible. But that is understatement.

[1] In the manner of the illustration on the title page of Hobbes's *Leviathan*, London, 1651. See ch. V, pl. XXVI.

II

PROVIDENCE

ONE of the crucial questions posed by *King Lear* is uttered by Albany, horrified, and bemused, at the curse Lear loads upon Goneril.

> Now, gods that we adore, whereof comes this?
> (1.4.312)

Albany addresses himself to a single and specific situation. But the question reverberates. It rises from particulars to encompass and to query all the awful business of the play, to ask: What is the root of unnatural conduct? Whence comes evil?

It comes in part from impiety. Its root is in the mistaking by man of his relation to the macrocosm, to the greater world which contains him. The Epicurean, to use Shakespeare's word, disallows the relation altogether. He is to the Renaissance, by virtue of his absolute naysaying, a scandalous and so an absorbing figure. Sir Philip Sidney, in the *Arcadia*, puts the characteristic words in his mouth:

> to thinke that those powers (if there be any such) above, are moved either by the eloquence of our prayers, or in a chafe by the folly of our actions; caries asmuch reason as if flies should thinke, that men take great care which of them hums sweetest, and which of them flies nimblest.[1]

The conventional discourse of the impious man, elaborated by Sidney, is adhered to by Shakespeare's Edmund, a generation later. Edmund scorns to 'make guilty of our disasters, the sun,

[1] *The Countesse of Pembrokes Arcadia*, vol. I of *The Complete Works*, ed. Albert Feuillerat, Cambridge, 1912, pp. 406f.

the moon, and the stars'. He sneers at heavenly compulsion, at spherical predominance. Like Cassius, he is emancipated:

> You know that I held Epicurus strong.
> (*Julius Caesar*, 5.1.77)

Like Iago, he is self-sufficient:

> 'Tis in ourselves that we are thus or thus.
> (*Othello*, 1.3.322f.)

He discountenances wholly a divine thrusting on. (1.2.128–49) He is audacious to do so. What is more, he is wrong.

> These late eclipses in the sun and moon
> portend no good to us.
> (1.2.112f.)

I do not think to confound Edmund with the opinion of Gloucester, who believes very much in sequent effects. Put with it, however, the opinion of Kent: men achieve great place because 'their great stars Throned and set [them] high'. (3.1.22f.) That they beget such different issue as the wicked sisters and Cordelia is because 'The stars above us, govern our conditions'. (4.3.35) Lear is of similar mind. He invokes the god Apollo. (1.1.162) He swears 'By all the operation of the orbs From whom we do exist and cease to be'. (1.1.113f.) He calls on Nature, presumably interested and possibly responsive, to hear him. (1.4.297–311) He is sure 'that in the pendulous air [plagues] Hang fated o'er men's faults'. (3.4.68f.) Even his denunciation of the forces of Nature as servile ministers (3.2.21) is rooted in a belief in causality, albeit malign.

One may argue, of course, that to Shakespeare and his audience, or to the more reflective persons in that audience, Edmund is wisely sceptical, and Gloucester, Kent, and Lear grossly superstitious. But aberrations in Nature, when recorded in the writings of Shakespeare and his age, and in the writings of the erudite man as well as the scribbler, do not get the laconic treatment Edmund accords them. King Richard II might have beaten down Bolingbroke's challenge had not his Welsh allies thought to read in signs and vaticinal sayings the futility of fighting any more:

> The bay trees in our country are all wither'd,
> And meteors fright the fixèd stars of heaven;

> The pale-fac'd moon looks bloody on the earth,
> And lean-look'd prophets whisper fearful change.
> (*Richard II*, 2.4.8–11)

Disaster on earth—the death of a king—requires celestial sympathy, for the heavens and earth are conjunctive:

> Comets, importing change of times and states,
> Brandish your crystal tresses in the sky.
> (*1 Henry VI*, 1.1.2f.)

Evil rampant on earth—man's ingratitude to man—requires celestial correction, a planetary plague hanging poison in the air over the high-viced city. (*Timon*, 4.3.108–10) The accomplished evil is scourged; evil to come—the bloody reign of Crookback—is predicted:

> The owl shrieked at thy birth . . .
> The night crow cried, aboding luckless time.
> Dogs howled, and hideous tempest shook down trees.
> The raven rooked her on the chimney's top,
> And chattering pies in dismal discords sung.
> (*3 Henry VI*, 5.6.45–48)

Similar omens accompany the birth, in 1612, of the Scottish hero Montrose, who is supposed, while still a sucking child, to have eaten a toad: an evil sign, infallibly, to the pious who happen also to be his opponents. But not only those whose wish fathers the thought find the course they must follow set for them by commotion in the heavens or in eccentric happenings on earth. When Charles V, lingering in Brussels, delays his promised abdication, a comet affrights him, portending war and pestilence and the overthrow of princes; and so like Hamlet he cries, 'My fate calls out!' and makes ready to depart.[1]

Richard III, *Richard II*, *Julius Caesar*, *Macbeth*, and *King Lear*: each abounds in reference to untoward disorders. Regan, whose evil business is accomplished out of season, threading dark-eyed night (2.1.121), embodies and announces them. Their significance is perfectly plain. The great and singular storm in *King Lear* means precisely the same as the great and singular storm

[1] For the story of Montrose see John Buchan, *Montrose*, London, 1949, p. 31n. Motley, *The Rise of the Dutch Republic*, I, 129, quoting a contemporary (1555) German chronicler, tells of Charles V.

which accmopanies the murder of Duncan and, if you will, the murder of Christ. It means that the heavens, as troubled with man's act, begin to threaten his bloody stage. (*Macbeth*, 2.4.5f.) Owen Glendower, who is only partly a fool, was sensitive to such threatenings. One is prone to sneer at Glendower, to mock, as Hotspur mocks, his prophetical powers. It is, however, Glendower who, overruled by prophecies, declines to do battle at Shrewsbury. (*1 Henry IV*, 4.3.18) The commonsensical Hotspur dies there.

What I would demonstrate is that the explicitly serious use of the portent as symbol is one of the most wonted conventions, not only in Shakespeare but in the Renaissance. Samuel Harsnett, on whose *Declaration of Egregious Popishe Impostures* Shakespeare probably drew for the names of the devils who lurk about Poor Tom, found 'all the sensible accidents . . . pendulous in the ayre'. The unknown author of *The Birth of Merlin* discovered them roofing our heads. Burton, in the *Anatomy*, laid corruption of the air, plagues, thunders, and fires, to the intervention of malevolent spirits. 'The air is not so full of flies in summer, as it is at all times of invisible devils.'[1] The Catholic polemicist, Noel Taillepied, understood that

> When some terrible political change is imminent, when a monarchy is tottering to its fall, or a kingdom is threatened by war, internal commotions, and republican sedition, such upheavals are frequently presaged by mysterious phenomena, by ghostly signs in the air, by prodigious happenings among the animal creation.[2]

Before the battle of Tippermuir—to cite a specific instance of change presaged by mysterious phenomena—airy armies contended, the sun shone at midnight, an unearthly choir sang, and a cannon shot, warning of invasion in the west, was heard over the whole kingdom.[3] Philip Melanchthon, Luther's distinguished and scholarly colleague—to choose at random a Protestant polemicist, to complement the Roman Catholic—

[1] See Harsnett, edn. 1603, p. 159; *The Shakespeare Apocrypha*, ed. C. F. Tucker Brooke, Oxford, 1908, p. 375 (4.1.220); *The Anatomy of Melancholy*, Pt. I, Sec. 2, mem. I, subs. 2. See also Harsnett on 'sparrow-blasting', p. 136; Edgar on 'star-blasting', *Lear*, 3.4.59f.; and Shakespeare's Sonnet 14, ll. 3f., 7f.

[2] *A Treatise of Ghosts*, Paris, 1588, tr. Montague Summers, London [1933], ch. XIV.

[3] Buchan, p. 148.

was sure that 'No year escapes that sees a blazing comet'.[1] Accordingly, he undertook to 'hold every man forewarned that one should not neglect divine tokens'. Luther himself manifests in his Table Talk (*Tischreden*) entire faith in portents. His opponent, the Anabaptist and rebel Thomas Münzer, cleaved with even more vigour to that faith. In 1525, on entering into battle, he spied out a rainbow and thus exhorted his troops: 'God declareth plainly by the similitude that he sheweth on highe, that he wyll aide us in the battell, and distroye the tyrauntes.'[2]

More often, the similitude does not hearten; it casts down. Gloucester's dark mutterings find a parallel, perhaps a source, in a pamphlet by the almanac writer, Edward Gresham. In *Strange . . . news which happened at Carlstadt* (1606), Gresham assures (and admonishes) his readers that

> The Earth and Moon's late and horrible obscurations, the frequent eclipsations of the fixed bodies . . . shall without doubt . . . have their effects no less admirable than the positions unusual.

Theodore Beza, Calvin's successor, entertained very much the same belief. It is the burden of his comment on the nova—a star grown suddenly bright—of 1572. He awaits with trepidation the approach of the time, presumably a vexing time, when 'theffects themselves shall show'. Fear of sequent effects ran also in the mind of the Englishman Grindal, Archbishop of York, who wondered if the earthquake of 1575 did not portend the death of Queen Elizabeth.[3] The lightning bolt which fired and consumed the steeple of St. Paul's on June 4, 1561, excited in Tom Nashe this ominous (and doggedly chauvinistic) observation: 'Did the Romans take it for an ill signe, when their Capitol was strooken with lightning, how much more ought *London*, when her chiefe steeple is strooken with lightning?' On June 8th, the Sunday following the fire, a sermon was preached

[1] 'Nulla aetas vidit flagrantem impune cometam.' Quoted James Howard Robinson, *The Great Comet of 1680*, Northfield, Minn., 1916, p. 8.

[2] Llewellyn M. Buell, 'Elizabethan Portents: Superstition or Doctrine?' *Essays Critical and Historical Dedicated to Lily B. Campbell*, Berkeley and Los Angeles, 1950, pp. 28, 30f.

[3] Beza, *Of the ende of this worlde*, tr. Thomas Rogers, London, 1577; John Strype, *The Life and Acts of Matthew Parker*, Oxford, 1821, II, 397; Buell, pp. 32f.

at Paul's Cross, in which the fire was seen as a warning to the realm of some greater misadventure to follow. In a published report of the burning, which appeared two days later, Jeremiah (as you might suppose) provided the prefatory quotation:

> I wyll speake suddenlye agaynst a nation, or agaynste a kyngedome, to plucke it vp, and to roote it out, and distroye it . . .

An insistence on design, however melodramatic, is explicit.[1] Holinshed's *Chronicles*, perhaps the work of reference to which Shakespeare resorted most often, is rife with the same moralizing of portents and prodigies. Even Lear's Fool, adverting to Merlin (whose prophecies Holinshed preserves), assumes the manner of a seer and foreteller of the future. Nor ought one to smile: divination was a flourishing business: in the *Catalogue of Printed Books in the British Museum*, twelve columns are given over to a listing of works dealing with Merlin.[2]

God's hand, then, is always raised to smite or reward, if only one has wit enough to see it. If a two-headed calf comes forth in Hampshire, or a strange fish is dragged from the Thames, God speaks in the event. When Luther and Melanchthon, joint authors of a chapbook attacking the papacy and the monastic orders, cast about for an emblem of their enemies, they find it in a dead monster fished from the Tiber in 1496, and in a calf with a dewlap, born at Freiburg-in-Meissen in 1522.[3] The enormously popular and prolific literature of the ballad

[1] Nashe comments in *Christs Teares Over Ierusalem*, London, 1593, Sig. Z2v. Some notion of the extraordinary impact an incident of this nature could make for may be gathered from the following beadroll of references to it: John Stow, *The Annales*, ed. Edmond Howes, London, 1615, pp. 646f.; Stow, *Survey of London*, Everyman edn., n.d., pp. 296f.; *Brief Discours de la Tempeste et Fouldre Advenue en la Cite de Londres . . . sur. . . . sainct Paul. . . .* Paris [1561]; ballads listed in *S.R.*, I, 202, 210, 263; and in Chappell, *Popular Music of the Olden Time*, I, 117. See also *The True Report of the burnyng of the Steple and Churche of Poules in London*, printed by William Seres on 10th June, 1561; and Jeremiah, xviii.

[2] Vol. XXXVI, cols. 249–60. The prevalence and importance of prophecy are illustrated further by the fact that, in 1541, Henry VIII felt compelled to declare a felony 'any false prophecy upon occasion of arms, fields, letters, names, cognizances, or badges'. Edward VI, in 1550, confirmed his father's prohibition. Elizabeth forbade explicitly the use of animal symbolism. The Catholic Church, too, felt the danger: in 1564, the *Index librorum prohibitorum* proscribed *The Prophecies of Merlin* on the authority of the Council of Trent, which condemned books on augury and divination. See Rupert Taylor, *The Political Prophecy in England*, New York, 1911.

[3] *Deuttung der czwo grewlichen Figuren*, Wittenberg, 1523; Buell, p. 29.

and broadside moralizes incessantly, throughout the sixteenth and seventeenth centuries, whatever is monstrous or bizarre.

> Strange Wonders God to us doth send,
> For to make us our lives amend.

Autolycus in *The Winter's Tale* may jest on ballads and credulity: Stephano and Trinculo in *The Tempest* are credulous. Even Montaigne is ready to read a moral in deformity. So is the Tudor physician John Hall who, in *The Court of Virtue*, finds a misshapen birth portentous. His contemporary, the author of 'A warnyng to England', discovers in the immorality of the mother the origin of 'The forme and shape of a monstrous Child, borne at Maydstone in Kent', in the autumn of 1568.[1] Everything untoward had its ascertainable cause. The sweating sickness or plague, which visited England in 1552, and claimed in one week, and in the city of London alone, the lives of eight hundred people, was so palpable a mark of divine displeasure that 'this nation', wrote a contemporary of Shakespeare's, 'was much afeard of it, and for the time began to repent & remember God, but'—and the sequel is characteristic, and endearing—'as the disease relented, the deuotion decaied'.[2]

The cosmology of the Renaissance not only agrees with, but very nearly enforces, the notion that God watches over and admonishes, even the least of His subjects. The Renaissance mind, when not perverted, beclouded, was full of His proximity. Caxton, following Ptolemy, undertook, in the encyclopedic *Mirror of the World*, to define it, to put it on paper, and so make it mathematically plain. Caxton's Universe was of course geocentric. That in itself is not a fact of overweening importance, if you hold with Sherlock Holmes that it is all one to us whether the earth revolves around the sun or the sun around the earth. The Ptolemaic theory is fraught, however, with this majestic consequence: represent the Earth as the centre of the Universe,

[1] See *The Pack of Autolycus*, ed. H. E. Rollins, Cambridge, Mass., 1927, pp. 139–45, 185–7; Sig. Nnlr in *The Essayes or Morall, Politike and Millitarie Discourses of Lo: Michaell de Montaigne . . . done into English By . . . Iohn Florio*, London, 1603; *The Court of Virtue*, Sigs. S4r–5r; and, for other ballads on similar subjects, *A Collection of Seventy-Nine Black-Letter Ballads and Broadsides*, London, 1867, pp. 194–7, 27–30, 45–48, 63–66, 112f., 145–7, 186–90, 201–04, 217–20, 243–6, and xvi–xviii (an introductory discussion on prevalence and meaning).

[2] Stow, *Annales*, p. 605. See also *Court of Virtue*, Sig. O7r; and *A boke, or counseill against the . . . sweatyng sicknesse. Made by Jhon Caius*, London, 1552.

and you make it thereby the centre of all God's concern, Encircling the Earth were the triple spheres of water, pure air, and fire. There followed next the seven spheres which housed the seven known planets. Beyond them extended yet another. This was the Firmament, containing the stars, 'Of whiche ben knowen pryncypally 47 . . . And of them ben taken 12 of the most worthy whiche ben called the 12 Sygnes [of the Zodiac].'[1] Enclosing the whole was the Primum Mobile; beyond it: the Blue Heaven, the Heaven Crystalline, the Heaven Imperial, abode of the angels, and last, the Heaven Celestial, where God sat His throne and viewed with a certain scepticism the self-sufficient posturings of Edmund.

It is one part of that self-sufficiency that Edmund should scoff at the stars. But here, in the mouth of Tecnicus, a character reminiscent of Shakespeare's Friar Laurence, in John Ford's *The Broken Heart*, is figured, not merely a more pious, but a more truly sophisticated position: 'Tempt not the stars; young man, thou canst not play with the severity of fate.' (I.3) Montaigne went further. He found 'the power and domination' of the stars to be exerted 'not onely upon our lives, and condition of our fortune . . . but also over our dispositions and inclinations, our discourses and wils, which they rule'. Edmund is incredulous, but here, in the preface to an ephemeral pamphlet, is his wisdom stigmatized for the foolishness it is: 'Among al sinnes, none is more odious before God, then is incredulitie: doubting both of divine promises and threatnings.' Finally, Edmund is impious. The terrible and all-embracing nature of his impiety, and just what it gives away, are made plain, I think, by this sentence of the Zwinglian theologian, Ludwig Lavater. Portents, asserted Lavater, come from God

> that we might understand that all these things happen not by aduenture [chance], without the wil & pleasure of God, but that life and deathe, peace and warre, the alteration of Religion, the exchaunge of Empires, and of other things, are in his power, that we might thereby learne to feare him, and to calle vppon his name.[2]

[1] London, 1480, Sig. m4v.

[2] See Florio's Montaigne, III, 205; Beza's *Of the ende of this worlde*; Buell, p. 262; and Lavater, *De spectris*, Zurich, 1570, tr. R.H.: 'Of ghostes,' London, 1572, II, xvi (ed. J. Dover Wilson and May Yardley, Oxford, 1929, pp. 164f.).

But to establish so much, that the men of the Renaissance, learned and unlearned, were pious in the old-fashioned way, is only, I daresay, to make a beginning. It is true, it gives one warrant to say or surmise how Shakespeare and his fellows must have treated the refusal of Edmund to endorse the notion of divine thrusting on. But it does not speak at all to the nature of that refusal, which is made, neither more nor less respectable by the headshaking of Edmund's contemporaries, however many of them one may bring forward. Truth does not turn on popular suffrage, nor is it qualified by the character of the man who gives it voice.

> Though all things foul would wear the brows of grace,
> Yet grace must still look so.

It is a fact that the geocentric universe is dead; and that the plagues which smote London and which John Stow described had as much to do in their arising with a lack of sanitation as with the displeasure of an ireful god; and that Münzer's peasant army, whatever the faith of its leader, went to the slaughter, even so. I do not mean to pretend, then, that the portent or prodigy are literal precursors of dreadful events. I suppose that Melanchthon and Taillepied, Harsnett and Nashe, describing them so, were deceived. It may even be true that man keeps the universe alone.

And yet the superstitious Gloucester, even conceding a universe from which the gods on whom he calls have all departed, remains more acute than his emancipated son. His belief in portents is to be construed as a kind of notation, a figure, resting on and expressing the acceptance of a principle of order and causality. The pious man of the Renaissance embodies that principle in the idea, if you like in the creation, of a personal and provident God. The embodiment itself may no longer compel assent or respect. But the principle the figure bodies forth, that every effect proceeds from its cause, that sequence and not chaos is manifest in the creation, remains compelling still. A man ignores or disputes it, to his cost. That at least is the assertion Shakespeare's play undertakes to explore and, in the event, to sustain. Edmund is in error, not because he goes counter to the conventional wisdom, but because his protestations are mocked in action, assayed and confounded by the course of the play. The plot is the testing of his egotism. It is the plot, the experiment, and not a cluster of apophthegms, which gives him the lie.

The Renaissance version of the universe we live in, however grossly it may err in particulars, is valid, is tenable, metaphorically speaking, in that, no less than *King Lear*, it declares for the contiguous nature of all things. That is why the engraver, designing a title page for Matthias Lobel's *Stirpium Adversaria Nova* (1570), is not content to represent the map of Europe alone: he must depict its near relation to the stars above us, forever fixed in their orbit beyond the planetary spheres, forever casting their influence, whether baleful or happy, on men. The printer John Day, when he chooses a title page for Foxe's *Book of Martyrs* (1570), does more than commemorate the heroic individual bearing witness to the truth. He wants also to express his author's vision, in its way more spectacular, of the indissoluble union of heaven and earth. For that reason he crowds together, all within one frame, the priest before the altar, the victim at the stake, the inspired prophet, a representation of the persecuted Church, and of the Church when it turns to persecution, the blessed in their glory, the cursed in their torment and, last and first, the figure of God, seated on the great globe itself, and addressing and attending to His people. Just so does the *Nuremberg Chronicle*, presenting in picture the universe described in *The Mirror of the World*, portray the great design, in all its meticulous detail, as conducting at last to God, enthroned at the apex of His work and participating in it still. That is the meaning of the many engravings of Jacob's dream of the ladder ascending to Heaven, a commonplace of emblem literature because it dramatizes with such clarity the faith of the Renaissance in contiguity.[1] To treat of the conjunction of things human and divine, as does the iconologist Cesare Ripa in depicting a man fallen on his knees and clasping a golden chain which hangs from a star in the Heaven is, essentially, to affirm the dependence of this upon that and of everything at last upon cause.[2] It is in that sense, and not as antique error, that one is to

[1] See, for example, the illustrations in Arias Montanus, *Humanae Salutis Monumenta*, Antwerp, 1571, under 'Humana Divinitas'; and in Strachan, *Early Bible Illustrations*, fig. 45.

[2] See Ripa, *Iconologia*, Padua, 1611, under 'Congiuntione delle cose Humane con le Divine'.

interpret the universe of Caxton and the belief in the operation of the orbs. The stars, declares the emblem writer, bend their mysterious power on men.[1] (Plate V) But that is only his way of speaking for sequence. The stars themselves are in fee to necessity.

The villainous persons in *Lear*, rejecting sequence, entertain no belief in Providence. All goes by chance. But the chanceful and the self made are equally fables. That is the pith of an emblem saluting David's conquest of Goliath. God's arm drives the stone from the sling.[2] Let a battle be joined: whatever the preponderance of power on one side, it is Providence that determines the issue. The hand of God, suspended, grasping the laurel wreath and the sword, appoints the victor.[3] (Plate VI) It does not follow that the victor can afford to grow rusty in what Shakespeare's Fluellen calls the disciplines of war. Despite the modest disavowals of Henry V, it is his superior direction, and not the intervention of the deity, that wins for the English at Agincourt. Nor is the triumph at Bosworth Field after all to be attributed to God.

> Miracles are ceased,
> And therefore we must needs admit the means
> How things are perfected.
>
> (*Henry V*, 1.1.67–69)

The unspectacular truth, to which the emblem testifies obliquely, admits those means. But its kernel is in the discovery that what a man is plays its part in what he does, in fact in what he can do. Richmond is not victorious over Richard III because he prays on the eve of battle. But his prayers betoken his equanimity, his harmonious relation to all the ends and purposes of his being. His is the unclouded mind on which good generalship depends. The guilty conscience of Richard argues,

[1] See Rollenhagio's gloss, in *Nucleus Emblematum*, Sig. B2v: 'Encor' que des Astres la celeste puissance, Verse dessus nos corps leur secrete influence.'

[2] Sig. F2v in Holbein's *Icones*, Lyons, 1549 (English version): 'Dauid castyng auuay Saul harnes, and tristing only in the pouur of God, vuyth a stone ouut of hys slyng kylleth Goliath.' David, 'Without being armed, in God confiding . . . chaseth auuay the Philistians.'

[3] Jacob Bruck glosses the emblem (*Les Emblemes Moraulx et Militaires*, Strasbourg, 1616, Sig. B4v): 'Cui Vult. Et le nombre de gens, & la force de bras, Et les lames luisant des tranchants coutelas Apportent au Colonel beaucoup grand advantage: Mais encor pour cela, il n'est victorieux Si Dieu ne luy ennoy' la victoire des cieux Dont à bon droit luy doibt faire honneur & hommage.'

conversely, a mind at sixes and sevens, incapable of making thoughtful provision. It is not the mind of the successful commander.

Providence describes the participation of character in the event. It dramatizes, further, the humbling proposition that man is not the measure of all things. Let a man outgo all others in accomplishment: still his puissance and knowledge are derivative. The sailors adrift in a rudderless boat—the theme of a French *tableau vivant*—do not founder. No doubt their seamanship is all that it should be. But their safety depends at last on the direction of the Queen, herself the vassal and vicegerent of Providence, enthroned on a rainbow in Heaven.[1] This is not to say that human enterprise is nothing, but only that it is not everything. That is the moral the emblem writer educes, in celebrating Drake's voyage around the world. All honour to Drake. But his triumph is not engineered, either fortuitously or of himself. From the clouds God's hand is extended. It clenches a girdle made fast to the *Golden Hind*, and so draws the vessel along. The motto: *Auxilio divino*: with the help of the Lord.[2] Sir Walter Ralegh, embarked on a more colossal voyage, the recording of the whole history of the world, discerns in that history a similar agency. The title page of his great work depicts those allegorical figures whose interaction makes up the story he would tell: Good Report, Notoriety, Experience, Truth, drawn naked—a convention to which I shall want to return—and above them all, observing them always, the eye of Providence.[3] (Plate VII)

The Heavens do participate. Order wields the world. 'The revenging gods,' says Edmund whimsically, ' 'Gainst parricides . . . [do] all their thunders bend.' (2.1.47f.) He is right. Only his whimsy is malapropos.

Jesters do oft prove prophets.
(5.3.72)

By the end of the play, Edmund is dead. The villainous Cornwall dies also. His death, says Albany,

[1] Kernodle, p. 95. The tableau was prepared for the entrance, in 1533, of Queen Eleanor into Lyons.

[2] Given in Whitney, *Emblemes*, Sig. C2r.

[3] For similar title pages, see H. Hammond, *A Practicall Catechisme*, London, 1646; L. Roberts, *The Marchants Mapp of Commerce*, London, 1638.

> shows you are above,
> You justicers, that these our nether crimes
> So speedily can venge.
>
> (4.2.78–80)

In the deaths of Goneril and Regan, Albany sees again 'This judgement of the Heavens'. (5.3.231) Kent is a good man, in part because he fears it (1.4.17), aware that the ungodly shall not stand in the judgement. Gloucester, tied to the stake, anticipates that judgement, looks to the winged vengeance (3.7.64f.), as the Psalmist looked to the lightning and the arrows of Jehovah, and the Latin poet to the red right hand of Jove.

In the nether world, all things are felt as manifesting design. Peter de la Primaudaye, a Frenchman who is also a popular preceptor to the English, embodies, in the wonted figure, that conviction of design: 'All things are guided and gouerned by the prouidence of God, who knoweth and ordereth casuall things necessarily.'[1] Gloucester's miseries are causal in their origin, not casual. Nor is Gloucester blinded because 'The gods . . . kill us for their sport' (4.1.38f.), but rather because

> The gods are just, and of our pleasant vices
> Make instruments to plague us.
>
> (5.3.170f.)

Thus Edgar, affirming and echoing the sentence of Cambria in the old play that lies behind Shakespeare's:

> The heauens are iust, and hate impiety.[2]

To put it another way: *propter hoc* and not *post hoc* is king.

[1] *The French academie*, London, 1618, p. 192.
[2] *The True Chronicle History of King Leir*, London, 1605, l. 1909.

III

KIND

THE gods dispense justice. But they do not dispense poetic justice. In the world of *King Lear*, the learned pate ducks to the golden fool. (*Timon*, 4.3.17f.) The usurer hangs not only the cozener but the innocent also. A dog's obeyed in office,

> Hooking both right and wrong to the appetite,
> To follow as it draws!
>
> (*Measure for Measure*, 2.4.176f.)

Strength is by limping sway disabled. Albany's hopeful saying,

> All friends shall taste
> The wages of their virtue, and all foes
> The cup of their deservings,
>
> (5.3.302–4)

is a piece of simplicity. Lear's 'Never!' confounds it. Cordelia, whose best meaning merits all honours, is not the first to find out an ignominious death. (5.3.3f.)

But—and here the critical point, which the plot is at pains to discover—though a good man's fortune may grow out at heels (2.2.164), a bad man's fortune will certainly do so, given only the passage of time. Shylock may die in his bed, with all his ducats restored to him (but not his daughter); or, like his fellow-villain Barabas, the Jew of Malta, may be tipped at last into the cauldron. This is to say: he may be lucky or unlucky: the spinning of the wheel is independent of good conduct or bad. But whether, in affluence or in penury, he will be found a man or a cipher, turns, decidedly, on conduct. For the gods are more than mere warders. They have given to man a fixed nature: the Elizabethans call it *kind*. If a man violates that nature, if he trespasses against kind, he is destroyed, not directly by the deity in the old melodramatic way, but rather by the deity acting through the man himself.

Sin debilitates the sinner. Because the plays are concerned, in the manner of plays, to be clear and dramatic, the consequence of that debility is apt to be physical, though it is no more terrible for being so, but only more startling, more readily apprehensible. The random spinning of the wheel is largely discounted. The sins of Mowbray, engaged to do combat against Bolingbroke, sit

> so heavy in his bosom
> That they may break his foaming courser's back
> And throw the rider headlong in the lists.
>
> (*Richard II*, 1.2.50–52)

The sins of the hero-villains, Brutus and Cassius, turn their own swords against their proper entrails (*Julius Caesar*, 5.3.94f.), as the strangling of the law brings Lucan's Romans with 'conquering swords [to lanch] their own breasts'. (*Pharsalia*, tr. Marlowe, ll. 2f.) The scheming Iachimo, in *Cymbeline*, is bested, not simply because he meets his superior in Posthumus, but because, as he is forced to acknowledge, the heaviness and guilt with which he is laden take off his manhood. (5.2.1f.) Self-indulgence is not to be censured *in abstractu*: an infringement of the tables. It is censurable because it is perilous. 'Our senses,' wrote Montaigne, glossing, in effect, one of Alciati's emblems, 'Our senses are not only altered, but many times dulled, by the passions of the mind',[1] and so neglect all office whereto our health is bound. (2.4.106f.) To give over the safer sense (4.6.81f.) is to dissolve the life that wants the means to lead it. (4.4.19f.) The choleric lion set upon by the hunters and their dogs, as he is enraged, works his own death: that is Alciati's point in depicting the emblem. Anger swallows up reason, makes the wrathful man a beast who, reckless of self-preservation, savages not another but himself. *Ira est mors*. The lion in Droeshout's emblem, attacking the dragon, is overcome by him, and this because, like the wrathful man, he gives odds to his opponent. (Plate VIII) Of

[1] *Emblemes d'Alciat. . . . A Lyon*, 1564, Sig. F4v, p. 88; Florio, IV, 70.

each it may be said: 'Their own wickedness hath blinded them.' (Wisdom, ii.21)

The sins of Lear wrench his frame of nature from the fixed place (1.4.290f.), and leave him prey to madness. The sins of Actaeon strip him of his manhood, convert him to the quarry he has trained his dogs to hunt. Sambucus, treating of Actaeon's demise, observes—a nice piece of meiosis—that 'Sensuality is full of troubles'.[1] Alciati appends as moral the single word, '*Desloyaute*': Actaeon, in the ultimate sense, has been false to himself.[2] He has turned his own reasons into his bosom like dogs upon their master (*Henry V*, 2.2.82f.), tearing the master. Whitney's reading is more explicit, and periphrastic: those who, like Actaeon,

> do pursue
> Their fancies fonde, and thinges vnlawfull craue,
> Like brutishe beastes appeare vnto the viewe,
> And shall at lengthe, Actaeons guerdon haue:
> And as his houndes, soe theire affections base,
> Shall them deuowre, and all their deedes deface.[3]

In precisely the fashion of Lady Macbeth, Actaeon, 'by self and violent hands', takes his life. It is not, as in the myth, that Diana wills it that way, or that the God of the Hebrews or Christians compels him to it. In the violent death of the wicked man there is more art, which is to say more economy, more decorum.

> Unnatural deeds
> Do breed unnatural troubles.
> (*Macbeth*, 5.1.79f.)

His life, like that of Cymbeline's wicked queen, being cruel to the world, is in its conclusion most cruel to himself (5.5.31–33), and this for constitutional reasons:

> As surfeit is the father of much fast,
> So every scope by the immoderate use
> Turns to restraint.
> (*Measure for Measure*, 1.2.130–2)

The evil a man does is inimical to what he is. Simply by virtue

[1] Sig. H8r, p. 128, in *Emblemata . . . Ioannis Sambuci*, Antwerp, 1564.
[2] *Emblemes d'Alciat*, Sig. E7v, p. 78.
[3] *Emblemes*, p. 15.

of his nature, his kind, he is unable to brook it. Man, in this sense, may be called the slave of nature. For 'there is no sinne', writes Primaudaye, 'that can auoide punishment, and that findeth not a Iudge euen in him that committed it, to take vengeance thereof, by meanes of the affections, which God hath placed in man to that end'.[1]

The malefactor bears his own cross. What is more, and more appropriate, he fashions it himself. It is Lear's own unkindness that stings his mind so venomously, that loads him with a sovereign shame. (4.3.43–48) There is dramatic propriety in the fact that, wherewith he sins, by the same is he punished, that it is his own imagination which torments him. (Wisdom, xi.16, xii.23) The engineer, infallibly, is hoist with his own petar, an irony the emblem books adumbrate over and over. Tyranny, to Boissard, is full of fear, and rightly: it looks to, and occasions, its own decay. With the same decorum the thief, in Whitney's emblem, is throttled by his plunder, and the Cyclops, the author of evil, made author also, and concurrently, of his own loss of sight.[2] 'Mischievous wickedness', writes Philemon Holland (after Plutarch), 'frameth of herselfe, the engines of her owne torment, as being a wonderful artisan of a miserable life.'[3] This is to say, with Desprez in the *Theatre des Animaux*, that the cozener is his own prime gull: '*Frauder le fraudeur*' (p. 23); and that the hunter, whose quarry is inhibited and out of warrant, preys on no one more than himself.[4]

Those who put off the nature belonging to them depart from the fountain which refreshes their being. They shall be written in the earth: the first wind that blows over them shall wipe away their names. (Jeremiah, xvii.13) 'That nature which contemns its origin,' says Albany,

> Cannot be bordered certain in itself.
> She that herself will sliver and disbranch
> From her material sap, perforce must wither
> And come to deadly use.
>
> (4.2.32–36)

[1] *The French academie*, pt. II, p. 506.

[2] See *Iani Iacobi Boissardi Vesuntini Emblematum liber*, Frankfurt, 1593, Sig. O2r, p. 91: 'Metus Est Plena Tyrannis'; Whitney, *Emblemes*, Sig. F1r, p. 41: 'Poena sequens'; *Emblemes d'Alciat*, Sig. N7v, pp. 206f: 'Iuste Vengence.'

[3] Quoted Campbell, p. 21.

[4] Sig. B1v, p. 10: 'Celuy qui chasse un autre, n'est mesme à repos.'

The image, expressive almost of the physiological imperatives of kind, is central to *Lear* and, beyond the play, to other work of the playwright, and further, to the Renaissance itself. Its function is to assert an organic relation between conduct and the consequences of conduct. Necessarily it defines nature: not a tissue of precepts but a fund of possibilities whose character and limitation are susceptible of testing. Shakespeare's play is such a testing. A tree cut away from its roots, which are the condition of its being, cannot survive. Neither can a man survive who repudiates his condition. The nexus between crime and punishment is that prosaic. The image derived from husbandry is met so often in the art and literature of the Renaissance because no other renders man more exactly nor with more implication.

> This is the state of man; to-day he puts forth
> The tender leaves of hopes, to-morrow blossoms,
> And bears his blushing honours thick upon him:
> The third day comes a frost, a killing frost,
> And when he thinks, good easy man, full surely
> His greatness is a-ripening, nips his root,
> And then he falls . . .
>
> (*Henry VIII*, 3.2.352–8)

The good easy man is Wolsey.

But the same image defines his master. When, in 1509, Henry VIII ascends the throne, not York and Lancaster, those abstractions, are united, but a white rose tree and a red. To represent the accession of Elizabeth, it is necessary only to add to the tree another branch. The genealogical tree, the civic counterpart of the Tree of Jesse, is the chief resort of street pageants and *tableaux vivants*, the convention to which they find it most natural to turn, when they would trace the noble lineage of some exalted person. So the ancestry of Louis XII is figured, on his entry into Paris in the closing years of the fifteenth century, by a *lis* on which are mounted the pictures of those kings who have gone before, leading to the reigning sovereign at the top. At a street theatre in Rouen in 1485 a revolving tree is made to present on different levels the ancient worthies; in its topmost branches an actor is enthroned as Charles VIII. In London in the middle of the following century two trees, growing out of Edward III, come together in the persons of Mary Tudor and Philip of Spain.[1]

The lofty place imputed to him flatters the monarch. But the image instructs him also in his condition, which is kindred, however splendid his degree, to that of the meanest subject. He is

> no more but as the tops of trees
> Which fence the roots they grow by and defend them.
> (*Pericles*, 1.2.30f.)

In nature the whole world is kin. The well-grown oak is more like than unlike the under shrubs that it crushes to splits in its fall. (Ford, '*Tis Pity*, 5.3) One emblem describes the noble and the liege man. Mirabel, the hero of *The Wild-Goose Chase*, wishes a long life in his father. He is

> none of these that, when they shoot to ripeness,
> Do what they can to break the boughs they grew on.
> (1.3)

His psychology, his kind, is that of the kingly protagonist of the old *Leir* play who, about to apportion his kingdom, addresses his daughters as

> florishing branches of a kingly stocke,
> Sprung from a tree that once did florish greene,
> Whose blossoms now are nipt with Winters frost.
> (Sc. 3)

D'Amville, Tourneur's hero in *The Atheist's Tragedy*, thinks his children

> as near to me
> As branches to the tree whereon they grow;
> And may as numerously be multiplied.
> As they increase, so should my providence;
> For from my substance they receive the sap,
> Whereby they live and flourish.
> (1.1)

Solyman, in Fulke Greville's *Mustapha*, knows that

> Flesh hath her buds, her flowers, her fruit, her fall.
> (2.2)

[1] See Kernodle, pp. 68, 76, 97f., 107. An illustration of Francis I, represented as the top of a tree, is given in Guigue, facing p. 16.

Shakespeare's imagery partakes of that knowledge. His greatest single source of imagery he finds in the countryside. When he would body forth human beings, he depicts them most often in terms of plants and trees. Juliet likens her love and Romeo's to a bud, in hope a beauteous flower. Rendered lifeless by the potion, she becomes the flower herself, blighted by an untimely frost. (2.2.121) Desdemona, when Othello mistakes her for the destroyer of their love, is altered from flower to weed.[1] (4.2.67) Achilles, in whom the seeded pride has flourished,

> must or now be cropped
> Or, shedding, breed a nursery of like evil.
> (*Troilus and Cressida*, 1.3.316)

The sonnets, from first to last, are instinct with the sequence of growth, perversion, and (*ipso facto*) decay.

> The summer's flower is to the summer sweet,
> Though to itself it only live and die,
> But if that flower with base infection meet,
> The basest weed outbraves his dignity.
> (Son. 94)

The image is more conspicuous still in the historical plays. It informs the only sustained passage in *1 Henry VI* that is worth pausing over: the emblematic scene in which the rival parties who will fight the civil war announce their division in the plucking of the white rose and the red (2.4); and also the one memorable line in the play, spoken by Talbot of his valorous son, who rushed into battle

> and there died,
> My Icarus, my blossom, in his pride.
> (4.7.15f.)

It is most conspicuous and most decisive in the gardening scene of *Richard II* (3.4), whose point the homilies had made familiar long before Shakespeare:

> Euen as a good gardiner is verye diligent about his gardeine, watering the good and profitable herbes, and rootyng out the vnprofitable wedes: So shoulde a kinge attende to his commen

[1] In the same way, the adultery of Vittoria, in *The White Devil* (1.2), is likened to the poisoning and blasting of herbs.

> weale, cherishing his good and true subiectes, and punishing suche as are false and vnprofitable.[1]

In *Richard III* the royal house figures explicitly as a tree. Those who comprise the house are so many branches, leaves, flowers, fruit. The idea of the tree being planted, storm tossed, grafted, rooted up, and withering at last, recurs constantly. It is levied on again in the later plays, by Posthumus, holding Imogen in his arms:

> Hang there like fruit, my soul,
> Till the tree die!
> (*Cymbeline*, 5.5.263)

and by Othello, intent on the murder of his wife:

> When I have plucked the rose,
> I cannot give it vital growth again,
> It must needs wither: I'll smell it on the tree.
> (5.2.13)

'I have begun to plant thee,' says Duncan of his greatest supporter, 'and will labour to make thee full of growing' (1.4.28f.), even as the Lord labours in planting the houses of his people. 'Thou hast planted them, yea, they have taken root: they grow . . . they bring forth fruit.' But, because of their perversity, the Lord kindles fire on the tree, 'and the branches of it are broken'. (Jeremiah, xi.16–17, xii.2) In the same manner when Macbeth becomes cankered, he is styled 'ripe for shaking'.[2] (4.3.237) Like Gloucester, assailed by Cornwall, his corky arms are bound fast (3.7.29): he has no marrow in them.[3] Like the dying Mortimer, in Shakespeare's first play, he is pithless,

> a withered vine
> That droops his sapless branches to the ground.
> (*1 Henry VI*;, 2.5.11f.)

The fall of such a man is not adventitious: it is organic. That is the point and the use of the image. Evil is felt as dessication.

> If so the stocke be dryèd with disdayne,
> Withered and sere the branch must needes remaine.
> (*Leir*, ll. 1242f.)

[1] Sig. Q4r, fol. 116, in William Baldwin and Thomas Palfreyman, *A treatyce of Moral philosophy*, London, 1564.

[2] So Edgar, in *Lear*: 'Know, my name is lost; By treason's tooth bare-gnawn, and canker-bit.' (5.3.121f.)

[3] Thus Harsnett, p. 23, writes of 'an old corkie woman'.

The process is sequential, admits of no gainsaying:

> The good soule graffeth goodnes, wher of saluation is the frute, but the euel planteth vices, the frute wherof is damnation.[1]

The tree infected: Lear's long-engrafted condition (1.1.300), is the right emblem of the wicked, who do violence on themselves. The tree, sound and whole, signallizes equally well health, which is virtue, in the man; long-maturing friendship between man and man;[2] continuity, a natural progression, in the state; and even the triumph of life over death. The sons of Edward III are felt as growing from their father: they are seven fair branches sprung from a single root. (*Richard II*, 1.2.13) Elizabeth also grows organically from that monarch, verifying the prophecy Robert Greene assigns to Friar Bacon:

> From forth the royal garden of a king
> Shall flourish out so rich and fair a bud.
> (*Friar Bacon and Friar Bungay*, 4.3)

(Plate IX) Henry VIII arises from Lancaster and York.[3] Jesse, who is the ultimate source of the figure, gives rise to all his descendants: 'And there shall come forth a rod [*virga*] out of the stem of Jesse, and a Branch shall grow out of his roots.' (Isaiah, xi.1–3) Sometimes the Virgin Mary (by confusion with *virgo*) is taken as the chief of those descendants; her *flos* or flower is Christ. And sometimes the rod or branch prefigures Christ himself. But the whole process, whatever its particulars, is seen always as the flowering of a single tree.[4] (Plate X) Even in the

[1] Thus William Baldwin, borrowing from Seneca (by way of the *Apophthegmes* of Erasmus), in *A treatise of Morall Phylosophie*, London, 1547, Sig. I6v. See also *Court of Virtue*, Sig. R8v.

[2] Friendship grows like a tree in Boissard, *Emblematum liber*, Metz, 1588, Sig. I1r, p. 65.

[3] See Edward Hall, *The union of the two . . . famelies of Lancastre & Yorke*, 1550, t.p.

[4] Many illustrations are given in Arthur Watson, *The Early Iconography of the Tree of Jesse*, Oxford, 1934. An article by the same writer, 'The Imagery of the Tree of Jesse on the West Front of Orvieto Cathedral' (pp. 149–64 in Fritz Saxl: *A Volume of Memorial Essays*, ed. D. J. Gordon, London, 1957), documents the use of the tree in religious architecture. In fact, all one need do to be impressed with the extent of the convention is to look at the representations in stained glass in almost any medieval cathedral.

charnel house, from the skeleton itself, the tree, signifying virtue, flourishes and springs.[1] (Plate XI)

> Only the actions of the just
> Smell sweet, and blossom in their dust.

Virtue, the pure conscience, is man's laurel tree, impervious to the lightning, the emblem of victory and joy.[2] The virtuous man plants his roots in the house of the Lord: he shall stand and flourish whatever storms come against him. (Plate XII) But to abdicate virtue is to tear up one's roots, to be slivered and disbranched, to wither—and I quote from Whitney's *Choice of Emblemes*—'like the blasted boughes that die'. (P. 67)

Our vices manifestly are made instruments to plague us. Men are punished with their own abominations.[3] Aquinas, who sums up with more eloquence and precision even than Hooker this conception of what may be called implicit Providence entertained by the Renaissance and dramatized in Shakespeare's play, finds

> The rational creature, man . . . subject to Divine providence in the most excellent way possible; it has a share of Eternal Reason, whereby it has a natural inclination to its proper end and act.

Because man is endowed with 'the light of natural reason—the imprint of the Divine light . . . he is able to discern what is good and what is evil'. It is this 'ineradicable habit or law of the mind', which must incite each man through the agency of conscience 'to good and [to] murmur at evil'. As man chooses the evil way, he himself 'accuses, rebukes, and torments' himself.[4] The evil man, that is to say, does himself to death. Let humanity commit vile offences, and it will fall—perforce: the decisive assertion—to preying on itself. (4.2.47–50)

The gods are provident, no question. But to bring them 'vpon the stage . . . thundring, clapping, and flashing out

[1] See also Horozco, *Emblemas*, Sig. M5r, p. 85. The emblems gloss, in some sense, the saying of Psalm xcii: 'The righteous shall flourish like the palm tree. . . . They shall still bring forth fruit in old age.' (12, 14)

[2] Conscience figures so in Sambucus, *Emblemata*, pp. 14f.; and in Whitney, *Emblemes*, Sig. I2r, p. 67.

[3] Thus Jeremiah, ii.19: 'Thine own wickedness shall reprove thee.'

[4] *Summa*, I–II.91.2; I.79.12, 13.

. . . the huge thunder cracke of adiuration',[1] as Shakespeare does in *Cymbeline*, is a piece of unnecessary crudeness. The gods are subtler than that, more cunning, more covert. They do not hurl thunderbolts. They work rather

> With windlasses and with assays of bias,
> [And so] By indirections find directions out.

They commend to the sinful man a poisoned chalice. (*Macbeth*, 1.7.10–12) He drinks it and dies. That is why Albany and Cornwall, who have borne hard rein against the old kind king (3.1.27f.), must fall to fighting among themselves. (2.1.11f., 3.1.19–21)

> Mark the high noises.
> (3.6.114)

That is why the usurpers quarrel in *1 Henry IV*, why Regan sickens, and Goneril must come to deadly use.

> I had rather lose the battle than that sister
> Should loosen him and me.
> (5.1.18f.)

If a man cannot be honest, neither can he be valiant, neither can he be capable. He is

> but naked, though locked up in steel,
> Whose conscience with injustice is corrupted.
> (*2 Henry VI*, 3.2.234f.)

That is why Albany grows full of alteration (4.2.3–11, 5.1.3f., 21–27), why Macbeth

> cannot buckle his distempered cause .
> Within the belt of rule.
> (5.2.15f.)

It falls out, as you would think, that 'The tyrant's people on both sides do fight' (5.7.25), that Malcolm and his English allies

> have met with foes
> That strike beside us.
> (5.7.28)

But there is in the fact this subtler truth: the tyrant is up-

[1] Harsnett, p. 108.

braided, not merely by his people but, more cruelly and decisively, by himself. Heavy conscience sinks his knee. (*Cymbeline*, 5.5.413) His senses are pestered. They cannot choose but recoil

> When all that is within him does condemn
> Itself for being there.
>
> (5.2.23–25)

Give appetite his head,

> And appetite, a universal wolf,
> So doubly seconded with will and power,
> Must make perforce a universal prey,
> And last eat up himself.
>
> (*Troilus and Cressida*, 1.3.121–4)

The emblem writer, no less than the dramatist, discovers evil eating up itself. That is how he interprets the fable of the fox and the eagle. The wicked, as they are powerful, insult over the weak. 'Yet soone, or late, the Lorde in iustice strikes.' The eagle that swoops down on the little foxes and destroys them finds its own nest and offspring consumed, *tôt ou tard.*[1] It needs, as I have said, only time. So Cordelia admonishes her sisters:

> Time shall unfold what plaited cunning hides.
> Who cover faults, at last shame them derides.
>
> (1.1.283f.)

In the event Cordelia is justified. Time, necessarily, reveals Truth. So profoundly does belief in that promised revelation impinge on the imagination of the Renaissance that the central fact of its theology, the epiphany of the divine principle on earth, witnesses—perhaps unconsciously—to it. In sixteenth-century religious art, Truth is unfolded when Mary unveils the infant Jesus. Dekker, in *The Whore of Babylon*, dramatizes the unfolding. In the dumb show preceding the play, Time and Truth banish falsehood: here, the plaited cunning of the Papists. In allegorical painting Rubens, in the sixteenth century, Poussin, in the seventeenth, attest to the triumph of

[1] *Fables D'Esope*, Paris, 1689, Sig. B4r, p. 23: 'Les méchans qui oppriment par leur puissance les miserables, périssent tôt ou tard.' For another representation, see Francis Barlow (1626–1702), 'Fox and Eagle', Oxford, Ashmolean Museum, engraved for Ogilby's *Aesopico*, 1668 (given in Woodward, pl. 32). The quotation is from Whitney, *Emblemes*, Sig. F1r, p. 41.

Truth.[1] Bronzino discovers Time and Truth tearing the specious cover from Luxury: whom shame at last derides. In a Renaissance tapestry (after Bronzino), Time rescues Truth and vindicates Innocence.[2] And so the twin functions of Time the Revealer are presented. Shakespeare describes them in *The Rape of Lucrece*:

> To unmask falsehood and bring truth to light.
> (l. 940)

Early in the sixteenth century, a Venetian printer embodies them in his emblem: Truth, attacked by the monster Calumnia, rises toward Heaven out of the abyss, assisted in her progress by Time.[3] Early in the seventeenth century, an English bookseller does the same: in his device, winged Time rescues Truth from a cavern as, in the device of Mary Tudor, Truth is brought by Time from the pit. The Catholic Queen dies, a Protestant succeeds, but the image and the understanding that informs it remain constant. When Elizabeth enters London, a street theatre offers for her instruction a tableau of two kingdoms, figured by hills, one prosperous, one failing. From the cave which divides them Time emerges with Truth, who carries in her hand and presents to the Queen the *Verbum Dei*, the Bible in English.[4] The darkness of the false faith is irradiated, in time, by the light of the true. Time unfolds what cunning hides.

Nor must one take the words as pious ejaculation, a poet's facile saw: Truth crushed to earth shall rise again. There is no

[1] Richelieu ordered from Poussin, *c.* 1641, a Triumph of Truth. G. B. Tiepolo executed drawings of Time and Truth, now in the Metropolitan Museum. François Le Moine painted Time revealing a naked Truth over a prone figure holding a mask (Wallace Collection, London). For a compendium of famous lines on Time revealing Truth, see under 'Time and Truth' in B. Stevenson, *Home Book of Quotations*, New York, 1934.

[2] Bronzino's 'Allegory' is in the National Gallery, London. It is from a cartoon of the London painting that the Florentine tapestry derives. Described *Studies in Iconology*, pp. 84, 86–91, and illustrated fig. 66. For a full discussion of the subject, see Panofsky's entire chapter, 'Father Time', pp. 69–93.

[3] Marcolino da Forlì's emblem for the Bottega della Verità is given, facing p. 199, in Fritz Saxl, 'Veritas Filia Temporis', *Philosophy & History: Essays Presented to Ernst Cassirer*, Oxford, 1936. The English reformer, an agent of Thomas Cromwell, who prepares a primer of 1535, draws also on medieval pictures of Christ's descent into Limbo in depicting the liberation of Christian Truth from Roman Catholic hypocrisy. Illustrated Saxl, p. 205.

[4] Kernodle, p. 97; Saxl, p. 207.

treacle, no mustering of spirits, no hint of Robert Browning at the window in the emblem that adorns an anonymous account of the Overbury murder: *Truth Brought to Light and Discovered by Time*. A tree laden with books and documents sprouts from the coffin.[1] (Plate XIII) The sense of the picture is patent: the identity of the murderer is certain to follow. The engraver of the title page is suggesting—after Rosalind, in *As You Like It*—that only Time is requisite, the old justice that examines all such offenders. He is content to let Time try. (4.1.203f.) But there is in his acquiescence, as in Cordelia's adjuring of her sisters, an intelligent, a reasoned confidence whose ground is more than wishing and willing. He does not suppose that God or His viceroy Time will pull a curtain to discover the murderer behind it. It is rather that the murderer will discover himself, on the analogy that poison, when it is quaffed, will commence, however slowly, to bite the spirits.

Shakespeare's work from the beginning, drawing on the analogy to dramatize the sequel of unnatural behaviour, conveys that assurance. What is more, it confirms it in action. Cardinal Beaufort, a wicked man, dying,

> whispers to his pillow . . .
> The secrets of his overchargèd soul.
> (*2 Henry VI*, 3.2.375f.)

The point of the scene from the very early play is remembered and recapitulated later, in a graver and more terrible context: 'Infected minds', says the Doctor, who ministers to Lady Macbeth, 'To their deaf pillows will discharge their secrets.' (5.1.80f.) Time's office and glory, asserts Lucrece—it is her comfort—is to work that discharge, at last 'To mock the subtle in themselves beguiled'. (l. 957) The murder of the Duke of Gloucester will be redressed, says Gaunt to the importunate widow, when Heaven sees the hours ripe on earth. (*Richard II*, 1.2.6–8) Isabella, cozened by Angelo, balked for the moment of justice, awaits the unfolding, in

[1] At the top, flanking the figure of King James beneath a curtain, are, left: naked Truth, surmounting Error with his crutch; and, right: Time, treading on the skeleton, the image of Death. John Droeshout's engraving is particularly interesting and much the more compelling in that it fuses the image of Truth and Time with that of husbandry.

ripened time
. . . [of] the evil which is here wrapped up
In countenance.
(*Measure for Measure*, 5.1.116–18)

So, conversely, with the goodness which Kent disguises in himself: the ill-suiting weeds in which he is attired are not to be doffed, the truth which he embodies is not to be known, until time thinks it meet. (4.7.6–11)

Truth, manifest in Goneril's letter to Edmund, will be revealed to Albany 'in the mature time'. (4.6.277–9) Edgar, the instrument of the revelation, will appear to confirm it, 'When time shall serve'. (5.1.48f.) Even Edmund bears witness to the empery of Time. For the evil he has done, he is sure that 'the time will bring it out'. (5.3.162f.)

His assurance is verified. 'He that covereth his sins, shall not prosper', but not because Polonius might have said so. Edmund's lines, and Cordelia's, and the Biblical Proverb (xxviii.13) on which her couplet depends are sustained by the action of the play. Time leads on the triumph of Truth.[1] (Plate XIV) Error, who is known by his crutch, cannot stand in that ultimate judgement. Nor is it the dramatist who tells you so, but the drama. Even Death is tumbled down, who lays his icy hand on kings. Time treads on the skeleton, in Droeshout's engraving. Death has no dominion over virtue, which is Truth.[2] (Plate XV) The gravamen of Boissard's image, in which the skeleton holds aloft an hour-glass as, in Bernini's tomb of Alexander VII, he raises toward the kneeling Pope a glass in which the sands have all run, is not that Death triumphs over humanity, but that Truth is triumphant over Time.[3]

For Truth, to the Renaissance, is Time's daughter and heir. (Plate XVI) *Veritas filia temporis.* Erasmus announces the relation. Bacon corroborates it. The private man and the sovereign agree in finding it valid. A minor English poet of the seventeenth century celebrates it in his verses. A sixteenth-

[1] At the top: emblems of the Trinity, Justice, Mercy, Nature, Love, Time and his daughter Truth, Nemesis mounted upon Pegasus. At the sides: two crowned women kneeling, one with two children, the other with what appears to be an infant. Beneath them: the New Jerusalem and the Ark. At the foot: Peace, Justice, and the author at the age of 31. [2] *Sola Vistus Est Funeris Expers* (Boissard). [3] Bernini's tomb (1671–8) is in St. Peter's, Rome.

century Italian is sure that 'Time . . . being the Father of Truth cannot and will not suffer her to remain hidden under any deceit or fraud'. Whitney's emblem communicates the same assurance. Truth may be fettered in a dungeon:

> Yet Time will comme, and take this ladies parte,
> And breake her bondes, and bring her foes to foile.

Time, to paraphrase a doggerel couplet by Thomas Kyd, 'Time . . . the author both of truth and right . . . will bring . . . [all] sins, all treachery to light'. Queen Mary, who has her own reasons for crying Amen, engraves the Latin motto on her coins and State seal, and takes it for the legend on her crest.[1] It is much more than ill mannered to misconceive or to call in question the relation which that legend announces. It is fatal. That is the conclusion which the denouement of *King Lear* enforces. Time brings in his revenges. Justice and Providence obtain.[2] But the agent is the peccant man himself.

[1] For Erasmus, see *Adagiorum opus*, Basle, 1526, p. 436; and Saxl, p. 200 n.: 'quendam veterum poetarum Veritatem Temporis Filiam vocasse, quod licet aliquando lateat, temporis progressu in lucem emergat.' For Bacon: *Works*, Ellis and Spedding, 1857, I, 191; and Saxl, p. 220: 'Recte enim Veritas filia Temporis dicitur, non Auctoritatis.' The English poet is Thomas Peyton (*The Glasse of Time*, 1620, the t.p. of which is reproduced here as pl. XIV). Anton Francesco Doni writes of Truth as Time's daughter in *La Moral Filosofia*, Venice, 1552. See Gertrud Bing, 'Nugae circa Veritatem: Notes on Anton Francesco Doni', pp. 304–12 in *Journal of the Warburg Institute*, vol. I, London, 1937, p. 306, and fig. 46a. For Kyd, see *Sp. Trag.*, 2.4.174f. Queen Mary is hailed by the Bishop of Winchester: 'Veritas iam proxima est.' Chew, pp. 69–90, cites Renaissance works in which Truth appears as Time's daughter.

[2] God—and let him be, at your pleasure, explicit, implicit—God lives and sees and, given time, will stretch forth his hand: *Dominus vivit & videt.* Whitney, *Emblemes*, Sig. f3r, p. 229, gives an emblem (available in *Shakespeare and the Emblem Writers*, p. 416) depicting Adam hiding in the garden, and thinking, oblivious of the sense of the Latin tag quoted here, to deny an answer to the voice that seeks him out.

IV

FORTUNE

Now if a man disputes the regnancy of law, manifest in portents and prodigies, and in the twin concepts of Providence and kind, if he says, with Edmund,

> Tut, I should have been that I am had the maidenliest star in the firmament twinkled on my bastardizing,
>
> (1.2.142–4)

he is not, paradoxically, freeing himself. He is fettering himself. It is true, I suppose, that Shakespeare, like Edmund, disbelieved in judicial astrology. Henry Cornelius Agrippa, defining that mock discipline, exposes sufficiently the vulgarity of its pretensions:

> There yet remaineth an other kinde of Astrologie, which is called Diuinatorie, or Iudiciall, the which entreateth of the reuolutions of the yeares of the world, of natiuities, of questions, of elections, of intentes and thoughtes, it teacheth moreouer to fore tell, to call backe, to auoide or flee the endes of all thinges that maie happen, and the secrete disposition of Gods prouidence.

Calvin despises astrology, and rightly.[1] So do his more thoughtful contemporaries. Gloucester, owing allegiance to a pseudoscience, is therefore not sophisticated but simple. Edgar's wonder, that his brother, whose professions he confounds with belief, should grow to a sectary astronomical, his incredulity, his amusement, are meet.

[1] For Agrippa, see Sigs. M8v–N1r, in *Of the Vanitie and Vncertaintie of Artes and Sciences*, tr. Ia. San [ford]. Gent., London, 1569. Calvin's disbelief is set forth in *An Admonicion against Astrology Iudiciall*, tr. G. G[ylby], 1561. See particularly Sig. B1r.

Do you busy yourself about that?
(1.3.155)

But tact is requisite here. Gloucester, making guilty of our disasters the sun, the moon, and the stars, seems to discountenance free will. Edmund, ostensibly, defends it.

> An admirable evasion of whoremaster man, to lay his goatish disposition to the charge of a star!
> (1.3.137f.)

But Gloucester's simplicity looks to the truth, albeit in superstitious ways.

> Blind fear that seeing reason leads finds safer footing than blind reason stumbling without fear.
> (*Troilus and Cressida*, 3.2.76–78)

Gloucester is purblind: he has got his hieroglyphics wrong. But, however obliquely, he perceives their existence. Superstition is not so mad as self-sufficiency. For it posits a cause.

Edmund is blind altogether. He owns to no agency. He conceives of man as a natural, in his sense a bestial, a wilful, phenomenon. He is therefore made thrall to a mechanistic psychology, to a kind of puerile determinism, from which he cannot possibly depart.

> Men
> Are as the time is.
> (5.3.31f.)

His apprehension is that crude, his freedom that circumscribed. Like Richard III, his predecessor in Shakespeare's gallery of self-made men, he is precisely the slave of nature. (1.3.230.) Characteristically, indeed inevitably, he apostrophizes Fortune (2.1.19), on whose wheel, now ascending and now turning downward again, the self-sufficient man, the individualist, must always climb.[1] (Plate XVII)

[1] Rollenhagio, Sig. A3r, glosses his emblem of Fortune: 'Le Sage cependant mesprisant sa puissance, S'esleue iusque au ciel par sa ferme constance.' For other emblems of Fortune, see Lydgate, *The Siege of Troy*, MS Royal 18 Dii, *c.* 1450, given in Farnham, *The Medieval Heritage of Elizabethan Tragedy*, facing p. 16; Campbell, p. 12; Howard R. Patch, *The Goddess Fortuna in Mediaeval Literature*, Cambridge, Mass., 1927 (12 plates).

It is a slippery business. For the wheel, endlessly turning, suggests not only its untrustworthy nature, but the insecurity of Fortune herself. Art and literature describe it. The goddess in whose service Edmund goes stands uneasily upon the sea.[1] One foot seeks for its stay, the plunging dolphin. Another 'is fixed upon a spherical stone, which rolls, and rolls, and rolls'. The veil that encircles her is bellied out by the winds. The mast is shattered to which she clings for support. Safety eludes her; danger is her constant companion. Like a ship at the mercy of the waves, she never knows to what haven, or peril, she will be carried. She is painted blind, with a muffler before her eyes. It follows, to Primaudaye, that 'They are very blinde, who, calling Fortune blinde, suffer themselves to be guided and led by her'. 'She is painted also with a wheel,' as Fluellen describes her, in *Henry V*, and this 'to signify to you, which is the moral of it, that she is turning, and inconstant, and mutability, and variation.' (3.6.31–38) This Fortune is a right whore. Whatever she gives

> she deals it in small parcels,
> That she may take away all at one swoop.
>
> (*White Devil*, 1.1)

The man is therefore Fortune's fool who calls himself Fortune's steward: as Falstaff does when his banishment is almost upon him. (*2 Henry IV*, 5.3.136f.) Only those who will not see found their hope and trust in Fortune.[2]

[1] See Corrozet, *Hecatomgraphie*, 1540, emblem 41; and *Shakespeare and the Emblem Writers*, p. 262. Fors Fortuna, the mutable goddess, appears in Ovid, *Tristia*, V. viii.15–18; Pliny the Elder, *Natural History*, ii.22; Horace, *Odes*, III.xxix.51f.; Juvenal, *Satires*, X.363; Virgil, *Aeneid*, vi. 748f.; Tibullus, I.v.69f.; Cicero, *Oration vs. Piso*, cap. x. See also Patch, *The Goddess Fortuna*, pp. 11–13, 121f., 150; and Patch, 'The Tradition of the Goddess Fortuna', *Smith College Studies in Modern Languages*, Northampton, Mass., 1922, III, 131–235. The Romans, conceiving of a goddess who rules the storm and guides or misguides the tossing vessel, paid homage to Fortune of the sea.

[2] Primaudaye, ch. 44: 'Of Fortune', p. 192. A similar contempt is the burden of the chapter entitled 'Of Fortune' in Baldwin-Palfreyman, edn. 1564, Sigs. X4r–6r. Seneca reflects constantly on the fickleness of Fortune. H. V. Canter compiles a catalogue of sententious references taken from the plays, in *Rhetorical Elements in the Tragedies of Seneca*, University of Illinois Studies in Language and Literature, Urbana, Ill., 1925, X, 97. Brant, *La nef des folz du monde*, Paris, 1497, Sigs. f3v–4v, includes a section on the mutability of Fortune, illustrated by a fine emblem of the wheel. Patch, *The Goddess Fortuna*, p. 38, lists invidious epithets and adjectives applied to Fortune, and current in Latin literature. He discusses and illustrates, on pp. 49–57, 164, the variable character of the goddess. The four figures who are

> What help can be expected at her hands
> Whose foot [is] standing on a rolling stone,
> And mind more mutable than fickle winds?
> (*Spanish Tragedy*, 1.2.28–30)

The intellectual acumen of Edmund is after all a pallid thing.

Now Kent also apostrophizes Fortune. (2.2.180; 5.3.280f.) He makes no question of her power to rain evil on the just and the unjust. But Kent—and the difference is absolute—Kent, like Banquo, keeps a bosom franchised. His equanimity in defeat matches that of King Edward in Shakespeare's early history, and rests on and betokens the same assurance.

> Though Fortune's malice overthrow my state,
> My mind exceeds the compass of her wheel.
> (*3 Henry VI*, 4.3.46f.)

Like Sir Thomas More (as Roper reports him), he understands that life and death are not within his keeping. More, announcing to his friends his refusal to attend the coronation of Anne Boleyn, is aware that his enemies, taking umbrage, may destroy him. 'It lieth not in my power but that they maye deuoure me.' That much any man, whatever his strength or present good fortune, must give away. The wise man adds, however, this condition: 'But god being my good lord, I will provide that they shall neuer deffloure me.'[1] The same condition is implicit in the behaviour and character of Kent. He may be cast down, like Cordelia. But in respect of those hardships that touch his own person, he is able, like Cordelia, to outfrown false Fortune's frown (5.3.6), and this because, like the Pompey of *Antony and Cleopatra*, he declines to be made the fool of Fortune. The decision is free, and his own.

> Well, I know not
> What counts harsh Fortune casts upon my face,
> But in my bosom shall she never come
> To make my heart her vassal.
> (2.6.54–57)

depicted, conventionally, as clinging to Fortune's wheel are called, significantly, *Regno, Regnavi, Sum sine Regno*, and *Regnabo*. The first, as the wheel turns, shall be last.

[1] William Roper, *The Lyfe of Sir Thomas Moore, knighte*, ed. Elsie V. Hitchcock, London, 1935, p. 59.

Choice is explicit; and choice, in this ultimate matter, Shakespeare never relinquishes. His tragic heroes enjoy, when all is said, no more security than Oedipus. Physically they are no freer than he, they see no further.

> But, oh, vain boast!
> Who can control his fate?

It is, however, Shakespeare's scheme, as it were his sole proviso, to image this saving conviction: that the will need not become the servant to defect, that man, who may be overthrown tomorrow, may die, at his own election, a free man or a captive. Choice is his: whether his neck submits to Fortune's yoke or his mind continues dauntless, to ride in triumph over mischance. (*3 Henry VI*, 3.3.16–18) That is all the volition Shakespeare compounds for; but it is everything.

> I will drain him dry as hay.
> Sleep shall neither night nor day
> Hang upon his penthouse lid.
> He shall live a man forbid.
> Weary sennights nine times nine
> Shall he dwindle, peak, and pine.

But though his bark may be tempest tossed, consigned from the moment of its putting forth to the malice and the whimsy of Fortune:

> Behold, he is in thine hand,

he cannot founder in his heart, the inmost place from which his current runs, unless he himself allows Fortune dominion there. Pericles, who bears a tempest which his mortal vessel tears, keeps his integrity inviolate. And so he rides it out. (4.4.29–31)

Agreed, that Fortune is sovereign in all the chances of this life. The man, in Gower's poem, who undertakes a voyage, may wonder and fearfully, 'If that fortuna with him stonde'. (*Confessio*, ii.2529) He never knows, nor can he know. Even Death, the last of all chances, is at the pleasure of Fortune. Sir David Lindsay gives to one of his characters the saying, 'I trow wan-fortune brocht me heir'—and 'heir' is the gallows, and the speaker is about to be hanged. (*Ane Satyre*, l. 4022) Fortune, then, may dog a man to death. The Biblical reservation: 'but save his life', is given away. So common is unmerited suffering that the Heavens have grown impervious to it. They can hear a good man groan, and not relent or compassion him. (*Titus*, 4.1.123f.)

But Fortune's dominion is not absolute, even so. Patience triumphs over Fortune.[1] Manly excellence or virtue, dressed out in the conventional accoutrements of Fortune, and standing on the waves with a dolphin for support, bears a striking but a specious resemblance to Fortune which, as it is specious, dramatizes more vividly the difference between them, and the superiority of the one to the other.[2] (Plate XVIII) Fortitude also, thriving on Fortune's malice, is represented as Fortune's superior.

> But in the wind and tempest of her frown,
> Distinction with a broad and powerful fan,
> Puffing at all, winnows the light away,
> And what hath mass or matter, by itself
> Lies rich in virtue and unmingled.
> (*Troilus and Cressida*, 1.3.26–30)

Fortune, as in Boccaccio's fable, having no portion in Poverty, is bested by Poverty.[3] Reason is proof against her blandishments, Nature having given us the wit to flout at Fortune. (*As You Like It*, 1.2.48f.) If the dwelling place of the goddess attests to her power in disposing of all temporal things, it is evidence also, to the reasonable man, that only bluntness of mind will offer to build happiness on them. For Fortune lives on a mountain, at the summit of earthly felicity.

> I have upon a high and pleasant hill
> Feign'd Fortune to be thron'd.
> (*Timon*, 1.1.65f.)

But the winds of chance assail that lofty place, and render everything that lodges there uncertain.

[1] 'La Patience triomphe de la Fortune.' Boccaccio, Lorenzo de' Medici, Froissart, Gower, Boethius, and others, moralize on the theme. See Patch, *Fortuna*, p. 83, n. 2; and Rudolf Wittkower, 'Chance, Time, and Virtue', *Journal of the Warburg Institute*, London, 1937, I, 316–21.

[2] The inferiority of Fortune to Wisdom is illustrated in Rollenhagio, emblem 97. A sword and palm are balanced on a winged ball and surrounded by a serpent, the emblem of eternity. The gloss (Sig. D4r): 'Victrix fortunae sapientia. Ce trencheant coutelas sur la boule volante, Et ce serpent couvert de palme triomphante, Vont demonstrans a l'oeil, comme par la vertue La fortune est vaincue, E son vol rabatu.'

[3] *De Casibus*, III, i, pp. 60ff.; and Patch, *Fortuna*, pp. 73f., 64, n. 1.

They that stand high have many blasts to shake them,
And if they fall they dash themselves to pieces.
(*Richard III*, 1.3.259f.)

(Plate XIX) More's youthful verses for the beginning of the *Book of Fortune* offer an alternative gloss:

Build not thine house on height up to the sky.
None falleth far, but he that climbeth high.
Remember, Nature sent thee hither bare;
The gifts of Fortune—count them borrowed ware.[1]

Those who bow their heads against the steepy mount, as Timon does, thinking to climb his happiness (1.1.77f.); who labour to the top, like the wicked Tamora, trusting thereby to be safe from Fortune's shot (*Titus*, 2.1.1f.), fall to their destruction

When Fortune in her shift and change of mood
Spurns down her late beloved.
(*Timon*, 1.1.86f.)

The conclusion you are to draw, and the course you are to follow, are set forth in Boethius, who furnishes the text and model for so many, like More, who come after him.

> He that would build on a lasting resting-place; who would be firm to resist the blasts of the storming wind . . . must leave the lofty mountain's top . . . The hill is swept by all the might of the headstrong gale . . . Let him fly the danger . . . let him be mindful to set his house surely upon the lowly rock. Then let the wind bellow . . . thy life will be spent in calmness, and thou mayest mock the raging passions of the air.
> (*Consolation of Philosophy*, II, Metrum 4)

Shakespeare is more succinct, but hardly less explicit. He witnesses to the casting down of Edmund. And the cause is not the nature of whoremaster man. It is that Edmund has given himself over to Fortune. But, after all, how should he not? If you disbelieve that B follows A, if you have no faith in sequence, where are you to go but to chance? how else are you to read life but as a lottery? But so to read is to misread, to say with Leontes, in *The Winter's Tale*,

[1] Quoted in R. W. Chambers, *Thomas More*, Ann Arbor, Mich., 1958, p. 157.

I am a feather for each wind that blows.
(2.3.154)

This is to give up volition, with which, the Renaissance was certain, each man is endowed. It is to let

the unthought-on accident . . . [be] guilty
To what we wildly do . . . [and thus to] profess
Ourselves to be the slaves of chance.
(4.4.548–50)

The result is predictable.

The wheel is come full circle, I am here.
(5.3.174)

One is not to trust to Fortune, that arrant whore (2.4.52), for Fortune is constant only in inconstancy. No faith inheres in her. She is, herself, maimed and incapable.[1] To Shakespeare, as to the Renaissance engraver (Plate XX)—and his conventional depiction tallies with a hundred others—she is

That goddess blind,
That stands upon the rolling, restless stone.
(*Henry V*, 3.6.27f.)

Those who rise as the wheel rises, fall as surely as it falls:

Base fortune, now I see, that in thy wheele
There is a point, to which when men aspire,
They tumble hedlong downe.
(*Edward II*, ll. 2627–9)

So Mortimer, in Marlowe's play, and before him, the emblem writers Sambucus and Whitney and Boissard. Seas alter, men die, the bravest ship goes down:

Which warneth all, on Fortunes wheele that clime
To beare in minde how they have but a time.[2]

The fickleness of Fortune, her giddiness, her blindness, these, I take it, are given:

[1] See Boissard, *Emblematum liber*, Sig. O3r, p. 93: 'Nvlli Prestat Velox Fortuna Fidem'; Horozco, *Emblemas*, Sig. P5r, p. 109: 'Pensier Auança Fortuna Manca.'

[2] See Whitney, *Emblemes*, Sig. B2r, p. 11; Sambucus, edn. 1584, Sig. C7v, p. 46; Boissard, *Emblematum liber*, Metz, 1588, Sig. D1r, p. 25: 'Humanae vitae conditio.'

> 'Tis common.
> A thousand moral paintings I can show
> That shall demonstrate these quick blows of
> Fortune's
> More pregnantly than words.
>
> (*Timon*, 1.1.89–92)

But to ebb and flow by the moon, to become a kind of shuttlecock, that is only a corner in the punishment reserved for those who do homage to Fortune. The empery of Fortune effects more than this: it works a metamorphosis in the man who avows its dominion, it overcomes his virtue, at last it gathers up his soul. The villain who announces his intention to play a part in Fortune's pageant (*2 Henry VI*, 1.2.66f.) chooses the exact metaphor. Enrolled in the pageant he becomes a man of wax, a lay figure whom others manipulate at their pleasure. Edmund, as he is Fortune's acolyte, is like a man made after supper of a cheeseparing. Goneril the whimsical is not herself any longer, but Vanity the puppet (2.2.36), as devoid of real substance as the wooden figures who act out the Morality plays.

> This' a good block!
>
> (4.6.185)

Brutus, who breaks at Philippi, is only another man fallen in the chances of life. Cordelia falls also. But Brutus, who is cozened by Cassius, who swallows the unconscionable saying that one must be cruel only to be kind, who undertakes the murder of a friend and finds reasons to cover it:

> In your bad strokes, Brutus, you give good words,
>
> (*Julius Caesar*, 5.1.30)

who, condemning suicide in Cato, ends a suicide himself, this Brutus is a man broken in more than body. That, at least, is how the emblem books moralize his story. *Fortuna virtutem superans.*[1] Suicide is censured. It is the last link—given its

[1] See *Andreae Alciati Emblematum Libellus*, Paris, 1536, p. 44; *Emblemes d'Alciat*, Sig. K2v, p. 148; and Whitney, *Emblemes*, Sig. I3v, p. 70. The sense of the latter is suggestively different. The 'noble harte' of Brutus, assailed by grief, scorns flight: 'my flighte with handes shalbee'. Addressing himself to suicide, Brutus, 'with courage great', discovers and announces that prowess waits on Fortune, and that 'fortunes force, maie valiant hartes subdue'. Whitney's Brutus is already the ambiguous figure of Shakespeare's play, at once overthrown and overthrowing.

antecedents, the necessary link—in a painful and ignominious chain.

How Shakespeare construed it is perhaps another matter—one, in any event, not responsive to easy apophthegms. Brutus, believing suicide cowardly and vile, resolves to arm himself with patience—Edgar's counsel to Gloucester—and look to the providence of those high powers that govern us below. (5.1.104–8.) But Brutus forswears his resolution, he plays the Roman fool, and this because—one is made somehow to feel—he bears too great a mind. Hamlet, acting on the gad, precisely as Macbeth does:

> The very firstlings of my heart shall be
> The firstlings of my hand,
> (4.1.147f.)

shoots his arrow over the house and hurts his brother. His punishment, and he perceives it, is the loss of his will. The Heavens make him their scourge and minister. Yet Horatio's farewell is just.

> And flights of angels sing thee to thy rest!

Antony, who gives himself to dotage, has lost his way for ever (*Antony and Cleopatra*, 3.11.3f.); and yet, palpably, not so.

Shakespeare I think has it both ways. His tragic heroes and villains commit themselves to Fortune, and so are altered, one would suppose irreversibly.

> But when we in our viciousness grow hard—
> Oh, misery on 't!—the wise gods seel our eyes,
> In our own filth drop our clear judgements, make us
> Adore our errors, laugh at 's while we strut
> To our confusion.
> (*Antony and Cleopatra*, 3.13.111–15)

But Shakespeare, perhaps unreasonably, allows a brief reprieve, a final welling up or recrudescence.

> Yet I will try the last.

Before the battle of Bosworth Field the rival captains address their troops: first (in Shakespeare's source) the evil Richard, and then, as the culmination, the pious and victorious

Richmond. Shakespeare deliberately reverses the order, and so makes more effective, and even attractive, the final speech of his villain.

> I have set my life upon a cast,
> And I will stand the hazard of the die.
>
> (*Richard III*, 5.4.9f.)

I suppose dramatic exigency, the irresistible attraction of that last efflorescence, to govern him here.

It does not always govern. Oswald is Fortune's fool, and Oswald dies still abused. He turns the wrong side out (4.2.9), a pretty thorough metamorphosis. Like Edmund, he repudiates causality. He does not believe that base conduct leads on to bad fortune. He is as duteous to the vices of his mistress as badness could desire. (4.6.258f.) In consequence, Nature disclaims in him: his soul is his clothes (*All's Well*, 2.5.48): he might have been made by a tailor. (2.2.59f.) He is unmanned, and this in accordance with the law which Mephistopheles, in a whimsical context, announces to Faust. A man is free to choose of the differing paths which present themselves to him (read: of this character or that). But having chosen, he must cleave to his choice. This is to say that, on his commitment, he is made the slave of nature.

> Das erste steht uns frei, beim zweiten sind wir Knechte.

Hence the terms with which Kent reviles Oswald. He is a servile cur, a kingfisher, a creature bereft of all volition, one of those who

> Renege, affirm, and turn their halcyon beaks
> With every gale and vary of their masters,
> Knowing naught, like dogs, but following.
>
> (2.2.84–86)

The halcyon smooths the commotion of the waves. He reaps the reward of peace and complaisance. *Ex pace ubertas.* (Plate XXI) He is, in iconography, a figure of peace. Turning his bill into the prevailing wind, he knows the weather well. The publisher, Fisher, who took the bird as his device because it punned on his name, and Boissard and Giovio, the contrivers of emblems, thought only to praise. Most Elizabethan writers—Gosson and Lyly, Lodge, Greene, and Nashe—are of the same mind: Happy the Halcyons.[1] Shakespeare turns the cat in the pan. His halycon is a type of the opportunist, the idolater of Fortune, whose wisdom, in proof, is no wisdom at all.

> The knave turns fool that runs away.
> The fool no knave, perde.

The halcyon's way, that of the follower-fool, is the way of Oswald, who might have survived the character of knave, beggar, and coward, and even the legacy descending to him as son and heir of a mongrel bitch; but who falters absolutely in his role as super-serviceable rogue. (2.2.17) For the man who seeks only to ascertain which way the wind blows that he may make himself the more conformable to it, this practical man, by a pleasant irony, is just the one whom the wind will capsize. Complaisance is not merely mean, but—more pertinent to the Oswalds and the Edmunds—it is poor policy. A sport, a weathercock, does not really look after itself. It has no autonomy. Only to snuff the wind or, to alter the metaphor, to catch hold of the wheel as it goes up the hill and so be drawn after (2.4.72–75), is to change an active, a man's role, for a passive, to become a sort of manikin, to be done to, not to do. The manikin, whose hallmark is passivity, complaisance, has got to take his chances. He—but gender is inapposite: sticks and stones have no gender—is the natural fool of Fortune. To serve without let is to please not oneself but some other. *Libera Mens Servire Negat.*[2] The ever-faithful servant is a perpetual ass.[3] 'And do not stand on quillets how to slay him' (*2 Henry VI*, 3.1.261) is the counsel a villain bestows on a fool.

Fortune's fool possesses no principles: these derive from the perception of sequence, the fit, the immitigable relation of

[1] See the printer's device in John Marston, *The History of Antonio and Mellida, The First Part*, London, 1602; William Meredith Carroll, *Animal Conventions in English Renaissance Non-Religious Prose (1550–1600)*, New York, 1954, pp. 105f.; and Paolo Giovio, *Dialogo dell' imprese*, Venice, 1562, for an emblem of the halcyon given in *Shakespeare and the Emblem Writers*, p. 392. Muir, in his edn. of *Lear*, p. 73n., cites complementary references in T. Lupton, *Tenth Book of Notable Things*; and *Jew of Malta*, 1.1.38f.

[2] See Whitney, *Emblemes*, Sig. N3r, p. 101: 'bondage is the Prison of the minde'; and Bruck, *Emblemata Bellica*, emblem 18, from which the quotation is taken.

[3] *Fidus servus perpetuus asinus*. This was the saying in old age of the Netherlander Vigilius, a time-serving politician who, through a long life, sacrificed his country to the Spaniards. See Motley, II, 287.

things. He cannot, consequently, discriminate between loyalty and slavishness. Oswald in a sense is loyal.

> My lady charged my duty in this business.
> (4.5.18)

But the man who does not ask, Who is my lady, and What is my duty, is not loyal but obsequious, and fatally so.

> Every good servant does not all commands:
> No bond, but to do just ones.
> (*Cymbeline*, 5.1.6f.)

The first command the sycophant follows, not thinking to poise and query it, makes him a captive.

> Freedom lives hence, and banishment is here.
> (1.1.184)

The last command kills him. For the rub is that principles are not a luxury, as the world likes to construe them, but indispensable. The unprincipled man never knows where he is. Aye and no is parlous divinity, alike for the courtier and the king.

> To plainness honour's bound
> When majesty stoops to folly,
> (1.1.150)

and not wholly for ethical reasons: to turn one's beak with each gale of the master is hardly to look after oneself.

The villain thinks otherwise. He confounds his passivity with forthputting behaviour.

> For my state
> Stands on me to defend, not to debate.
> (5.2.68f.)

But the look of the thing requires a gloss. Really to defend my state may require that I chastise it, resign it even. 'Wherein I am false, I am honest; not true, to be true.' (*Cymbeline*, 4.3.42) Debate, the poising of alternatives, marks the self-conscious man, mere reflexive action the puppet. To say, blandly:

> Now then, we'll use
> His countenance for the battle,
> (5.1.62f.)

or

That eyeless head of thine was first fram'd flesh
To raise my fortunes, (4.6.228f.)

or

All with me's meet that I can fashion fit, (1.2.200)

to say, in effect, that human beings are so many ciphers, their sum a *point d'appui* 'To raise my fortunes', is to make a cipher of oneself. For if a man cannot perceive the operation of sequence, if he miscalls it flux presided over by a blind and whimsical goddess, what is he then but a prisoner in flux.

The wise man for his part perceives that chance and caprice are only the façade of things. So perceiving, he turns his back on Fortune.[1] (Plate XXII) He understands, with Plutarch, that 'as for the power of Fortune . . . it bringeth downe those men that of their owne nature are cowards, fearefull and of small courage'.[2] He knows that, in all last things, Fortune's power is conditional.

> Neither must we attribute cowardlinesse to misfortune, nor valure and prudence to Fortune, who is not able to make a man great without vertue.

And the corollary: neither can Fortune make a man mean without his connivance. 'There is no time so miserable but a man may be true.' (*Timon*, 4.3.461f.) Fortune's sway encompasses everything, except the thing itself: the nature or definition of a man. It holds no power there unless a man, warring on himself, makes a breach in his own defences, unless, as the metaphor has it, he elects to climb on the wheel. Primaudaye is right: it is 'great blockishnesse to attribute . . . all casuall mishaps, both generall and particular, to certaine second causes'.[3]

For Fortune is after all a minor goddess, like the stars in fee to necessity. Fortune rules the rim of the wheel. God sits at the centre.

For Juno is the tresourere,
And fortune hir awmonere.[4]

[1] *Expers Fortunae Est Sapientia.*
[2] *The French academie*, ch. 44: 'Of Fortune', p. 196.
[3] *The French academie*, p. 136.
[4] Lydgate, *Reson and Sensuallyte*, ll. 1350f.

In *The Rape of Lucrece*, it is Time who turns the giddy round of Fortune's wheel. (l. 952) In the earliest known Spanish engraving on metal, Time, controlling Fortune, is himself controlled with reins held in the hands of God. To Boethius and to Dante, to Chaucer and Lydgate and Shakespeare, Fortune or Chance is a handmaiden merely, like Providence and the images derived from husbandry and Time a kind of notation, serving to make clear and dramatic and pictorial the way in which the evil man eats up himself.[1] Fortune is a metaphor, describing what happens after the important decisions have been made. The empery of Fortune is exercised always, after the fact. That is why wisdom (which is freedom), disbelieving in Fortune, is founded on the perception of necessity. Or, if you prefer another text, the beginning of wisdom is the fear of the Lord.

[1] See Chew, p. 9; and Patch, *Fortuna*, pp. 18f., 28f., 31f.

V

ANARCHY AND ORDER

THE last and most terrifying role played by the impious man is that of an anarch.

Blow, wind! Come, wrack!

But Lear offers the best example. He is unkind. Fortune in consequence makes his heart her vassal. And so he is buffeted; and so at last he despairs,

Bids the wind blow the earth into the sea,
Or swell the curlèd waters 'bove the main;
(3.1.5f.)

calls upon the thunder to

Smite flat the thick rotundity o' the world!
Crack nature's moulds, all germens spill at once
That make ingrateful man!
(3.2.7–9)

To read through all of Shakespeare, and then to return to passages like these, is to understand, I think, that he expresses in them his sense of the ultimate horror. Whenever he wishes to get at the nadir of human experience, he uses language of this kind. It is the same in the very early plays and the very late. Clifford, one of the principals in Shakespeare's second historical drama, discovers the dead body of his father:

Oh, let the vile world end
And the premisèd flames of the last day
Knit Earth and Heaven together!
(*2 Henry VI*, 5.2.40–42)

Timon the misanthrope speaks, in what is presumably the last of Shakespeare's tragedies:

> Piety and fear,
> Religion to the gods, peace, justice, truth,
> Domestic awe, night-rest and neighbourhood,
> Instruction, manners, mysteries and trades,
> Degrees, observances, customs and laws,
> Decline to your confounding contraries,
> And let confusion live!
>
> (4.1.15–21)

Florizel, the young hero of *The Winter's Tale*, seeking fit punishment for what is most heinous and least possible, is ready, if his faith should ever fail, to

> Let Nature crush the sides o' the earth together
> And mar the seeds within!
>
> (4.4.488f.)

The rebel Northumberland, informed of the death of Hotspur, his son, turns desperate:

> Let Heaven kiss earth! Now let not Nature's hand
> Keep the wild flood confined! Let order die!
>
> (*2 Henry IV*, 1.1.153f.)

The murderous Macbeth bids the Witches make answer, even though the waves

> Confound and swallow navigation up;
> Though bladed corn be lodged and trees blown down;
> Though castles topple on their warders' heads;
> Though palaces and pyramids do slope
> Their heads to their foundations; though the treasure
> Of nature's germens tumble all together,
> Even till destruction sicken.
>
> (4.1.53–60)

To trace the concept of Nature's germens, *rationes seminales*, the basic seeds of all living things, the stuff of creation, from St. Augustine through Sts. Anselm and Bonaventure, Albertus Magnus and Roger Bacon and Aquinas, is to be impressed, not so much with the antiquity of that concept as with the reverence accorded to it; and so with the magnitude, the more than desperate abandon of the curse. The metaphor which gives substance to the maledictions of Lear and those who share the abyss with him expresses the totality of their despair to the degree that it summons up the long-continuing and deeply disquieting sense of evil, for the dramatist and for his contemporaries, with which anarchy, the tumbling of Nature's germens, is invested.[1] Shakespeare's play evokes that sense of evil, neither for the first time nor the last. This is to say that in its evocation it is conventional, of its time, save of course, and always, for this: that no other play mirrors with such clarity or terror the horror attaching to anarchy, to the abdication of order and degree.

Great horror turns on great conviction: for who, without standards, will decry, or recognize even, a departure from the norm? In this case of *King Lear*, the central witnessing is to the primacy and rightness of order. Shakespeare, exalting order, appeals to sanctions almost mystical on their face but, in essence, prosaic, entirely practical. Intelligence divines the necessary: order is necessary if life is to be sustained: chaos, the antithesis of order, is also the abrogation of life. When the Renaissance anatomizes man, and the commonwealth in which he is subject, and the universe in which he moves, it professes to see everywhere gradations and connexions; it admits of no interstices, of nothing capricious. It is, in its reading, not Epicurean but Stoic. Bacon's *Advancement*, Caxton's *Mirror of the World*, *Batman upon Bartholemew*, *The Kalendar and Compost of Shepherds*, the catalogues of Lobel, Gesner, and Turner, Robert Recorde's *The Castle of Knowledge*, the elaboration of detail on the title pages of Elizabethan books: these attest to the same impulse, are done in the same faith.

Often the result is tedium, a pedantic (inapplicable) heaping up of detail. But the ordered vision of Hooker and the careful articulation of much of Shakespeare's verse—I have in mind particularly Queen Margaret's nautical similitude before the battle of Tewkesbury (*3 Henry VI*, 5.4.3–36), Canterbury's analogy of the honey bees in the first act of *Henry V*, Falstaff's disquisition on sherris, Menenius Agrippa's metaphor of the body—these are also a result.

[1] The traditional view of anarchy as the ultimate disaster is treated by W. C. Curry, *Shakespeare's Philosophical Patterns*, Baton Rouge, La., 1937, ch. II: 'Tumbling Nature's Germens', pp. 29–49.

> Oft have I seen a timely parted ghost,
> Of ashy semblance, meagre, pale, and bloodless,
> Being all descended to the labouring heart,
> Who, in the conflict that it holds with death,
> Attracts the same for aidance 'gainst the enemy;
> Which with the heart there cools and ne'er returneth
> To blush and beautify the cheek again.
>
> (*2 Henry VI*, 3.2.161–7)

When, in subsequent decades, men learn to prefer before all temples the upright heart and pure, the vision breaks and the sinews of poetry slacken. But not yet. To Shakespeare (as to Topsell and John Gerard and Thomas Cooper and Primaudaye) everything is at bottom contiguous; one explores the connexions.

Lear, striving in his little world of man to outstorm the wind and rain (3.1.10f.), is seen expressly as the microcosm, an abstract or model of all other things, a faithful rendering in little, agate-like, of the macrocosm, the greater world, which contains him. Here is Bacon, in *The Advancement of Learning*, on man figured as the microcosm, a kind of metonymy but engrossed: one part implying but also including the whole:

> Of all substances which nature hath produced, man's body is the most extremely compounded. For we see herbs and plants are nourished by earth and water; beasts for the most part by herbs and fruits; man by the flesh of beasts, birds, fishes, herbs, grains, fruits, water, and the manifold alterations, dressings, and preparations of the several bodies, before they come to be his food and aliment. Add hereunto, that beasts have a more simple order of life, and less change of affections to work upon their bodies: whereas man in his mansion, sleep, exercise, passions, hath infinite variations: and it cannot be denied but that the Body of man of all other things is of the most compounded mass.[1]

Ulysses, in *Troilus and Cressida*, analysing the dissension which frustrates the Greeks, isolates it—to use Bacon's phrase—in one 'exact or compendious image':

> Kingdomed Achilles in commotion rages
> And batters down himself.
>
> (2.3.185f.)

[1] Book II, pp. 109f., Everyman edn.

King John, beset by the claims of conscience and the wicked desire to achieve his cousin's death, finds in himself a civil tumult reigning,

> in the body of this fleshly land,
> This kingdom, this confine of blood and breath.
>
> (4.2.245–8)

Not man, generically (as Falstaff conceives of him), is warmed and exhilarated by wine: rather is the little kingdom of man incited by it to arm. 'And then the vital commoners and inland petty spirits muster me all to their captain, the heart, who, great and puffed up with this retinue, doth any deed of courage.' (*2 Henry IV*, 4.3.116–21)

It is, to alter the analogy, reminiscent of a nest of Chinese boxes, this Renaissance notion of part within part, and of the matchless congruence which this part displays in its connexion with and dependence on that other. The Ptolemaic universe is one emblem of that congruence. Copernicus, who begins its destruction, finds nevertheless 'a wonderful symmetry in the universe, and a definite relation of harmony in the motion and magnitude of the orbs'.[1] The hierarchy which obtains in the well-ordered state offers a second emblem:

> For government, though high and low and lower,
> Put into parts, doth keep in one consent,
> Congreeing in a full and natural close,
> Like music.
>
> (*Henry V*, 1.2.180–3)

The family has its dependencies: the man is the head of the woman. To dispute the relation, as Henry's queen Margaret does, who hampers and dandles her husband like a baby, makes against what is congruous. Thus the (scandalous) occasion of the proverb: 'Most master wear no breeches.'[2] (*2 Henry VI*, 1.3.148f.)

When Albany steps forward, to defend, in legal and churchly phrases, the right of his wife to marry the half-blooded fellow:

> 'Tis she is sub-contracted to this lord,
>
> (5.3.87)

[1] *De revolutionibus orbium celestium*, lib. I, cap. 10.
[2] 'The woman wears the pants'.

the impact of the tableau, which is, significantly, the moment of peripeteia, derives from one's awareness that the canons of church and law, now insisted on, however sardonically, have been scanted throughout the play by Edmund and Goneril and Regan. It is they who mimic, and not Albany, and we who recoil at the mimicry. When—another tableau—Goneril and Edmund play at chivalric romance:

> Yours in the ranks of death,
> (4.2.24)

their brute lust is made the more manifest by contrast with the character it seeks to assume. One's sense of the convention is never more acute nor more strongly asserted than when that convention is guyed.

> And, farewell, friends.
> Thus Thisby ends.
> Adieu, adieu, adieu.

Physiology also, and husbandry, furnish analogies. *King Lear* levies on all these, at once to dramatize what happens when the ideal is destroyed, and to set forth, by inference, the seals or spells which make good the destruction. It is a play about the relation of parent and child, husband and wife, master and servant, health and sickness, custom and the breach of custom, convention and aberration, the natural and the perverse, the use and the misuse of power, loyalty and sycophancy, chaos and concord.

The right relation lapses. The strong and manifold bond (2.1.49f.) no longer ties parents and children. Paternity is disavowed.

> I never got him.
> (2.1.80)

A daughter's dower is her father's curse. (1.1.207) Children make their parent an obedient parent, act towards him in the tender of a wholesome weal. (1.4.230)

> Old fools are babes again.
> (1.3.19)

A daughter, who knows or knew once the offices of nature, the bond of childhood (2.4.180), traduces her father to his vassal. (2.1.91–95) The father who thinks, like Ferardo in Lyly's *Euphues*, to reap comfort for his care—and the assumption is laconic: that is its point—finds obstinacy paid for obedience and, for duty, the dereliction of duty. A son-in-law, who is also a liege man, denies to speak with the king, his wife's father. It is as if the fixed stars no longer held to their courses.

> The images of revolt and flying off.
> (2.4.90)

The kingly father, necessarily, is counselled:

> You should be ruled and led.
> (2.4.149)

He must kneel, for mere necessities, to the child. This father makes his daughters his mother. (1.4.187f.) That other becomes as ward to the son. (1.2.73f.)

Aeneas, 'our great ancestor', on whose shoulders the wearied Anchises, his father, is brought safely out of Troy (*Julius Caesar*, 1.2.112–14), is the honoured and conventional emblem of loyal and natural behaviour. (Plate XXIII) *Pietas filiorum in parentes*. Shakespeare approves and dramatizes the legend in the person of young Clifford, who bears the body of his father 'As did Aeneas old Anchises bear'.[1] (*2 Henry VI*, 5.2.62) Edgar, disguised as Poor Tom, as he leads and supports the blinded Gloucester (4.1), enacts the familiar emblem. Edmund, who is called loyal and natural, distorts it to parody. In the world of *King Lear*, Edmund is the new Aeneas.

> The younger rises when the old doth fall.
> (3.3.26)

The child-like office for which he is praised is not the succouring of age, but its confounding with idle bondage and oppression. (2.1.106) But as he confounds—again, the wonted economy of the play—so is he confounded. Absalom also, the archetype of filial ingratitude as Aeneas is of filial duty, Absalom, like Edmund, misconstrues the relation of parent and child.[2] (Plate XXIV) The mistaking of each is the destruction of each.

[1] Whitney also, *Emblemes*, Sig. X2r, p. 163; and Horozco, Sig. R3r, p. 123, moralize the piety of Aeneas. Bernini memorializes it in a statue of 1618–19 in the Galleria Borghese, Rome. And see Green, p. 191; and Alciati, *Emblematum Libellus*, p. 73.

[2] The Death of Absalom is given also in Bocksperger, Sig. Glv.

No doubt it is a foolish father who sees his son a gentleman before him (3.6.13f.), who gives everything to the son and, in his waning age, sets foot under his table. (*Taming of the Shrew*, 2.1.402–4) But the son is more foolish, to build on the father's ruin.[1] And not because the homilies say so. Of course, it is precisely what they do say. 'We ought to have for our parents in their old age, the same care that they had for us in our childhood.'[2] So the good commonplace. The model of that recommended care is Cordelia. Like the kind son of Sidney's unfortunate king (*Arcadia*, 11.10), the only remnant of her happiness is to do a service to her parent.

> It is thy business that I go about.
> (4.4.24)

But if one assents to Aesop's saw, and Cordelia's devotion, and the unexceptionable saying of Corinthians that love 'seeketh not her own things' (1.xiii.4–5), it is not from vague piety alone, a merely sentimental concurrence. It is from the conviction that he's mad who tears the hand that feeds him. (3.4.15f.) Filial ingratitude is suicide. It reflects, most dramatically because most personally, the rash indifference to natural law—which is only the codification of the possible—that reaches its apogee in the disordered state, and culminates, willy-nilly, in chaos.

> Intestine strife, is fearefull moste of all.
> (Plate XXV)

That is why, at the beginning of his career, Shakespeare presents, as the right emblem of the civil warfare his early histories explore, the mortal conflict between fathers and sons.

> England hath long been mad, and scarred herself—
> The brother blindly shed the brother's blood,
> The father rashly slaughtered his own son,
> The son, compelled, been butcher to the sire.
> (*Richard III*, 5.5.23–26)

The conflict waxes. Not only great folks, despite the grave digger in *Hamlet*, have countenance to do themselves hurt. The

[1] Brant, Sigs. p 1v–2v, includes in his catalogue of fools those who withhold honour from their parents.

[2] *Fables D'Esope*, p. 221. Storks figure in Aesop's emblem as a corroboration of the central point: they are supposed to help one another in flying. See Ripa, *Iconologia*, under 'Commertio della Vita humana'.

I

II

III

IV

V

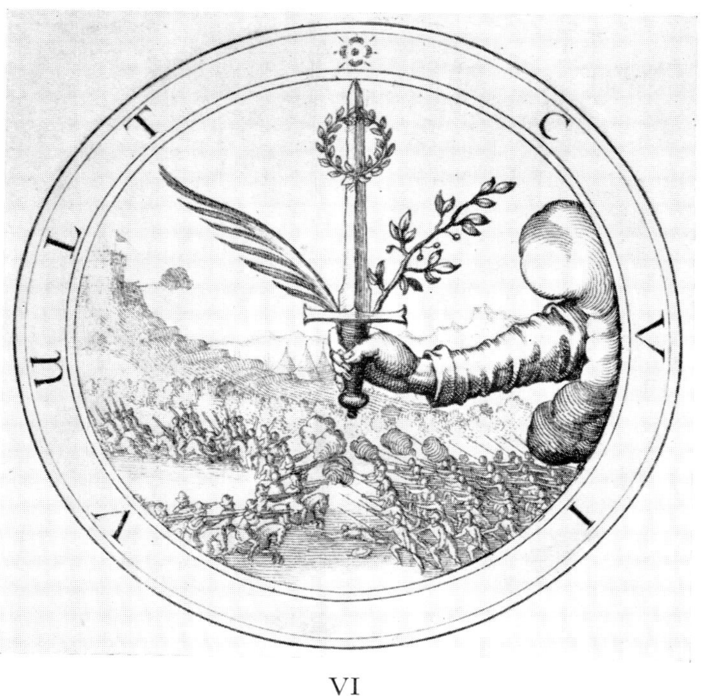

VI

PROVIDENTIA
FAMA BONA
FAMA MALA
THE HISTORY
OF THE WORLD
MAGISTRA VITÆ
TESTIS TEMPORV
EXPERIENTIA
NVNCIA VETVSTATIS
LVX VERITATIS
VERITAS
VITA MEMORIÆ
OBLIVIO
MORS
At London Printed for WALTER BVRRE.
1614

VII

Vngue Leo fisus credit tenuisse Draconem,
sed, quia iustus, eum iam Draco fecit ouem.
Hoc docet exemplum breuiter violenta perire,
solaq; in æternum viuere iusta solent.
Iustus ut palma
LVSITANIA LIBERATA
ab injusto Castellanorum dominio;
RESTITVTA
Legitimo Principi Serenissimo IOANNI IV.
Lusitaniæ, Algarbiorum, Africæ, Arabiæ,
Persiæ, Indiæ, Brasiliæ, &c. Regi Poten-
tissimo.
Summo Pontifici, Imperio, Regibus, Rebus-pub-
licis, cæterisq; orbis Christiani Principibus.
DEMONSTRATA.
Per D. Antonium de Sousa de Macedo Lusitanum, aulæ
Generosum; Regij ordinis Christi equitem, ac com-
mendatarium; in supremo Lusitaniæ Senatu Senato-
rem, Expeditoremq; grauaminum, atq; appellationum.
OPVS
Historico-Juridicum.
HAEC
VICIT.
Stemma Lusitan.
Insigne Regis Ioan. II.
Ordo Regius Lusit.
Insigne Regis Emanuel.

VIII

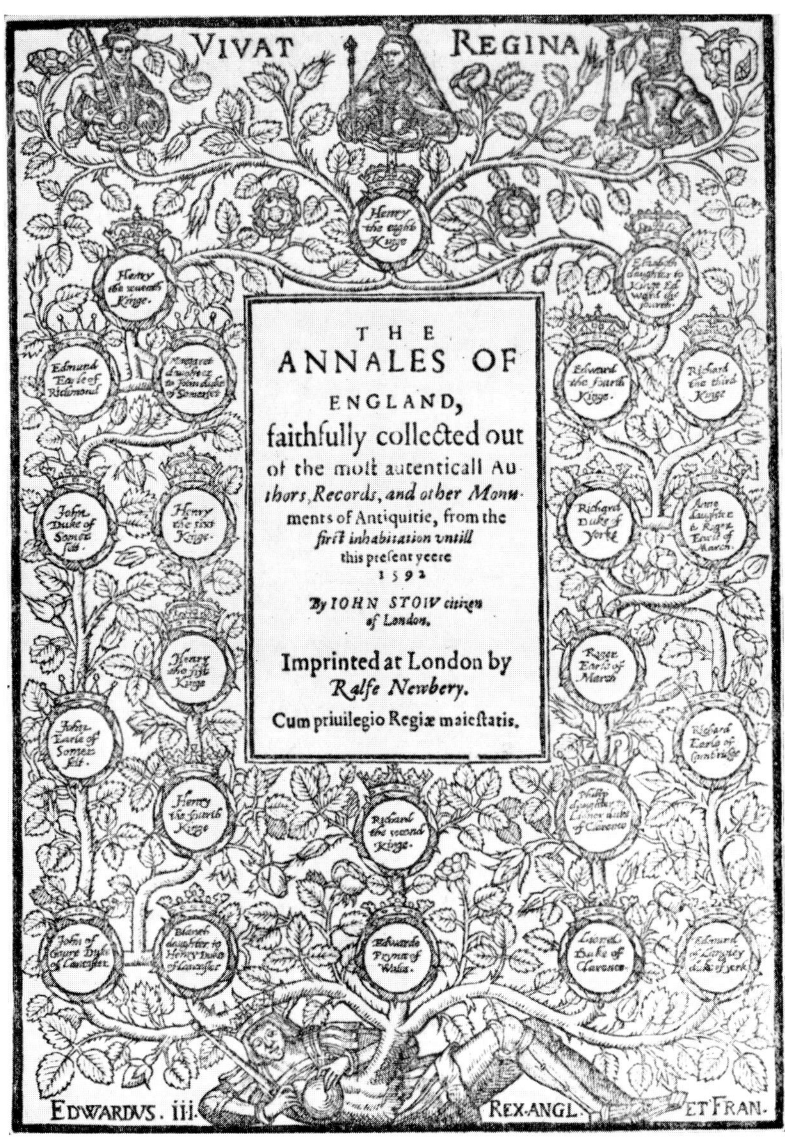

VIVAT REGINA

THE
ANNALES OF
ENGLAND,
faithfully collected out
of the most autenticall Au-
thors, Records, and other Monu-
ments of Antiquitie, from the
first inhabitation untill
this present yeere
1592

By IOHN STOW citizen
of London.

Imprinted at London by
Ralfe Newbery.

Cum priuilegio Regiæ maiestatis.

EDWARDVS. iii. REX.ANGL. ET FRAN.

IX

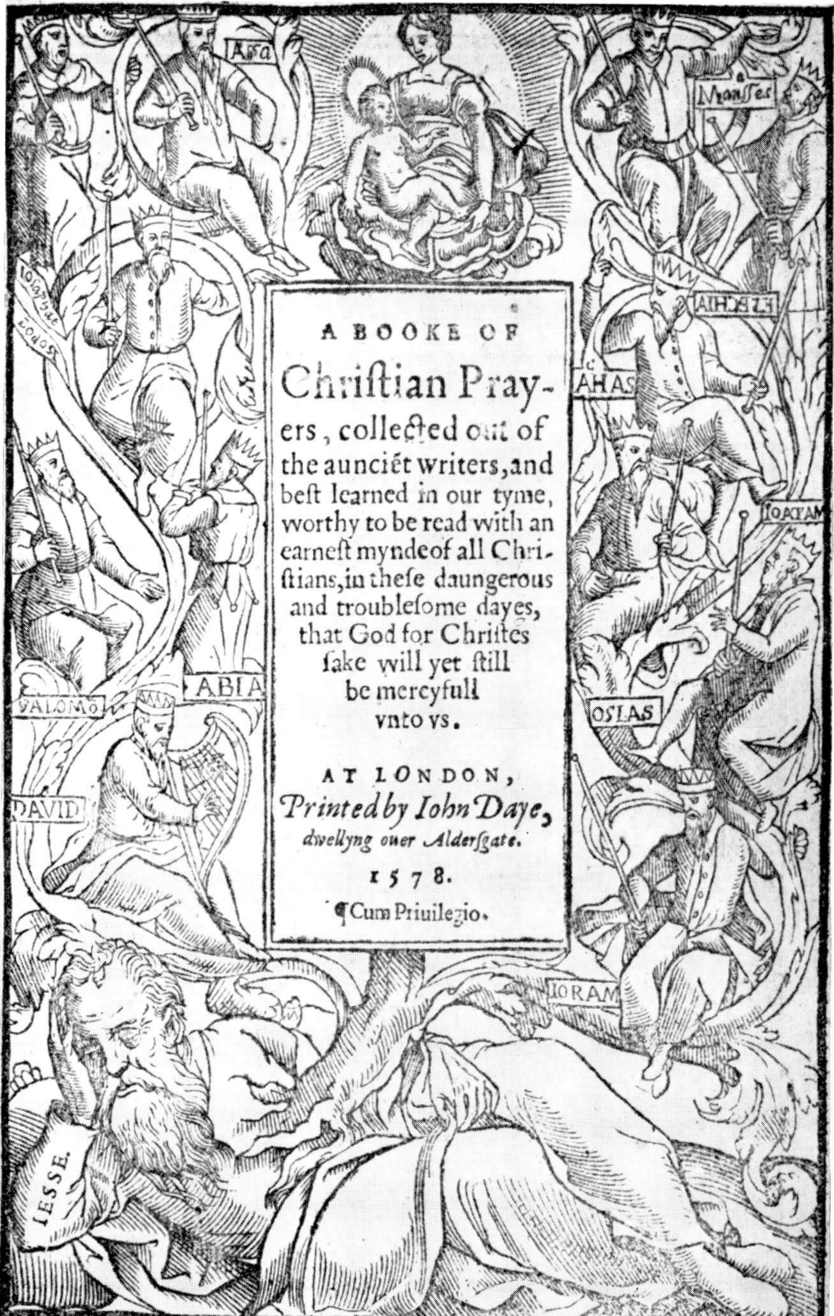

A BOOKE OF

Christian Prayers, collected out of the aunciet writers, and best learned in our tyme, worthy to be read with an earnest mynde of all Christians, in these daungerous and troublesome dayes, that God for Christes sake will yet still be mercyfull vnto vs.

AT LONDON,

Printed by Iohn Daye,

dwellyng ouer Aldersgate.

1578.

¶Cum Priuilegio.

ETSI
MORS,
INDIES
ACCELERAT
POST FVNERA VIRTVS
VIVET TAMEN
I.D.

XI

XII

TRVTH
Brought to light and
discouered by
Time
or
A
discourse
and
Historicall Narration
of the first XIIII yeares
of King Iames Reigne
London
Printed by Richard Cotes and are to be Sold by
Michaell Sparke at the Blew Bible in
Green 1651 Arber Iohn Droeshout sculp: Lon

XIII

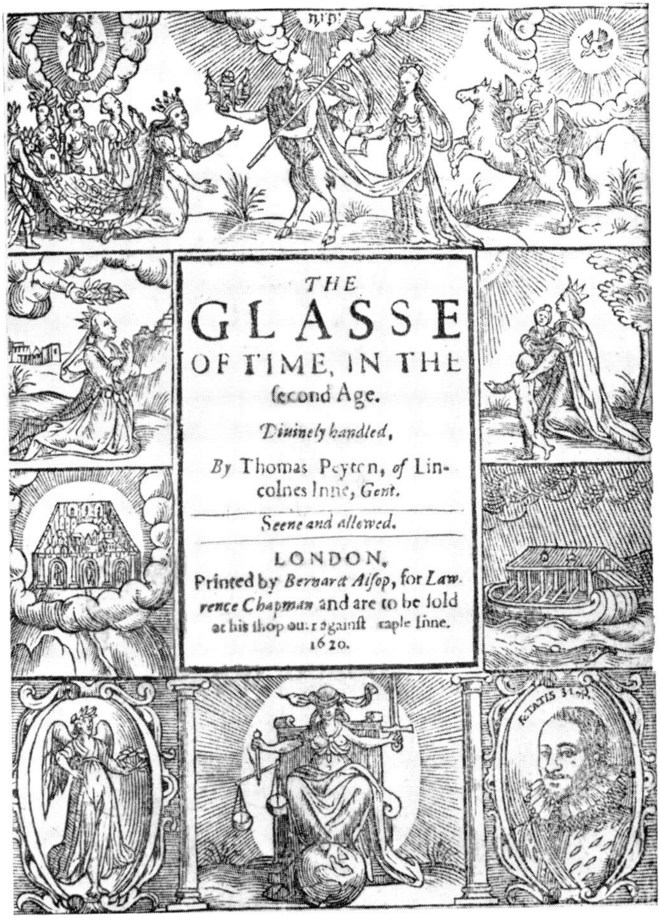

THE
GLASSE
OF TIME, IN THE
second Age.

Diuinely handled,

By Thomas Peyton, *of* Lincolnes Inne, *Gent.*

Seene and allowed.

LONDON,
Printed by *Bernard Alsop*, for *Lawrence Chapman* and are to be sold at his shop ouer against Staple Inne.
1620.

XIV

XV

XVI

XVII

XVIII

XIX

SVPERBIA & IVSTICIA AVARICIA

VNIO

DISSIDENTIVM, OMNIBVS unitatis & pacis amatoribus utilissima, ex præcipuis Ecclesiæ Christianæ doctoribus per Hermānum Bodium diuini uerbi concionatorē eximium selecta, & iam denuo aucta & locupletata: uerum ea diligentia curaq; à nobis nunc ab innumeris mendis ita repurgata, ut priores æditiones quantūuis adcuratas longe tamen uincat. Nam infinita penè loca malè citata restituimus, corrupta emendauimus, mutila suppleuimus. Quod facile deprchender, quisquis hanc cum prisinis editionibus cōtulerit.

¶ Doctores ex quibus hæc unio selecta est uersa indicabit pagella.

PRVDENCIA SPES

INVIDIA FORTVNA SVSPITIO

XX

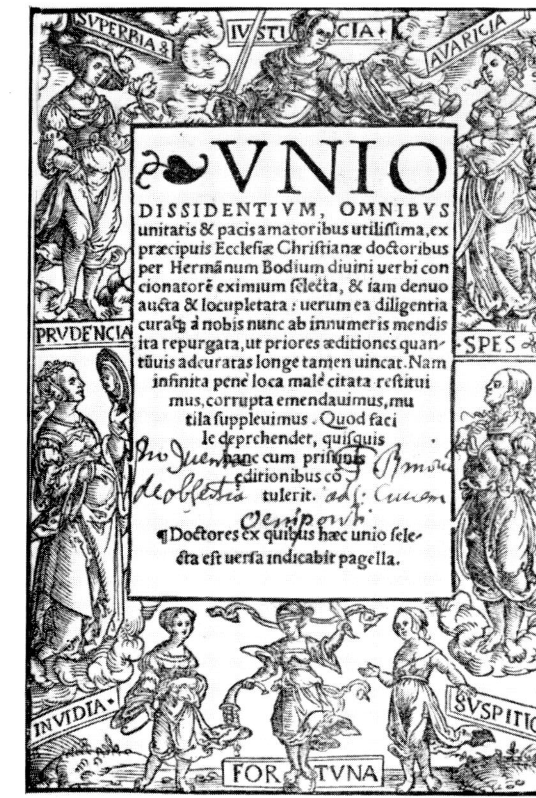

XXI

XXII

XXIII

XXIV

XXV

mere servant rises, the prelude to his fall, declines to serve his royal master, declines to acknowledge his existence.

> My lady's father.
> (1.4.87)

But the lackey, in his wilful disputing of decorum, has a pattern before him to study. He is urged to rebel by the mistress who ought to restrain him.

> What grows of it, no matter.
> (1.3.23)

Nor is the mistress content to corrupt the apprehension of a servant. As he is enfranchised by her—the enfranchisement of Caliban:

> Freedom, heyday!
> (*Tempest*, 2.2.191)

so is her husband, by agreement her master, depressed:

> Pray you, content.
> (1.4.336)

Wives and daughters in *King Lear* change their thimbles into gauntlets, their needles to lances, their gentle hearts to bloody inclination. (*King John*, 5.2.156–8) A servant betrays his lord, and so at last himself; a lord betrays his servant, and himself. The worthy arch and patron (2.1.61), who owes and professes good will to his fief:

> My noble friend!
> (2.1.88)

confounding expectation—again, the source of the horror—does upon him the most terrible ill. So all things find out their contraries. The intervention of a menial, who stabs the master he has served ever since he was a child (3.7.72), answers to, and pays home, that master's unkindness. It functions also as the final notation in the paradigm, disorder. Nor is the yoking of the words, so diverse in connotation, inapposite, really. Oswald with a lorgnette, the card or calendar of gentry, Albany at the distaff, Goneril with a drum, and Regan a baton, and the Duke of Cornwall put down by a peasant: oxymoron is the figure for *Lear*.

Society has its norms; so does the body. The breaking of hierarchy is the antithesis of the one. Disease is the antithesis of the other. Each is seen as usurpation, the disputing of what ought to be. Tragedy is the ultimate usurpation or incongruity. It involves in its working out, the destruction of the good. That fact, as it is monstrous, is either denied (the appeal to sentimentality), or palliated by the absurd suggestion that the good deserve their misfortunes (the appeal to the Elizabethan World Picture). Juliet and Desdemona are said to be wilful: after all, they disobey their parents. What! My foot my tutor andsoforth. Cordelia's silence is said to be self-indulgent: she shows herself headstrong like the king. But the metaphor from sickness enforces an understanding of the rigour of tragedy that is neither timorous nor fanatic, that has nothing to do with justice or injustice. Given its fevered origin, the issue of tragedy is necessary, but in altogether impersonal ways:

> Before the curing of a strong disease,
> Even in the instant of repair and health,
> The fit is strongest. Evils that take leave,
> On their departure most of all show evil.
> (*King John*, 3.4.112–15)

Contagion catches the good man. It taints the life of the commonwealth, also. Rebellion, a constant in the Lancastrian plays, engendered in the sick brain of the malcontent, grows to a dangerous distemper in the whole body of the kingdom. Rank diseases menace its heart.[1] The melancholic Jaques, who follows the deposed Duke of *As You Like It*, discovers the world, topsy-turvy as it is, on a sick bed: he would cleanse its foul body of infection. (2.7.59–61) Richard II, deprived also of his right, likens the depriving and its issue to a boil, pustulous with sin, which

> gathering head
> Shall break into corruption.
> (5.1.58f.)

The lords attending on King John find out his evil purpose in his face. It reveals, in its malign alterations, a 'passion . . . so

[1] 'The English state, the universe of this play [*2HIV*], is an unhealthy body which needs a drastic purge, which may, indeed, be incurable': Traversi, *An Approach to Shakespeare*, N. Y., 1956, p. 29; and see p. 36.

ripe it needs must break. And when it breaks,' avers Pembroke, anticipating the murder of Arthur,

> I fear will issue thence
> The foul corruption of a sweet child's death.
> (4.2.79–81)

Gloucester rationalizes the treachery he imagines in Edgar, once a son, 'Now outlaw'd from my blood' (3.4.171)—not, I think, a legalism only: Edgar, now attainted, but a physiological description: Edgar, now wasted, corrupted, diseased. Lear, baffled by Goneril's unkindness, must see her behaviour, not as wilful but involuntary, a disease in the flesh, a swollen boil,

> A plague sore, an embossed carbuncle,
> In my corrupted blood. (2.4.225–8)

Sanity cannot abide any other explanation. And when that other comes, its entail is madness, figured also as rebellion, usurpation:

> down, thou climbing sorrow!
> Thy element's below. (2.4.57f.)

But Lear is mad before. Careless of precedence, he is kinder to his toe than to his heart. (3.2.31f.) Enter to him, admonishing, Menenius Agrippa. Blind to use and wont, he disclaims, with that other kingly anarch, Leontes, all paternal care (1.1.115), esteeming only 'our forceful instigation'. (*Winter's Tale*, 2.1.163) He is, as he plumes the will, indifferent to the sanctions and prohibitions of custom, not, in his simplicity, the antique face of plain old form (*King John*, 4.2.21f.), but shrivelled to the dust on antique time. He craves permission to sweep it away. (*Coriolanus*, 2.3.125f.) After all it is Lear who gives Edmund, the decrier of custom, his charter. Custom is a plague. (1.2.3) Enter Coriolanus, raving.

> Let me o'erleap that custom.
> (2.2.140)

To do so is, however, to make a mortal breach in oneself. That is why York, in *Richard II*, counsels his master to respect the prerogative of a subject. To despise it is to

> take from Time
> His charters and his customary rights.

The result of that usurpation is tragedy, to the sovereign and to his subject:

> Let not to-morrow then ensue to-day;
> Be not thyself; for how art thou a king
> But by fair sequence and succession?
> (2.1.195–9)

For custom is neither affectation nor idle ceremony. It is the sign and flag of conduct which most nearly fulfills and agrees with human nature or kind. Philip II, reproving a subordinate for sacrificing an interest to a ceremony, is answered and rightly: 'How a ceremony? Your Majesty's self is but a ceremony!' What is customary and ceremonious has to do with what is feasible in nature. Custom is in fact our vice-nature. So John Donne, in 'Love's Deity' and, before him, the Elizabethan homilist: 'Custome is as it were an other nature.'[1] It follows that the breach of custom is breach of all. (*Cymbeline*, 4.2.10f.) Who pays allegiance to custom

> Hath good assurance long to dure,
> And who the same to rente is ryfe,
> Regardeth neither helth nor lyfe.[2]

Edmund, who overleaps custom, as he is less in blood than others, wrongs others the more. (5.3.167f.) He is the bastard, who would top his legitimate brother. (1.2.20f.) He is the son and the subject, who would undertake the murder of both father and king.

Now, as Providence is the emblem of order in the universe, and Fortune of disorder in the disposing of all temporal business, so, in the commonwealth, the emblem of order is the king.

> What is the body when the head is off?
> (*3 Henry VI*, 5.1.41)

Like the imperatives of kind, the duties owed to a king are, not prescriptive but organic. When, in *King John*, the repentant rebels determine to pay those duties once more, they see and render themselves, and their relation to the sovereign, in terms of natural phenomena.

> We will untread the steps of damnèd flight,
> And, like a bated and retirèd flood,

[1] Sig. Dd2r in Baldwin-Palfreyman, edn. 1564.
[2] Hall, *Court of Virtue*, Sig. R1v.

Leaving our rankness and irregular course,
Stoop low within those bounds we have o'erlooked
And calmly run on in obedience
Even to our ocean.

(5.4.52–57)

The ocean is the king. He enfolds all his people. As Providence towers over the world, so the king, who is the deputy of Providence, however unworthy in himself (*2 Henry VI*, 3.2.285f.), towers over the kingdom, contains it in his person. (Plate XXVI)

Lear, alive belatedly to the magnitude of his charge, is more than angered at the stocking of his messenger. He is incredulous: men do not exist who will work such violent outrage on respect. (2.4.24) And yet, as it is he who gives warrant to Edmund, so is it he who, mistaking his own place (2.4.12), emboldens Cornwall and Regan to engross the mistake. To shake all cares and business (1.1.40) is not the business of a king. The tenor of Leir's resigning in the old play is instructive in that it communicates a slackening of fibre:

Oh, what a combat feeles my panting heart,
'Twixt childrens loue, and care of common weale!

(Sc. 3)

When, less than a decade before Shakespeare was born, the king and emperor Charles abdicated his throne, he did so to great applause. It was not, however, his ambition, merely to slough a burden. He sought to exchange it for another, more onerous. That, at least, is the myth, the conventional reading. Lear is culpable, not because he abdicates, in any case not in that alone, but because of the manner in which he gives over. It is so fatuous and irresponsible, so patently self-indulgent, blind pride going before the inevitable fall. Lear's abdication is a kind of mean charade:

Unburdened [to] crawl toward death.

(1.1.42)

In that sense abdication is felt as 'sloth and want of courage', and so Philemon Holland, translating the *Moralia*, construes it.[1]

[1] P. 383. Quoted Campbell, p. 182.

But if a man divests himself of rule (1.1.50), he must agree to be ruled, henceforward to bear his ass on his back.[1] (1.4.176f.) Lear grudges his assent: it was not what he meant at all. And so he seeks to reassume, at least the privilege of kingship. But he can no longer manage what he has given away. Sovereignty is indivisible.

> What, hath the firmament more suns than one?
> (*Titus*, 5.3.17)

The analogy from nature is common.

> One Sonne ruleth over the day, and one Moone over the nyghte: and to descende downe to the erthe, in a litell beest whiche of all other is moste to be marvayled at, I meane the Bee, is lefte to man by nature, as hit semeth, a perpetuall figure of a iuste governaunce or rule: who hath amonge them one principall Bee for theyr governour, who excelleth all other in greatnes.

But the primacy and indivisibility of a king rest also on Biblical sanction. Again, Sir Thomas Elyot is apposite:

> And if any desireth to have the governance of one persone proved by histories, let hym fyrste resorte to the holy scripture: where he shall fynde that almyghty god commanded Moses only to brynge his elected people out of captivite, gyvynge onely to hym that authoritie, without appoyntynge to hym any other assistence of equall power or dignitie . . . And bicause Dathan and Abiron disdayned his rule, and coveyted to be equall with hym, the erthe opened, and fyre issued out, and swalowed them in.[2]

The impact of the story, attested to by its currency, derives from the conclusion it enforces. When Mary Stuart returned from France in 1561, the citizens of Edinburgh, to impress on her their hatred of idolatry: more gods than the one true god, represented in a *tableau vivant* the destruction of Dathan, Abiram, and Corah. Earlier in the century, Holbein reflected on their protest and its answering. The Erastian propagandist who composed *The Pilgrim's Tale* saw also any challenge to undivided authority as bringing with it immediate requital. He cited also as his exemplum the lot of Dathan and Abiram who, 'for resistinge moses . . . sonk vnto hell'. The emblem writers for their part are alert to the moral, explicit (they would

[1] See Plate XLIX, ch. VIII.

[2] Elyot, *The boke named the Governour* London, 1531, Sigs. A7v, A8v.

say) in the fate of the Reubenite chieftains: the king's prerogative is single.[1] It is one of the ironies of the play that Lear, a king and no king, should be answered out of his own mouth, should find his passionate protest annulled in dispassionate ways. The buckler that defends him so long as he wears it, an impersonal thing, shows him its other face when he hands it to another. The buckler, the office, is no more partial than roan Barbary, who bears King Richard today and, Richard dismounting, King Bolingbroke tomorrow.

The king, putting off his prerogative, is guilty. That is a given, and verified and requited in proof: at Pomfret, at Dover. But the successor, usurping the prerogative, or using it only to abuse it, is also guilty. His punishment follows.

> So shaken as we are, so wan with care.
> (*1 Henry IV*, 1.1.1)

Macbeth steals the ruler's garment. It does not fit: he is a dwarfish thief whose robe hangs loose about him (5.2.20–22), an insufficient pretender on whom the cloak of office

> lies as sightly . . .
> As great Alcides' shows upon an ass.
> (*King John*, 2.1.143f.)

For that reason his imposture is discovered. It is a measure of his puerility that he does not appreciate his own slightness. His case is mirrored faithfully in that of the pigmies, who presume on their master Hercules, sleeping.[2] Macbeth creeps on Duncan, asleep, and Caliban on Prospero, and the mongrel Oswald and his betters on Lear. The sleeping king betrays his trust.

> I, thus neglecting worldly ends.
> (*Tempest*, 1.2.89)

But those who move against him under cover of that betrayal nod also.

> So doves do peck the falcon's piercing talons.
> (*3 Henry VI*, 1.4.41)

[1] See Boissard, *Emblematum liber*, Sig. T3r, p. 149: 'Sacerdotes honorandi'; Kernodle, p. 69; *Icones*, Sig. E1r; *The Court of Venus*, ed. R. A. Fraser, Durham, N.C., 1955, p. 104, l. 9.

[2] See Whitney, *Emblemes*, Sig. B4v, p. 16: 'Quod potes, tenta.'

Lear's indignant cry, 'I think the world's asleep' (1.4.51f.), is approved in a double sense. There's a divinity that hedges the office of the king. (3.7.57)

The divinity that wards, and the sacrosanct flesh are, like Providence and Fortune, symbolic merely. The Elizabethans, or some of them, mistook the symbol for literal fact. If no one makes that mistake any longer, if the outwall or symbol has been corroded to rubbish with time, the imperatives it was fashioned to express remain, at least viable, still. Degree is not the specious mask of thrones to bear down Nature: the eccentric proposal Fulke Greville allows to a character in one of his plays (*Mustapha*, 4.4) It is the line of demarcation that separates disparate things, and so preserves the integrity, and efficiency, of each. When Shakespeare wants an emblem of disorder, he offers the firm soil winning of and losing to the watery main, an interchanging of states which cancels the autonomy of either.[1] (Sonnet 64) That is why Laertes, hastening against the king, is seen as the ocean, eating at the flats, overpeering of his list (*Hamlet*, 4.5.99–105): in sum, taking to himself, not simply what is interdicted: there is no force, after all, in arbitrary prohibition; but rather, taking to himself what is inimical to himself, what is subversive of, and contrary to, his nature. And the striking effect of the analogy in that particular scene in *Hamlet* is not diminished but engrossed by the fact that its application is deeply incongruous. The king in question is the shadow of a king, a cutpurse of the title. But when Claudius says,

> There's such divinity doth hedge a king
> That treason can but peep to what it would,
> (4.5.122–5)

his almost blasphemous enunciating of what may be called the proper reticulation of things is made the more compelling of acknowledgement, just in proportion to the element of falsity in the speaker, a clown in regal purple dressed. The exception affirms the rule. Milton's Satan is a parody of God, and Sycorax a parody of Prospero; and the parody, the simulacrum, heightens one's understanding of, and reverence for, the thing itself. We mind true things by what their mockeries be. (*Henry V*, 4. Prologue) The parody enforces discrimination.

[1] And see *2HIV*, 1.1.62f.; *TC*, 1.3.111–13.

To say, then, with the homilist: As well assault the heavens as the throne, is to utter a similitude, expressive of the notion that no man is omnicompetent, nor—the other face of the coin—entirely negligible, either. The saluting of another's prerogative is the condition of the saluting of prerogative in oneself. The relinquishing of a portion of my freedom is the condition of my freedom. The Renaissance, endorsing the proposition, is, characteristically, oblique, analogical. It figures order in the heavens, embodies order on the throne, and then brings forward Capaneus, in contempt of both. Capaneus assails the ruler and challenges the god.

Trout for factitious bait.

He ends as you would think, consumed with the lightning in scaling the walls. (Plate XXVII) Marsyas, the satyr of Phrygia, essays the same challenge. He avows himself, in music, Apollo's superior: he is bested by Apollo and bound and flayed alive. (Plate XXVIII) Niobe, despising divine privilege—and, the moralists would interpolate, privilege divinely appointed—is bereft of her children and turned into stone.[1] As men 'puffe them vp with pride', so does the frog, a homelier anarch, a more vulgar kind of fool, who would rival the ox in size as the addle-pated commoner would rival the king. The result is substantially the same, and also the moral: *Arrogance renversée.*[2]

Phaeton, to whom Shakespeare likens the reckless king Richard II (3.3.178f.); Icarus, whom John Higgins in the *Mirror for Magistrates* describes inferentially in terms of the foolish parent of King Lear;[3] Ixion, for his attempt on the Queen of Heaven, one of the four chief sinners punished in Hades; most conspicuously, Prometheus, not the aspiring hero of Shelley but the overreacher of Alciati and Aneau who finds out his just deserts: these, to the Renaissance, are the most popular archetypes of usurpation and its issue. Phaeton, playing at the role of Apollo, is hurled for his incapacity from the chariot he rashly assumes.[4] (Plate XXIX) Icarus, as he shuns the good

[1] See Whitney, *Emblemes*, Sig. B3r, p. 13.

[2] See Desprez, *Le Theatre*, Sig. A4r, p. 7.

[3] Ll. 37–39: 'A fethered king that practisde for to flye and soare: Whereby he felt the fall God wot against his will, And neuer went, roode, raignde nor spake, nor flew no more.' Quoted Muir, p. 238.

[4] *In Temerarios* (Alciati).

sense of the saying, *Noli altum sapere*,[1] makes one of those who 'paste theire reache doe mounte'. He is incompetent; he falls to his decay.[2] As Lear, for his sins, is bound to the wheel of fire (4.7.46f.), so Ixion, for taking to himself the prerogative of a god, revolves in perpetual torment on the wheel.[3] (Plate XXX) For the concord which pervades the cosmos must expel, as foreign to it, all that is discordant, a man who claps on wings, a man who looks into the sun. This is to paraphrase Bradley (whose master is Hegel) on the nature of Shakespearean tragedy. But the notion is an old one, and familiar to Shakespeare. Its root is in Pythagoras and his disciples. Plato and Cicero expound it. Pliny likens the sun to the intellect of the universe, and discovers it routing the darkness, not only from the sky but even from the minds of men.[4]

Dispute the primacy of the sun, and darkness mantles the reason. Caliban casts out Ariel. The reign of Jack Cade or Jack Straw commences: the reign of chaos and old night. It is Catiline, in Jonson's play, the classic figure of the rebel, who calls on chaos. Thus the admonition of Erasmus: 'The thynges that be aboue vs belonge nothynge vnto vs . . . it becometh not Iacke strawe to reason of princes matters.'[5] The same words are seized on by Alciati to moralize the punishment of

[1] See the printer's device in T. Morton, *Apologia Catholica*, London, 1605: a scroll on which the words, *Noli altum sapere*, appear, and beneath which an old man is standing, is secured to the branches of an olive tree. The device was used originally by the Parisian printer, Charles Estienne (1551–61). With Estienne's motto, compare the saying, *Nimium sapere*, applied explicitly to the flight and fall of Icarus by Sambucus, *Emblemata*, Sig. B8v, p. 32. Phaeton is depicted also in *Emblemes d'Alciat*, Sig. F2v, p. 84; Green, pp. 285f.; and by Michelangelo in three chalk drawings, intended to denote his own presumptuousness in addressing himself to Cavalieri. See *Studies in Iconology*, figs. 162–4, and p. 219n. for a list of traditional allegorical interpretations of Phaeton as overreacher.

[2] For representations of Icarus, see *Emblemes d'Alciat*, Sig. I4r, p. 135; Whitney, *Emblemes*, Sig. D2v, p. 28; Alciati, *Emblematum Libellus*, p. 57; and Green, pp. 288f.

[3] Rollenhagio, Sig. C2v, glosses the crime and punishment of Ixion: 'Sequitur sua poena nocentem. De l'homme impenitent le forfaict execrable, Ne demeure impuni, ains tousiours miserable Il sent la main de Dieu, qui avec pieds boiteux Exige tost ou tard un tourment rigoureux.'

[4] *Timaeus; Somnium Scipionis; Natural History*, II.5. J. A. K. Thomson, *Shakespeare and the Classics*, London, 1952, pp. 142f., quotes the latter passage and offers additional documentation.

[5] Sig. C4r in Richard Taverner, *Proverbes or Adagies, gathered oute of the Chiliades*, London, 1552. See also Taverner's trans. of *Flores . . . sententiarum*, under 'Socrates'; and Greene, *Friar Bacon*, I.2, in which the clown Miles speaks of 'the fable of the Fox and the Grapes; that which is above us pertains nothing to us'.

Prometheus, the great breaker of concord, the master thief of what belongs to another.[1] (Plate XXXI) The pain he suffers, he solicits. That is why the emblem writer finds the tearing of Prometheus analogous to the self torment of a guilty conscience.[2] Prometheus is consumed by the gnawing vulture of the mind. (*Titus*, 5.2.31) It is he himself, another Lear, who, abjuring his place, the vestment or outward sign of his nature, ties to him sharp-toothed unkindness, like a vulture. (2.4.135f.)

The Renaissance, because the result of challenging order is so clear and acutely disagreeable, never stints in celebrating its virtues.

> In every thyng is ordre: and without ordre may be nothing stable or permanent: And it may nat be called ordre excepte it do contayne in it degrees, high and base, accordynge to the merite or estimation of the thynge that is ordred.[3]

Neither does the Renaissance tire of representing the torment inflicted by the vulture of sedition, to take a phrase from *1 Henry VI.* (4.3.47) In a classical mood it will refer you to the punishment of Tityus who, for presuming to attack Latona, the mother of Apollo and Diana, must acquiesce, eternally, in the eating of his liver, the seat of his unlucky aspiration. In a whimsical mood it will seek out in the bestiaries its emblem of presumption and the ills attending on it. Case in point: the raven. He looks hard at himself, and discovers there the puissance of the eagle; and so finds out the reward of all myopic creatures, a place in tomorrow's bill of fare.[4]

Take but degree away.

The entire action of Shakespeare's two historical tetralogies dramatizes the wisdom of Ulysses, the pertinence and rightness of his warning.

[1] *Qual supra nos, nihil ad nos.* The torture of Prometheus is given also by Boissard, *Emblematum liber*, Metz, 1588, Sig. C1r, p. 17, under 'Periculosa scrutatio'; Aneau, *Picta Poesis*, Lyons, 1555, p. 90 (in Green, p. 267); *Emblemes d' Alciat*, Sig. I3v, p. 134 (in Green, p. 266, who draws from different edns.: Lyons, 1551, and Antwerp, 1581); and, in painting by Rubens. See *Stud. in Icon.*, fig. 161.

[2] Whitney, *Emblemes*, p. 75.

[3] Elyot, *The Governour*, Sig. A3v.

[4] Michelangelo (in a chalk drawing) and Titian depict the torture of Tityus. See *Stud. in Icon.*, figs. 159, 160. The raven and eagle appear in Desprez, *Le Theatre*, p. 16: 'Ne cherche point les choses plus hautes que toy.'

> Take away ordre from all thynges, what shulde than remayne? Certes nothynge finally, except some man wolde imagine eftsones, *Chaos* . . . where there is any lacke of ordre, nedes muste be perpetuall conflicte . . . whan . . . [a man] hath distroyed that wherewith he dothe participate by the ordre of his creation, he hym selfe of necessite muste than perisshe, wherof ensuethe universall dissolution.[1]

Degree must obtain, else man will prey on man, and chaos, Elyot's 'confuse mixture', come again.

Chaos is the absence of the justice which is order. When justice lies hidden, all earthly things fall in confusion.[2] The emblem of that confusion is Doomsday, the promised end (5.3.263), the commingling of land, sea, and sky, the confounding of light and dark, the warring of the elements, the collapsing of the Earth about the Poles.[3] (Plate XXXII) Chaos, 'that indigest' (*King John*, 5.7.26), as it is the negation of form, is necessarily the annulling of life. The abhorrence of it is accordingly proverbial, as with most things that are deeply felt:

> The man I hate
> Worse than confusion.
> ('*Tis Pity*, 2.3)

Seneca, whose tragedies afford to the Renaissance a general conspectus, dilates on it in the *Hercules Oetaeus*:

> A day will come when all the laws of the universe will be overthrown: the South Pole will crush all Libya, all the land of the nomad Garamantes; the North Pole will crush all that is beneath it and that the dry Boreas beats down upon; and the trembling Sun will be dislodged from the sky, bringing light to an end; the heavenly palace in its fall will bring down East and West, all the gods will perish and collapse in the general chaos. Last of all, Death will pronounce the final sentence of extinction against itself.
>
> (ll. 1102ff.)

[1] Elyot, *The Governour*, Sig. A2v. Tillyard, *The Elizabethan World Picture*, ch. 2, draws in his discussion of order on Elyot, Spenser, Hooker, Chapman, and Shakespeare.

[2] 'Est Mundanarum talis confusio rerum. Quo Regina latet Tempore Iustitia.' So Aneau, *Picta Poesis*, p. 49 (in Green, p. 449).

[3] Bocksperger's emblem glosses Revelation, vi.12–13. For another representation of Chaos, see Whitney, *Emblemes*, Sigs. Q1v–2r, pp. 122f. (in Green, p. 450).

The Scriptures also are taken as announcing that chaos follows the suffocating of degree. (*Troilus and Cressida*, 1.3.125f.) It is of Matthew xxiv that Gloucester is thinking when he cites his dark prediction and finds it fulfilled. (1.2.112–24) Degree being honoured, men come within their awful banks again. (*2 Henry IV*, 4.1.176) But given, the choking of degree, and the waters make head against the kingdom of the shore. Cataracts and hurricanoes rain on the world. (3.2.2) Nature, contemning its origin, is no longer bordered in itself. (4.2.32f.) Once law contained it, folded it—the phrase is Sidney's—'within assured bounds'. Those bounds past, 'mans nature infinitely rangeth'.[1] The end of all things Kent and Edgar and Albany discern in the close of Lear's story.[2] It is conceived in anarchy, the ultimate gainsaying of kind. It fulfils, in its close, the pledge of its beginning.

Now to qualify a little. There is a considerable gulf—rather, a universe opens between Shakespeare and the mere preceptors whose constant business is to deprecate rebellion, whatever its terms. It would be a simple matter, and to a degree entertaining, to eke out the saws and sayings of Richard Taverner with those of William Baldwin and Thomas Palfreyman, who also redacted Erasmus;[3] and Robert Crowley, whose concern was to stigmatize those 'manye abuses, that maye and ought to be put away';[4] and John Hall who, in *The Court of Virtue*, concurred enthusiastically with the injunction:

> Let no man from his calling fall,
> But eche man in his state remayne:
> Let not the common people deale
> With matters highe of common weale.[5]

Never a man's thought in the world keeps the roadway better than theirs. Even Ovid, than whom, I suppose, no more amoral writer ever lived, is made to jog along with them and so to proclaim the same forced and unlovely conclusions. The witty changes he treats of are seized on by moralists like Arthur

[1] Sidney, 'Arcadia', in *Works*, ed. Feuillerat, II, 195.

[2] See Bradley, *Shakespearean Tragedy*, London, 1904, p. 328n.

[3] In *A treatise of Morall Phylosophie*, London, 1547; 'augmented, & . . . enlarged', 1557 *et seq.*

[4] *One and thyrtye Epigrammes*, London, 1550.

[5] Sig. M5r. And see Baldwin-Palfreyman, edn. 1564, Sig. Q4r.

Golding and Thomas Peend to illustrate and to popularize the virtues of circumspection and humility. Golding, in his translation of the *Metamorphoses* (1567), extracts a moral lesson from each of the fifteen books. His allegorical misreading is anticipated in Peend's *Pleasant Fable of Hermaphroditus and Salmacis* (1565). When, earlier in the century, another Hall, the chronicler Edward, doing his loyal but insufficient best to prove the righteousness of Henry in every particular, insisted suavely that 'the affayres of Princes be not ordered by the commen people, nor were it convenient that all thynges be opened to theim',[1] Shakespeare, reading that passage, as I imagine he did, must surely have nodded, in a more or less perfunctory manner, and passed on.

For the context is everything. Shakespeare's conventional contemporary would no doubt have given his immediate suffrage—a muted suffrage, however, for the conventional person abhors vociferating, is bland if he is anything—to the public peace and quiet, whatever the context. Shakespeare, caring also for stability, and with a passion entirely unconventional, is concerned just by virtue of that passion to look further and determine whence genuine stability comes. He does not execrate the plebs in *Coriolanus* because they are rank smelling (well, not chiefly for that), or—and this is the mistaken saying of most of those who comment on the play—because they clamour for liberty; but rather because, like Coriolanus himself, who is also Shakespeare's butt, and on whom also and impartially he loads his contempt, they would bury all which yet distinctly ranges. This is not to be enamoured of liberty, but licence, and the hero of the play, more than any other, is given to confounding the two. True liberty is beyond his ken. The king sits his throne. He does not sit on the people.[2]

The conventional Elizabethan, who reads or has read to him the florilegia, and who gives back without reflection or qualification the servile commonplaces heaped up in those volumes, would have raised his hands in horror, to the degree that he took seriously the summons to obedience, at the usurpation of

[1] *The Triumphant Reigne of Kyng Henry the VIII*, ed. Charles Whibley, London, 1904, II, 197.

[2] See Boissard, *Emblematum liber*, Sig. D2r, p. 11: 'Libertas Vera Est Affectibvs Non Servire'; and Rollenhagio, emblem 55, glossed Sig. C2v: 'Consensu populi regnum subsistit'.

Bolingbroke or Henry Tudor. Richard of Bordeaux was after all anointed king. So for that matter was Crookback. And as Charles I might well have exclaimed, 'Not all the water in the rough rude sea'—but every schoolboy (as they say) knows the rest.

Shakespeare, concurring, appends however two qualifications. When King John, whose throne is menaced by the claims of Constance and Arthur, steps forward to assert, with the requisite pomp, 'Our strong possession and our right for us', Shakespeare does not concede that really there is no more to say. He gives to Queen Elinor the rugged retort, 'Your strong possession much more than your right, Or else it must go wrong with you and me'. (1.1.39–41) And so it proves, and does. The career in part belongs to the talents. David would do well to be superior to Absalom, and Moses to the Reubenites, and Harry to Hotspur, not only in title but, more crucially, in fact. The title is supposed to betoken the fact.

And the second proviso: a king's prerogative extends only so far as reason gives scope. To plead that prerogative, as the king in *Pericles* does, to justify the murder of his guest:

> It fits thee not to ask the reason why,
> Because we bid it, (1.1.157f.)

is to forfeit prerogative altogether. Kingly privilege is tethered, not infinite. Despotism and sovereignty do not jump together. They are not the same but antithetical.

> Boundless intemperance
> In nature is a tyranny.
> (*Macbeth*, 4.3.66f.)

The captain whom Edmund solicits to murder Lear and Cordelia, and who is content to abide the saying of his chief, 'Thy great employment Will not bear question' (5.3.32f.), is just such a man as the critics, elaborating and, as I think, misconstruing, the Elizabethan psychology, hypothesize. Lucio describes him, in *Measure for Measure*. He is a motion generative, a masculine puppet. (3.2.119) The good servant does not say, when murder is commanded of him:

> My commission
> Is not to reason of the deed, but do't.
> (*Pericles*, 4.1.83f.)

He says rather, with Pisanio in *Cymbeline*, a servant who keeps his wits and hence his virtue about him:

> If it be so to do good service, never
> Let me be counted serviceable.
>
> (3.2.14f.)

Obedience is a virtue only in so far as the thing commanded of one is a good thing. Thus Fulke Greville, in *Mustapha* (2.1):

> And while none dare shew kings they goe amisse,
> Even base Obedience their corruption is.

To obey without let is to forfeit the human condition, to

> float upon a wild and violent sea
> Each way and move.
>
> (*Macbeth*, 4.2.21f.)

The complaisant man is a weathercock. Kent is not complaisant, and so he keeps his autonomy to the end. Gloucester, who must relieve Lear, 'If I die for it' (3.3.18f.), whose duty, the apposite word, cannot suffer him to obey his master's injunction (3.4.152f.); the old man, who must relieve Gloucester, 'Come on 't what will' (4.1.50); the servant who bars the way to Cornwall—and so of course violates degree: these men read obedience and the bounds of obedience aright. Edmund, who perseveres in a dubious course of loyalty (3.5.2f., 21f.), and Oswald, a cruder sycophant, and the captain, responsive to any order so long as it is man's work (5.3.39): these men forget the nature of a man, and what he can do with impunity, and what, in the doing, destroys him.

> That thou mayest rightly obey power, her bounds know;
> Those past, her nature, and name is chang'd; to be
> Then humble to her is idolatrie.

The servile man and the merely fractious are one. In Caliban, now grovelling before his master and now seeking to paunch him with a stake, the two are met. It is easier of course (and more convenient) to censure fractiousness than servility. But to look nearer is to see that there went but a pair of shears between them.

VI

REASON AND WILL

EVIL, culminating in absolute confusion, rises from man's mistaking of his relationship to the greater world of which he is part, and to whose laws he must render allegiance. But whence comes the mistaking itself? Why, like Edmund, does man lapse in error? The answer—it is Hamlet's to Gertrude—is that reason panders will. Man is flawed, and tending always to fall. When Gower, in his role as Chorus to *Pericles*, comes on stage to introduce the play, he, whom the dramatist has brought to life again, describes himself, not simply as taking human shape, but as 'Assuming man's infirmities'. The phrases are felt as implying one another. When Prospero, in *The Tempest*, admonishes Ferdinand: 'The strongest oaths are straw to the fire in our blood' (4.1.52f.), it is his own embittered history to which he is appealing.

> We are all men
> In our own natures frail and capable
> Of our flesh.
>
> (*Henry VIII*, 5.3.10–12)

There is a

> taint of vice whose strong corruption
> Inhabits our frail blood.
>
> (*Twelfth Night*, 3.4.340f.)

The indwelling taint is an abstraction. The Renaissance, instinctively dramatic or pictorial, embodies it in the figure of a fettered slave, symbolic of the unregenerate soul made captive, in Milton's phrase, by foul exorbitant desires. In that manner

Michelangelo, in the Tomb of Julius II, represents the tension between reason and will. Edmund Spenser, in the second book of *The Faerie Queene*, chooses a more audacious image. Man is a living disjunction: 'th'eternall Lord in fleshly slime Enwombed.'[1] The antithesis between the two principles, one conducting to fulfilment, the other to destruction, is sharpened in *King John*. To Shakespeare, in that play, a man's 'purpose and his conscience', enemies, by definition, are 'two dreadful battles' or armies. (4.2.77f.) War is open and unceasing between them. Man, on such a reading, is neither angel nor devil, but a poignant commingling of each. That is the burden of Fulke Greville's great lament:

> Oh, wearisome condition of humanity,
> Born under one law, to another bound;
> Vainly begot, and yet forbidden vanity,
> Created sick, commanded to be sound.

Lear calls man a centaur (4.6.126), and the image, despite Lear's misanthropy, is apt: horse and rider indivisible, reason armoured in grace astride ebullient will. It is Machiavelli's metaphor also, though he, also, misconstrues it.[2] Friar Laurence discerns in man two kings for ever warring—the scruple of ill, the form of plausive manners—and the issue of their contest is the business of Shakespearean tragedy. The issue is so often a quarry of the slain because man is prone, by the accident of birth, by 'the imposition Hereditary ours'—I quote Polixenes, in *The Winter's Tale* (1.2.74f.)—to lust after evil, and so work his own decay.

> We are all frail.
> (*Measure for Measure*, 2.4.121)

But frailty, capability, which is proneness, argue the existence of alternatives: the cramping and denial of proneness.

[1] Michelangelo's use of the symbol is anticipated by Antonio Federighi's Holy Water Basin in the Cathedral at Sienna. See *Stud. in Icon.*, p. 194, fig. 138. For Spenser, see *F.Q.*, Bk. II, Canto x, Stanza 50, ll. 2f.

[2] Freud, in *The Ego and the Id*, pours old wine in new bottles: 'In its relation to the id . . . [the ego] is like a man on horseback, who has to hold in check the superior strength of the horse.' John F. Danby, *Shakespeare's Doctrine of Nature: A Study of 'King Lear'*, London, 1958, pp. 32–34, cites Bacon, Launcelot Andrewes, and Spenser on the duality of man's nature, symbolized not only by the figure of the centaur but by that of the half-bestial Pan and the Mermaids of the Bestiaries.

It is true, the perverted will is one part of a man's endowment. In some sense it is natural that one should follow its soliciting, and this whatever the importunities of the reason. Hume's maxim is therefore worthy of endorsement: every man should, in principle—I would add, in policy—be held a knave. It is salutary to be aware of the enemy within: awareness begets vigilance, a looking to one's defences, and so lessens the chance of usurpation. For that reason, what is natural is identified with what is evil: man is encouraged to stiffen up the sinews. And hence it is useful to see in Caliban, in whom rude will is ascendant absolutely, a type of the natural man; and in Gonzalo's Utopia, whose motto is passivity and the absence of law, the condition of 'mere' Nature. Prospero, the artificer, the civilized man who manipulates Nature, is the more likely to be realized if he is confronted with the wild man, Nature's slave, and forced to acknowledge in him an alternative version of himself. The wise man will put off ease, he will arm himself in rigour, to the degree that what is abhorrent is supposed to be natural or easy.

But to scrutinize more carefully the controlling word, natural. If disorder is natural, whence comes order? If our discontents are the price we pay for civilization, what inclines us to honour the account? To survive, it is clear, one must coerce his nature; and yet as clearly, to survive one must enlarge and express it. Nature errs in Othello; it does not follow its bent. (1.3.62) Because it does not, the hero is destroyed. Because it does, in *As You Like It*, the hero is fulfilled. It is his kindness, his nature, that cause him to save his wicked brother's life. (4.3.129f.) Nature, given scope, turns a rebel from rebellion in *1 Henry VI*. It is said to make him suddenly relent. (3.3.59) Edgar and Cordelia, not Edmund and the sisters, are Nature's servants or stewards. If, then, passion and reason self-division cause, the enmity between them does not infer two natures in man, the one counterpoising the other. The image of man as microcosm is illuminating here: the organism, compounded as it is of varying constituents which may even contend with one another, is most nearly itself when harmony obtains, the basis of which is subordination, when this party, whose pretensions to lead are approved by experience, is brought forward and given hegemony over the others. Though the differing voices which speak to a man's inner ear urge him in different directions, they are not equally compelling or substantial. It is not that reason is master of more eloquence than will, but that the course of action it commends is seen, in the event, to be superior. Reason's counsel, accepted, conduces to good. The counsel of the will is catastrophic. To accept the dictates of reason is therefore natural or kind in that they enable a man to survive. After all to plume the will is unnatural, abnormal, because it is destructive of the self. The claim of virtuous conduct to be identified with natural behaviour is essentially pragmatic. It is supported in proof. The good man is therefore the natural man.

Edmund will not have it so. To him the saying of the Lord Chancellor in *Henry VIII*, of Viola in *Twelfth Night*, of Angelo in *Measure for Measure*, is a tepid and a partial saying. Edmund abhors qualification. Like Machiavelli, he takes the potential for the thing itself. When, announcing his evil bias, he summons Nature to his support (1.2.1), it is a wholly maleficent goddess he apostrophizes, if you will the Setebos of Caliban, in whom the possibility of good does not inhere. Lear also invokes Nature. (1.4.297) His appeal is a horrid one, the conveying of sterility on his child. But, however perverse, it depends on the equating of what is natural with what is kind. A daughter has wronged him. It is Nature's part to punish the daughter, and so to redress the wrong. Implicitly, Lear's prayer defines Nature.

Edmund disputes the definition.[1] His whoremaster man dwells in a universe presided over, neither by God nor by Satan, but, more prosaic than either, by self-interest, incarnate, and very narrowly construed. Edmund's Nature is made of the old stock which Hamlet hypothesizes, which virtue cannot inoculate. (3.1.118f.) Nor is that Nature self-consciously evil, as Lucifer is, who had in him the power of election. To treat of good or evil is to speak beside the point. Men are as the time is. They cannot well be otherwise. When Lear withholds his hand from Gloucester:

Let me wipe it first,
(4.6.136)

[1] The play may be taken as an essay in discrimination. 'The words "nature", and "natural", "unnatural" occur over forty times in *King Lear*' which, moreover, 'incorporates the living parts of both *Ecclesiastical Polity* [represented by "the Lear party"] and *Leviathan* [represented by Edmund].' So Danby, pp. 18f.

he manifests, in his madness, the psychology that Edmund, rather more phlegmatically, has announced from the beginning. Man comes crying hither. He is a whited sepulchre; a verminous fellow crawling between heaven and earth; a ruined piece of Nature, who is herself a ruin.

Shakespeare does not pay homage to the sentimental creed of total depravity. But he is not concerned either to scant the possibility of evil.

> Oh, undistinguished space of woman's will!
> (4.6.278)

I do not know that he believed with Samuel Harsnett in the literal existence of devils. Nor does it matter very much. I am sure that he found them, at least a suitable metaphor for the wickedness latent in the heart.

> Demand me nothing. What you know you know.
> From this time forth I never will speak word.

It is Iago who vows silence. Presumably he is true to his promise. And the chill it engenders is in the impression it creates of a knowing of evil which staggers comprehension, and ought to be beyond it, and is not. Iago is a demi-devil, and also, like Edmund, a Machiavel, whose popularity on stage is traceable, perhaps, not to strange oaths or to esoteric cruelty but, more suggestive and more appalling, to his essential blandness of manner. Aaron, the wicked Moor of *Titus Andronicus*, is an early version of Iago and Edmund. Aaron is a passionless rogue. His pursuit of evil is artistic in that it is disinterested.

> Oh, how this villainy
> Doth fat me with the very thoughts of it!
> (3.1.203f.)

But Shakespeare, imitating but in unpractised ways the awful whimsicality of Barabas in *The Jew of Malta*, takes the audience too palpably by the lapels. And so Aaron's lipsmacking at the prospect of murder and rape makes, not for shuddering but hilarity. Iago is not given to smacking his lips. His villainy is altogether laconic. Evil is a word he does not know how to gloss. The melodramatic villain is a figure of fun.

> Chop off his head, man—somewhat we will do.
> (*Richard III*, 3.1.193)

The self-conscious villain one can assimilate also: Angelo, Claudius. But the monster one boggles at, who rubs a quat to the sense, or undertakes a murder, with the same efficiency and, worse, the same phlegm. The sulphurous pit opens in him, a potential of evil which the dramatist discloses, I think almost with astonishment.

> Ask me not what I know.
> (5.3.161)

When Goneril speaks those words and, with neither joy nor trepidation, without a grain of remorse, gives herself over to death, it is as if Shakespeare plumbs the Lake of Darkness, and is bemused.

> Who is't can read a woman?
> (*Cymbeline*, 5.5.48)

Lear seeks to explore and to anatomize the darkness. The images of bestiality which abound in the play[1] are all of them analogues, essays in definition, of man's horrid potential. Goneril, like the she wolf, is ravenous for prey (1.4.330) and, like her—a wry conjunction of Lear's epithet and natural lore—chooses a mate that has made itself foul in pursuing the female.[2] She is one with the kite and the vulture: like them, she snuffs up decay.[3] (1.4.284; 2.4.137) Venomous, subtle, and treacherous, she finds her emblem in the serpent who, despite Lepidus and Antony, is not bred in the earth, but in the body of a man.[4] (2.4.163; 5.3.84) Adam and the serpent are one.

> This thing of darkness I
> Acknowledge mine.
> (*Tempest*, 5.1.275f.)

Lear's daughters are doghearted daughters (4.3.47): full of

[1] *Lear* contains 133 separate references to 64 different animals. See Muir, pp. lx–lxi.

[2] See *The Whole Works of Roger Ascham*, ed. J. A. Giles, London, 1864, III, 153; *The Life and Complete Works in Prose and Verse of Robert Greene, M.A.*, ed. A. B. Grosart, London, 1881–6, IV, 132; Carroll, pp. 119f.

[3] See Sidney, *Arcadia*, I, 79, 470f.; Carroll, pp. 108, 119.

[4] So Edward Topsell, *The History of Four-footed Beasts and Serpents*, London, 1658, p. 595: '*Pliny* affirmeth [serpents] to be engendered of the marrow in the back-bone of a man.' See also Pliny, *Natural History*, tr. H. Rackham, Loeb Classics, Cambridge, Mass., 1938–40, III, 411, 413; *The Works of Thomas Nashe*, ed. R. B. McKerrow, London, 1904, II, 138; Carroll, p. 114.

envy, currish, contemptible in nature.[1] They share his slyness with the fox (1.4.340f.), and his ferocity with the boar (3.7.58), and his inscrutable cruelty with the tiger.[2] (4.2.20) Like the pelican they tap out and drunkenly carouse the blood of their father. (3.4.76f.) Lear repasts them with his blood; they offer death for life.[3] (Plate XXXIII)

The pious sacrifice at which Shakespeare glances in *King Lear* is recapitulated, not only in the drama of his contemporaries, but in emblem literature, in painting and engraving, in colophons, and in the *tableaux vivants*. Leir, in the old chronicle history, is

> as kind as is the Pellican,
> That kills itselfe, to saue her young ones liues.
> (sc. 6)

The patriot, like the king, is a sacrificial figure. The emblem in each case is the same. When, in 1582, the Duke of Anjou is invested as sovereign of the Netherlands, a splendid allegory is enacted before him in which Patriotism is personified by the pelican. The new prince is congratulated; he is also advised. For the pelican, in the words of Cesare Ripa, 'never stirs from her young, and when Nourishment fails, she feeds them with her own Blood'. To restore them to life, to quote Bartholomeus, she 'smiteth herself in her side, that the blood runneth out, and sheddeth that hot blood upon the bodies of her children, and by virtue of the blood the birds, that were before dead, quicken again'. That is why Mantegna and Breughel the Elder picture Charity with a pelican, whose young are sustained by feeding on its flesh. To Ripa the pelican is the emblem of Charity, the wonted companion of Good Nature and Compassion. In 1568, William of Orange, beginning his campaign to drive the Spaniards from his country, emblazons on the banners of his

[1] See *A Petite Pallace of Pettie His Pleasure*, ed. H. Hartman, New York, 1938, pp. 186, 206f., 216; *Coriolanus*, 1.1.28; *Othello*, 5.2.361; Carroll, pp. 99f.

[2] See Topsell, p. 221; Carroll, p. 104 ('fox'). For the boar: Wilson, *Arte of Rhetorique 1560*, ed. G. H. Mair, Oxford, 1909, p. 171; Carroll, p. 94. For the tiger: *The Works of Thomas Deloney*, ed. F. O. Mann, Oxford, 1912, p. 90; Carroll, p. 117.

[3] See also *The Holy Bible*, London, printed by Robert Barker, 1611, t.p.; A. F. Johnson, *A Catalogue of Engraved and Etched English Title-Pages . . . to . . . 1691*, Oxford, 1934, under Droeshout, no. 10; Whitney, *Emblemes*, Sig. L4r, p. 87; Camerarius, *Symb. et emblematum, &c.*, 1596, p. 87; Reusner, *Emblemata*, 1581, Book II, p. 73; Carroll, p. 112; Epiphanius, *Physiologus*, printed Christopher Plantin, Antwerp, 1588, p. 30 (quoted Green, p. 394); and Muir, pp. 118f.

army the figure of a pelican who tears its breast to nourish its offspring. John of Gaunt likens Richard II to those offspring, spilling a parent's blood.[1] (2.1.126f.) The metaphor, in fact, is applicable to all men, by virtue of the primal sacrifice of Christ, whom Dante describes as *nostro Pellicano.*

Like Christ, and the good king who is Christ's vicar, the pelican is kind. The Renaissance, in representing her piety, fashions an emblem of natural behaviour. It is clear that the emblem does not answer to the definition which Edmund, by his conduct, implies. It repudiates that definition as insufficiently catholic. Neither does it infer, like the image of husbandry, the limits which environ bad conduct. It is not negative or circumscribing. Its function is to body forth inclination and the conduct it begets (read: natural behaviour), when reason, ensinewed by grace, has triumphed over will. The nature the emblem purports to describe—given, the achieving of that triumph—is manifest in self-abnegation.

The business of the emblem is altogether with the sacrifice of the parent, and not with the reception of the sacrifice. The parent is kind. The behaviour of the offspring, whose survival turns on that kindness, is no part of its concern. Shakespeare, however, as he inverts the praise of the halcyon—not an image of peace but servility—assimilates to his own purpose the sacrifice of the pelican. The emblem dramatizes the norm. The exalting of self in Goneril and Regan is made the more terrible, to the degree that it is felt as divergence from the norm. Their revolt assumes thereby the proportions of another fall of man. (*Henry V*, 2.2.141f.) In Shakespeare's lexicon, the sacrifice, if it illustrates natural behaviour, functions also as an emblem of parricide. The offspring of a loving father are rendered as cannibals, consuming the father.

But the inversion is just, in the ironic way of *Lear*. It is the father who invokes first the myth of Thyestes: 'he that makes his

[1] Motley tells of Anjou and Orange, III, 521, and II, 244. The engraving attributed to Breughel is reproduced in René van Bastelaer, *Les Estampes de Peter Breughel*, 1908, no. 134. And see Ripa, under 'Bonta' and 'Compassione'; Ripa, London edn., p. 14; Kernodle, p. 67; *Bartholomeus de Proprietatibus Rerum*, bk. xii, 829, tr. J. Trevisa, London, 1535 (quoted H. W. Seager, *Natural History in Shakespeare's Time*, London, 1896, p. 239); the colophon of Sebastian Brant's *La nef des folz du monde*, Paris, 1497; and Praz, I, 67, for an illustration from Typotius, *Symbola*.

generation messes.' (1.1.119) This is to say that bestiality is not peculiar to Lear's wicked daughters. The king, disclaiming propinquity, figures as the dragon (1.1.124), like man in general an ambiguous and manifold emblem: the chief of creatures and the sum of all ill.[1] His abjuring of kind finds a complement in Gloucester's. And hence what was felt as perverse in the beginning becomes in the end almost conventional. Humanity dissolves: animality displaces it.

> The strain of man's bred out
> Into baboon and monkey.
> (*Timon*, 1.1.259f.)

The state itself is gored. (5.3.320) The masters who have its leading, turn it to a shambles. But the masters also are turned or bemonstered:

> You men, you beasts.
> (*Romeo and Juliet*, 1.1.90)

Edmund, the chief among them, is toad-spotted (5.3.138): it is the venom of the toad Edgar glances at in him.[2] Unaccommodated man, divested of nurture, is kin to the animal; at last he is an animal himself. (2.4.269f.) Kent, reduced, is a fellow to the monkey. (2.4.7–9) Gloucester, reduced, goes down to the bear pit. (3.7.54) Edgar, in the character of a madman, is hog, fox, wolf, dog, and lion (3.4.95–97), all of them fit terms for the old stock, the thing itself.

Shakespeare is not singular in spying out in man the capacity of all ill, which stripes may move but not kindness. The Seven Deadly Sins, whose sum is man in what Hobbes called the condition of mere nature, find their appropriate and conventional emblem in the brutish creatures to whom Poor Tom compares himself.[3] The monstrous caricatures of human beings, animal-like, vegetable-like, nightmarish in what they are and

[1] Wilson's *Arte of Rhetorique*, p. 197; Carroll, p. 101.

[2] Topsell, *The Historie of Serpents*, London, 1608, pp. 187–9. Beast images to describe a traitor, the character assigned Edmund here, are frequent in Shakespeare's early histories, and in particular in 2 and 3 *Henry VI* and *Richard III*. See Spurgeon, pp. 228–30, 232f. *Timon of Athens*, among later plays, resorts conspicuously to animal imagery, and for the same reason, I suppose, that one finds such imagery so conspicuous in *Lear*: the unsparing nature of the vision.

[3] See Morton W. Bloomfield, *The Seven Deadly Sins*, East Lansing, Mich., 1952; and especially Appendix I: 'The Association of Animals and Sins.'

what they do, in the pseudo-Rabelaisian *Songes drolatiques*, hint broadly, I suppose, at the fund of strange and bizarre possibilities in man. The image in medieval art of an ape or monkey in chains betokens the state of man before the New Revelation. In the art of the Renaissance, the same image depicts the quelling of man's latent bestiality. The ape, who resembles man without the stiffening and distinguishing mark of reason, is taken as the symbol of everything sub-human in man. That is his use in Renaissance sculpture, to dramatize the debased condition of the soul enslaved by matter.[1]

Cousin to the ape is the wild man or woodwose, a semi-human creature of great antiquity, pre-Christian in his origins, who is believed to inhabit the forests. When Edward Hall chronicles the coronation of Anne Boleyn, he remarks particularly 'a foyst or wafter full of ordnance'—a barge on the Thames,

> in which was a great dragon continually moving and casting wild fire, and round about the foyst stood terrible monsters and wild men, casting fire and making hideous noise.[2]

Those wild men, those wilful men, seem almost to haunt the imagination of the Renaissance. They appear in the homilies, in plays like *The Tempest* and poems like *The Faerie Queene*, and on the title pages of Elizabethan books. Cloten in *Cymbeline*, 'this civilized Caliban', as Granville-Barker called him, an uncertain mixture of human and beast, a creature partly comical but sinister also, is one attempt on Shakespeare's part at representing the wild man. He enters the drama in a medieval Whitsun play which bears his name.[3] *Gorboduc*, the first English tragedy, introduces him to the Elizabethan stage. He appears in the dumb show which prefaces the first act of the play; and also as Bremo in the comedy of *Mucedorus*. As a participant in English and continental street pageants, he was a familiar and, by intention, a deeply disquieting figure. In 1610, a St. George's

[1] As in Michelangelo's tomb of Julius II, in which the ape accompanies a slave. See *Stud. in Icon.*, pp. 195f. and n., fig. 142 (for a seventeenth-century engraving of the ape as an emblem of the subjugation of evil); and Ripa, under 'Sensi' ('Gula') and 'Sfacciataggine'.

[2] Quoted in Theodore Maynard, *The Cross and the Crown*, New York, 1950, p. 91.

[3] The *magnus ludus de homine salvatico*, put on by the citizens of Padua, and performed in 1208, 1224, and (in Switzerland) 1399.

procession in Chester was led by a pair of hideous wild men, whose black hair and beards were tangled in ivy, and whose hands wielded clubs and scattered fireworks before them.

Wild men and women were admitted also to the *tableaux vivants*, as at Bruges in 1515. When the Emperor Charles V was entertained at a street theatre in that city, savage creatures stood guard before it. They intruded their malformed—or, more precisely, unformed—presence in romances like *Valentine and Orson*, in *Gawain and the Green Knight*, and the *Roman de la Rose*, and in Sir Thomas Malory's *Morte d'Arthur*. Hans Sachs in a moment of eccentricity sentimentalized them, anticipating the naïve celebration of the primitive which Shakespeare, in *The Tempest*, puts into the mouth of Gonzalo. Even the Court knew them. In commemoration of Twelfth Night, they danced before Henry VIII in the Great Hall at Greenwich. To divert Elizabeth, during her stay with Leicester at Kenilworth Castle, one of their number, taking advantage of a pause in the chase, emerged from the shrubbery to address an incongruous compliment to the Queen. Two centuries before, and on more than one occasion, they took part in festivities at the Court of Charles VI of France. Swiss tapestries of the fifteenth century include them as a necessary part of the whole. The wild man, like Caliban, is villainous to look on.

> But, as 'tis,
> We cannot miss him.
> (*Tempest*, 1.2.310f.)

This is to say: we cannot do without him. It is that unpalatable truth which Prospero communicates to Miranda.

Heraldic devices of the early Tudor period represent the wild man. In an English Book of Hours, he indulges his characteristic vice of raping women. Less sensationally, in *Don Quixote*, and also in *The Tempest*, he is set his characteristic task of performing heavy labour. Piero di Cosimo paints him. Breughel the Elder, in a woodcut, depicts the Play of the Death of the Wildman. His ancestors are Pan and Silenus; his kindred are fauns, centaurs, and sylvans. He is begotten by a satyr, whose commitment to disorder is similar to his own, and who excites in the Elizabethans the same abhorrence and the same compulsion to keep him before their eyes as a warning or cautionary tale. Thus the contract for the building of the Fortune requires columns carved with satyrs, and not only for the two columns at the front of the stage but also for those which surround the frame of the theatre.[1]

Woodwoses, crouching satyrs, bestial termini, sagittaries: the goatish disposition which is plenary to Edmund but only partial to others, finds its outwall in them.[2] (Plates XXXIV–XXXVI) They are, compounded, the beast in man, the roaring lion of St. James, latent in every human being, the thing of darkness to which even the best man is yoked. Unsophisticated nature and the wild man are one.

> Allow not nature more than nature needs,
> Man's life's as cheap as beast's.
>
> (2.4.269f.)

Take from nature what Edmund, reasoning the need, would designate her accoutrements, expendable at will, and man is worse than a beast. He is crueller because more capable; but that is not it: he is crueller because an apostate. The cuckoo that bit off the head of the sparrow (1.4.235f.) is sickening to contemplate. But it does not know any other law. One is merely sentimental to call it ungrateful. The copulation of the polecat, the wren, the gilded fly (4.6.114f., 124f.) is (it may be) disgusting; but Lear, who calls it lechery, is wrong. Only man is an ingrate and lecher.

[1] See *F.Q.*, I. vi (for the tale of Una, the Satyrs, and Satyrane), and VI, iv; Richard Bernheimer, *Wildmen in the Middle Ages*, Cambridge, Mass., 1952, pp. 51, 59, 62, 67, 86, 93f., 100, 113, 146f., 156–68, 176–85; Robert Withington, *English Pageantry*, Cambridge, Mass., and London, 1918, I, 72–77, and illustrations facing pp. 74 and 102; Kernodle, pp. 64, 73, 134; Chambers, *Eliz. Stage*, II, 437. The fourteenth-century Taymouth Book of Hours is in the B.M., fol. 61v–106v, and is illustrated in Bernheimer, fig. 26, who gives also an illustration of Breughel's woodcut, fig. 16. Illustrations of wild men in heraldic emblems of Henry VII are given in Erna Auerbach, *Tudor Artists*, London, 1954, plates 8 (1517) and 9 (1518).

[2] The motif of Plate XXXV occurs in the work of R. Chaudière I, printer at Paris, 1516–51, and Philippe Pigouchet, bookseller and printer, 1486–1512. See also Berjeau, no. 8; and W. Dunbar, *The Ballad of Lord Barnard Stewart* [1508]. The termini in Plate XXXVI are copied from the frame of a portrait of Erasmus, supposed to be by Holbein, and engraved by Hans Lützelberger. See also H. Braunschweig, *The noble experience of the vertuous Handy Work of Surgery*, Southwark, 1525 (in which a male and female woodwose are used as the printer's device); T. Blenerhasset, *The Seconde part of the Mirrour for Magistrates*, 1578, t.p. (upheld by crouching satyrs); R. Whittington, *De sillabarum quantitate*, 1519 (sagittary and greyhound upholding Caxton's mark); R. Brathwaite, *Natvres Embassie: or, The Wilde-Mans Measvres*, 1621, t.p. (dance of naked satyrs).

Ingratitude is more hideous, more sharp, in the child than in the sea monster or serpent (1.4.281–3, 310f.), because the child, by definition, is the pattern of gratitude. That is what is meant by the offices of childhood. A woman, by definition, by nature, is comely. That is why deformity shows more horrid in her than in the fiend. (4.2.60f.) Gloucester, apprised of the treason of his son, is hardly capable of the wild surmise of belief.

> He cannot be such a monster.
> (1.2.102)

Edgar's supposed opinions are unnatural to his father, a whole man; they are natural, only to a fragment like Edmund.[1] Gloucester calls them brutish, and then, on reflection, 'Worse than brutish!' (1.2.82) 'Let Aesop fable in a winter's night': to praise or blame an animal is to spend one's breath to no purpose. And yet even the brute, the head-lugged bear in his torment (4.2.41f.), does not manifest such cruelty as man. 'All cruels else subscribe' (3.7.64), which is to say, I take it:

> Th'unkindest beast more kinder than mankind.
> (*Timon*, 4.1.36)

Only man is not pregnant to pity.

That is how the story of Arion is moralized. At the great entertainment at Kenilworth in 1575, a man appears before the Queen in the character of Arion, riding the back of an enormous dolphin.[2] The point in which Elizabeth is supposed to be instructed is the same in the *tableau* as in the numerous emblems which redact it.

> No mortall foe so full of poysoned spite,
> As man, to man.[3]

Arion embarks on a journey by sea. The sailors, whose business it is to transport him, choose in their wickedness to throw him over the side. It is left to a dolphin to bring him safe to land.

[1] Kent evinces the same disbelief as Gloucester, and for the same reason. He is unable to conceive of Oswald as a natural phenomenon. (2.2.59f.)

[2] Withington, I, 69, quoting Strutt, *Sports and Pastimes*, London, 1801, pp. xxxiif.

[3] Whitney, *Emblemes*, Sig. Q2v, p. 124. And see Alciati, *Emblematum Libellus*, p. 15; *Emblemes d'Alciat*, Sig. H3r, p. 117; Whitney, Sig. S4v, p. 144; *TwN*, 1.2.15; Ovid, *Fasti*, II. 79f.

Animals show a man greater kindness than his fellows. Man himself is a wolf to man.[1]

The sailors who give their passenger to the sea, in a sense do not know what they do. Their wickedness is a kind of mistaking. It rises from ignorance, which Alciati describes as the origin of evil, and which I take to be an expression and also a condition of man's perverted will. Like its emblem, the woodwose, ignorance is ugly to look on.[2] (Plate XXXVII) It ought, of itself, to proclaim and attest to its own ugliness. 'O thou monster Ignorance, how deformed dost thou look!' But the speaker is Holofernes, the foolish pedant of *Love's Labour's Lost.* (4.2.23) What he descries and cries out on in another, he fails to see in himself. The mariners are purblind also, which is to say wilful. No more than Holofernes do they see their own deformity. But the darkness in which they labour is not, necessarily, perpetual darkness. Given, the accession of knowledge, and evil is discovered for the misshapen leaven it is.

> Their understanding
> Begins to swell, and the approaching tide
> Will shortly fill the reasonable shore
> That now lies foul and muddy.
> (*Tempest*, 5.1.79–82)

If ignorance is the curse of God, knowledge is the wing wherewith we fly to Heaven. (*2 Henry VI*, 4.7.78f.) Ignorance is dissipated, knowledge is attained to, as man silences the darkening counsel of the will. The conditional relationship is precisely that which the emblem of the pelican is intended to mirror. Enlightened behaviour may be made natural behaviour,

> If with the sap of reason you would quench,
> Or but allay the fire of passion.
> (*Henry VIII*, 1.1.148f.)

Art and good learning stead a man in the endeavour. Jack Cade the rebel in *2 Henry VI* is knavish and foolish, only because

[1] *Homo homini lupus.* And see Bruck, *Emb. Bellica*, emblem 2 (a cock fight, complemented by men battling one another), glossed Sig. B2r in *Les Emblemes Moraulx*: 'Miserables humains, miserable leur vie, L'homme à l'homme est un loup plus cruel qu'une harpie.'

[2] 'Telle figure a l'ignorance'. And see Alciati, *Emblematum Libellus*, p. 50.

he makes himself their enemy. That is Shakespeare's point in exploiting the comedy of Cade's rebellion. Vulgar error misreads sophistication, discovering in it a distorting of human nature. But sophistication supplies what is wanting in nature.

> Diligence, maie make the crooked righte.[1]

It sponsors and strengthens those human, those reasonable impulses that might otherwise be overborne by the will. The sophisticated man and the natural man, in the ultimate sense are the same. Art, whom the emblem writers figure as Mercury, improves upon Nature, refines and instructs her. Time brings forth crude matter. Mercury and fire perfect it. In that manner alchemy is rationalized, in an allegorical engraving of 1569.[2] Mercury, in whom art and application are wed, tunes the broken lute, in an emblem dating from the year of Shakespeare's birth. The legend: industry corrects nature.[3] Art is sure: Mercury rests on a cube. Fortune (as you would think) is uncertain: Fortune's stand is a ball.[4] To leave to chance or fortune the task of impressing form on what is, in the beginning, amorphous, is to insure that a man will be no more than half made up. Art is the bestowing of form, a fair woman who supplies the stake which makes good the defects and weaknesses of Nature by supporting the tender plant entwined around it. (Plate XXXVIII) Romeo, made sociable again, made witful, by Mercutio, receives the approbation of his friend: 'Now art thou Romeo; now art thou what thou art, by art as well as by nature.' (2.4.92–95) Nature, left to itself, does not suffice: it is uncouth, malformed. It is however amenable. It may, by reason,

[1] Whitney, *Emblemes*, Sig. M2v, p. 92.

[2] By Hieronymus Olgiatus, who illustrates the inscription, *Hoc monstrum generat, tumperfecit ignis et Azoch*, with the figure of a beautiful winged man enveloped by a serpent and surrounded also by the Zodiac and by attributes of cosmic power. See *Stud. in Icon.*, pp. 72f., and fig. 37.

[3] *Industria naturam corrigit.* See Sambucus, *Emblemata*, Sig. D5r, p. 57; and also Whitney, Sig. M2v, p. 92; and Green, pp. 256f.

[4] So the two are represented under the motto, *Ars Naturam adiuuans*, by Alciati, edn. 1557, given in Green, p. 255. See also *Emblemes d'Alciat*, Sig. H8r, p. 127. In Renaissance iconography, Fortune is often contrasted with Virtue with the words: 'Sedes Fortuna rotunda; sedes Virtutis quadrate.' See Ripa under 'Fortuna' and 'Instabilità'; and *Stud. in Icon.*, p. 225. Rollenhagio, emblem 1, poses a wise man with one hand on a book and the other grasping a globe, against a figure of Death playing with the sceptre and crown: 'Vivitur ingenio, caetera mortis erunt.'

by learning, be licked into shape, as the bear cub is given shape by its mother.[1] (Plate XXXIX)

Cordelia, unlike Edmund, is not content with uncultivated nature. She compels it, becomes

a queen
Over her passion, who most rebel-like
Sought to be king o'er her.
(4.3.15–17)

The image, man as a commonwealth or microcosm, in which passion, the usurper, essays to lead the way, speaks precisely to Shakespeare's chief preoccupation: the war between the rebel and the ruler. Unlike Marlowe, in *Dr. Faustus*, and the masters of the Morality play, he does not extrapolate. There are in his work no good or evil angels, wrestling. The conflict is contained within the man himself.

Poor soul, the centre of my sinful earth,
Thrall to these rebel powers that thee array.

In the well-governed commonwealth, as in the man rightly led, rebellion is not suffered. It breaks down the pales and forts of reason; it makes the reason pander to its own unhallowed purpose: the case of Brutus, Othello, and Macbeth.

The Genius and the mortal instruments
Are then in council, and the state of man,
Like to a little kingdom, suffers then
The nature of an insurrection.
(*Julius Caesar*, 2.1.66–69)

The mortal instruments: my sinful earth, are not to sit down with the Genius, whose highest part is reason (*nous* or *logos*), in determining the course of man's little kingdom.[2] They are to

[1] 'Ingeniũ Doctrina et Literis Formandũ'. The she bear licks her cubs in Vaenius, *Amorum Emblemata*, emblem 29; Guillaume La Perrierè, *Le Theatre des bons engins*, emblem 98 (with the saying: 'L'homme par estude acquiert science et civilité'); Crispin de Passe, *Emblemata Amatoria*, 1596, fol. 2 (in Green, p. 349); and de Passe, *Thronus Cupidus* (in Praz, I, 108). Titian takes the emblem as his device, with the motto: 'Natura potentior Ars.' Perhaps tradition is thinking of the unlicked bear cub in making bears the closest associates of the wild man. See Bernheimer, p. 59; Praz, I, 96f.; Carroll, p. 93.

[2] The metaphor, and the psychology it expresses, enter the Renaissance through the writings of Aristotle and Plato, whose debt is probably to the Pythagoreans. See Thomson, p. 146.

be rated from the council board. Their presence is a usurpation, their business is the murder of a friend, to be sure under colour of necessity.

I must be cruel only to be kind.

Albany, who, like Cordelia, has an eye for decorum, acknowledges the primacy of reason. He forbears to tear his wife. It is not fit to let his hands obey his blood. (4.2.63–66) The others, Lear initially, Goneril, and Cornwall, give rein to the heyday in the blood. Lear cannot support Kent's monition, either in his nature or in his place. (1.1.173f., 302f.) His indulging of caprice in the opening scenes of the play enacts the proposition, 'For what I will, I will, and there an end'. (*Two Gentlemen*, 1.3.65) Goneril, offering necessity, the tyrant's plea, bids the will avouch all. (1.4.232f., 268f.) Cornwall, whose disposition will not be rubbed or stopped (2.2.153f.), like Macbeth enjoins his power to do a courtesy to his wrath. (3.7.25f.)

But Lear is not static but dynamic. He learns to forbear; he coerces the headier will. (2.4.109f.) In that achievement the tragedy is mitigated and the tragic protagonist redeemed. The achievement is unhappily peculiar to him; in that fact the tragedy is confirmed. Goneril and Cornwall, who ought to banish the Caliban, to shut him up in perpetual durance, choose instead to enlarge him. His scope is their captivity, his life their death. It is also the death of the good, who suffer willy-nilly for the choice of the wicked.

Whiles lions war and battle for their dens,
Poor harmless lambs abide their enmity.
(*3 Henry VI*, 2.5.74f.)

Thus the tragedy differs from the homily.

Then bridle will, and reason make thy guide,
So maiste thow stande, when others doune doe slide.[1]

The moralist abhors, and rightly, the triumph of will over reason. He discovers in that triumph the confounding of the fool who gives his countenance to it. The dramatist, who sees more, and who, faithful to his vision, sets down what he sees, is necessarily the more austere, and much the more impassioned.

[1] Whitney, *Emblemes*, Sig. A3v, p. 6.

In the usurpation of the will he discovers the overthrow of the just with the unjust. When the blood begins to rule the safer guides, not only Lear falls—that is, if you like, poetic justice—but Cordelia. In her fall there is no justice. *Terras Astraea reliquit.* There is only fidelity to fact.

VII

SHOW AND SUBSTANCE

REASON is sovereign. Will is a liegeman. Reason's office is to hedge round the will. But reason panders will. Reason is beguiled by the façade of things. It confuses show with substance. Reason is purblind.

A man's equipment, by virtue, I suppose, of the imposition hereditary ours, is clearly not all that it might be. The child who is attracted by the checkered skin of a snake is stung because his senses respond to its beauty; the passengers whom the crocodile snares with his tears have their inborn compassion to thank. Their mistake seems to turn on what they are, by definition. Man, whom all agree in describing as fallible, is necessarily a creature who squares his guess by shows. (*All's Well*, 2.1.153) He is liable, therefore, to draw false conclusions from the evidence available to him. Shakespeare's plays dramatize the mistreadings that follow, and the iron consequence those mistreadings involve.

> See how belief may suffer by foul show!
> (*Pericles*, 4.4.23)

It is, to say the least, very hard. But Queen Margaret's analogies in *2 Henry VI* (3.1.226–30) of the innocent child and the crocodile who appears to be mournful are not genuinely apposite. The plays do not have to do with children, or with technical matters on which only Pliny is competent to pass. They are concerned with the reading of human situations by adult persons who are or ought to be sophisticated, fully fledged, and hence qualified to judge of what they see. Shakespearean tragedy, if it confesses man's weakness, insists also, and more emphatically, on his strength. It posits in its heroes and villains an understanding of alternatives. They are not constrained to mistake an indefinite, a lesser good for the one good. Their ignorance, though an inheritance to them, is not beyond their controlling. It is felt, therefore, as culpable ignorance. There is no thought in the plays of mocking a man by requiring perception of him and yet depriving him of sight. The mock is rather that a man should have the use of eyes, and yet see the way of blindness. (*Cymbeline*, 5.4.194–5) No blind men stumble in Shakespearean tragedy; only seeing men. No children or idiots or uninitiated men make the wrong choices because they do not know any better; only the self-conscious are permitted to choose. The bad choice or faulty inference is felt to be avoidable, and so to merit, commiseration certainly, but also indictment. If man is prone to misread, he is free and also able to read aright.

It is because of that putative ability that blindness, which disuses it, is stigmatized, by convention. To the medieval moralist, blindness 'conveys to us only something negative and nothing positive, and by the blind man we generally understand the sinner'. Error, Fury, and Prodigality, as Cesare Ripa depicts them, are blind. The blindness of Cupid, an attribute created for him by the Middle Ages, attests, not to his caprice, but to the medieval abhorrence of profane love. In an engraving of the seventeenth century, it is Fortune who puts out the eyes of Cupid. The indicated response to both figures, standing together on the ball, is contempt: both are blind. But Cupid, in a painting by Lucas Cranach the Elder, who removes the bandage from his eyes while standing on the works of Plato, excites not contempt but admiration: his newfound knowledge makes him over. He becomes an emblem of clear seeing or genuine love.[1] Blindness is badness; the restoring of sight is the emergence of good.

Now Gloucester is blind. He affects to delineate the quality of nothing. (1.2.34f.) He plumes himself on his opacity.

[1] See Petrus Berchorius, *Dictionarii sev repertorii moralis . . . pars prima-tertia*, Venice, 1583, under 'Cecus, Cecitas'; and 'Blind Fortune Blinding Cupid', p. 157 in Otho Venius, *Les Emblèmes de l'Amour Humain*, Brussels, 1667. Cranach's 'Cupid Unblinding Himself' is in the Philadelphia Museum of Art. See also *Stud. in Icon.*, 'Blind Cupid', pp. 95–128, and figs. 105 (Venius) and 106 (Cranach).

Gloucester needs no spectacles. (1.2.36) And so you may draw him, as Hamlet draws Polonius.

Very like a whale.

Sight is given him; he disdains it: sight is taken from him.

Pluck out his eyes.
(3.7.5)

The King is blind also.

See better, Lear.
(1.1.160)

The darker purpose he wishes to express is more than the division of a kingdom. (1.1.36) It is nothing less than to plunge the scarabs in his eyes. Like Gloucester, he himself bereaves himself of sight.

That such a king should play bo-peep.
(1.4.184)

Unlike Gloucester, he does not wear the stigma of his blindness: the case of eyes. (4.6.147) He does not have to. To mark him would be superfluous. His blindness has been patent from the first: 'he hath ever but slenderly known himself.' (1.1.296f.) But self-knowledge is mandatory. So, unluckily, is a knowledge of others. It is as fateful to err in ignorance as in cunning. (*Othello*, 3.3.49) To think men honest that but seem to be so—Edgar's case, Othello's case—is to take hands with Edmund and Iago. On the foolish honesty of a credulous man, the plots of a villain ride easy. (1.2.197f.) Edgar, like his father, is blind.

But so, paradoxically, are Edmund and Goneril. 'Madman, thou errest,' says Feste the Clown to Malvolio. 'I say, there is no darkness but ignorance, in which thou art more puzzled than the Egyptians in their fog.' (*Twelfth Night*, 4.2.46–48) Edmund, in his ignorance, confuses mere sight with perceiving.

I see the business.
(1.2.198)

He takes the symbol for the thing itself. Goneril is ignorant also. She offers the symbol for the thing. She understands that the one does not jump with the other. She thinks only to make the imposture go down. That is the sense of her hypocrisy. The love she tenders Lear is dearer than eyesight. (1.1.56) But to practise on others is to hoodwink oneself. ' "Fly pride," says the peacock' (*Comedy of Errors*, 4.3.81), the incarnation of pride and so the emblem of hypocrisy, but also, and necessarily, of self-deception. Goneril's ignorance is as efficacious as Edmund's: imposition turns on evil purpose: to address oneself to evil is to warp one's nature to it. The dyer's hand acquires the colour of the dye. The face and the vizard at last are the same. Show is at last not to be distinguished from substance.

And knowing what I am, I know what she shall be.
(*Othello*, 4.1.74)

The credulous assertion is Iago's, who, as he is the prime hypocrite, is *ipso facto* the prime gull. His greatest punishment is not the torture to which he is consigned. It is to believe good of no one. Goneril, who cozens others at hoodman blind, infallibly is cozened herself. The hypocrisy she ventures on is in fact dearer than eyesight.

Do you see nothing there?
Nothing at all, yet all that is I see.

Goneril also is blind.

Cordelia and Kent, Edgar in good time, do not make the mistake of Malvolio. They do not take the symbol for the thing itself.

Nothing that is so is so.
(*Twelfth Night*, 4.1.9)

Nor do they offer that symbol in lieu of the thing.

Love, and be silent.
(1.1.62)

Cordelia's love is more ponderous than her tongue. (1.1.79f.) Her poverty, read thoughtfully, argues munificence: for want of a speaking eye, she is the richer. (1.1.230f.) Kent professes to be no less than he seems. (1.4.14) That is a measure, of his goodness, surely; but more than that: in the root sense, it describes his integrity. The hypocrite dismembers, and so disables, himself. He is a fraction.

I am not what I am.

Kent, concurrently, is more than he seems. (3.1.44f.) He wraps up his great quality in concealment (4.3.53):

> More valour in me than my habits show.
> (*Cymbeline*, 5.1.30)

That is a measure of his cunning: he pays the debt he never promised. Edgar, a fugitive, knows himself contemned. That is better than to be contemned and flattered. (4.1.1f.) Edgar, who seems wretched, has the victory of Edmund, who pledges more than he possesses. (5.1.42) It is a dangerous kind of vaunting, likened by the emblem writer to that of the ostrich, whose wings are fair enough and broad enough but, put to the proof, unavailing.[1] *Nil Penna, sed Vsus.* They have only the look of the thing. Edmund's case is the same. His appearance gives him out to be substantial; he is as little substantial as a worm-eaten nut. The rags of a carl put to shame the gilded arms of a retainer. (*Cymbeline*, 5.5.4) The rude Guiderius in *Cymbeline* shames Cloten the prince. Posthumus, the drudge of Nature, outfaces Iachimo. (5.2.4f.) Oswald, who wears a swashing and a martial outside (*As You Like It*, 1.3.122), is bested by Edgar, in the character of a peasant and slave. (4.6.235, 241) Oswald, as he is less than his outwall, cannot conceive of a man who is more. Oswald is fooled to the top of his bent.

Ignorance is not bliss, but the courting of disaster. To see the innocent flower but not the serpent beneath it is to go the way of King Duncan. To be the serpent and yet resemble the flower, is to go the way of Macbeth. (1.5.66f.) The king and the murderer fall equally from ignorance. Each is the gull of appearances. Duncan does not revel in his ignorance. His time is abridged. Macbeth, as he is given greater scope, is the more dramatically transformed. His nature, as it waxes in evil, wanes in the capacity of spying out good. Thus it speeds its dissolution. Only the beautiful soul perceives beauty. Goneril is deformed. Her punishment follows:

> Wisdom and goodness to the vile seem vile.
> (4.2.38)

Rank corruption is not static. Progressively, it mines everything

[1] Rollenhagio, *Nucleus Emblematum*, emblem 36. See also Whitney, *Emblemes*, Sig. G2r, p. 51.

within. So far from discerning error, one grows to adore it.

> He that is giddy thinks the world turns round.
> (*Taming of the Shrew*, 5.2.26)

The mildness of a husband begins to seem a harmful mildness; his gentle course becomes the occasion of irony and blame. (1.4.364–7; 4.2.1, 12f.) Thus the hard are hardened, the blind are blinded more. They strut to their confusion.

Surrey, in the last of Shakespeare's histories, as he is deformed, heaves the gorge at beauty:

> All goodness
> Is poison to thy stomach.
> (*Henry VIII*, 3.2.282)

The Elizabethan homilist is more memorable than Shakespeare's Wolsey: 'Put not meate into a pyspot . . . Caste not good sentences in to the mynde of a wycked person.'[1] Shakespeare, in *As You Like It*, makes the proverb presentable: 'to cast away honesty upon a foul slut were to put good meat into an unclean dish.' (3.3.35f.) Good counsel is squandered on evil behaviour. Evil savours only itself. King Lear, as he does evil, seels up his eyes. The result follows, and predictably. He confuses the foul disease and the physician. (1.1.166f.) He kills the physician. The disease kills him. He confuses show and substance, invests Albany and Cornwall with power and pre-eminence, retains for himself only the name and additions, which is to say the titles, pertaining to a king. (1.1.132–41) In Gloucester's phrase, he is 'Confined to exhibition!' (1.2.25) Then—and this, and not the act of abdication is the kernel of his fault—he would continue to manage the authorities he has given away. (1.3.16–18) But like his fellow monarch in Sidney's *Arcadia*, who loses his function to a bastard son, he comes to discover that, before he is aware, he has left himself nothing but the name of a king.

His greatest blunder is of course to misconstrue Cordelia, the epitome of the unprized that is precious. (1.1.262) To find that misconstruction improbable, is one thing. It is improbable; it has to be. To seek to gloss it over is, however, to miss the heart of the matter. Coleridge, contemplating uneasily the incredible

[1] 'Cibum in metellamne immittas.' See Sigs. I8r–v in Taverner, *Prouerbes or Adagies, gathered oute of the Chiliades*, 1552.

business of the opening scene, strives to rationalize it and so to make it credible by finding 'some little faulty admixture of pride and sullenness in Cordelia's "Nothing".'[1] In fact one wants to heighten and not to suppress the element of the bizarre in the rejection of a daughter neither prideful nor sullen but altogether guiltless. The less probable that rejection, the less credible, the more does it tell you of the monstrous nature of Lear's behaviour. The words of Perillus, who counsels Leir in the old play, are apt:

> Ah, who so blind, as they that will not see.
> (sc. 6)

King Lear will not see, though he has his own lantern to light him. (*2 Henry IV*, 1.2.52–54) Coleridge was right: the love test, as the spring of all that follows, is fantastic. Rymer was right: *Othello* hinges on a cheap trick of melodrama. But the beginning of *Lear* and the decisive complication of *Othello* are what they ought to be. Their eccentricity lights up what is at issue, what ordinary realism would serve only to obfuscate.

> Trifles light as air
> Are to the jealous, confirmations strong
> As proofs of Holy Writ.
> (*Othello*, 3.3.322–4)

Cordelia's refusal to utter hyperbole:

> I cannot heave
> My heart into my mouth,
> (1.1.93f.)

approves the Biblical saying, 'The heart of fools is in their mouth: but the mouth of the wise is in his heart.'[2] But Lear does not concur. He does not see, as France sees, that Cordelia is most rich being poor, most choice when forsaken, most loved, and loving, when despised (1.1.253f.); that, to paraphrase Corinthians, she has nothing, and yet possesses all things. By a kind of ghastly irony, he calls her himself the little-seeming

[1] See Coleridge, *Lectures and Notes on Shakspere and Other English Poets*, London, 1883, p. 335; and Bradbrook, *Themes and Conventions*, p. 40.

[2] Ecclesiasticus, xxi. 26. See the saying ascribed to Plato in Baldwin, *Treatise*, London, n.d., Sig. N7r: 'The tongue of a wise man is in his heart, but the heart of a foole in hys tong.'

substance (1.1.201); he rejects her solid quality, because it is unapparelled, for the hollow protesting of Goneril and Regan. The wicked sisters apparel vice like virtue's harbinger. (*Comedy of Errors*, 3.2.12) They are as rich in promise as an alehouse painted sign. (*Titus*, 4.2.98) But rich honesty is not richly apparelled. It dwells like a miser in a poor house. (*As You Like It*, 5.4.63f.) Truth also, as the Renaissance bodies her forth, is unapparelled, like Cordelia.[1] (Plate XL) Cunning is plighted, not candour. (1.1.280) Evil hides in pleats of majesty. (*Lucrece*, l. 93) Truth is stripped naked, clad only in itself. (4.3.44)

Lear, perversely blind, identifies nakedness with lack of substance. He makes the mistake of the medieval artist who, depicting a contest between Nature and Reason, clothes the higher principle and leaves Nature, the lesser, unclothed. Mantegna also, painting the two Venuses, indicates by her nakedness the inferiority of Aphrodite to Urania. But the right reading is otherwise. The lesser figure, Kent as Caius in Shakespeare's play, is wrapped up in concealment. He is known and honoured, his truth is made manifest, only as he puts off his mufflings. (4.3.53–55). Conversely, Man the hero, in Henry Medwall's *Nature*, as he puts on those mufflings, is diminished. His nakedness, initially, denotes his freedom from taint. In the interlude, the innocence of the hero is established; in the tragedy, the redemption of the hero is prefigured, in the denuding of either.

> Off, off, you lendings! Come, unbutton
> here.[2] (3.4.112f.)

Edgar also, stripped of his Persian attire, as he enacts 'the naked fellow' is made, not less but more. For nakedness is not the badge of inferiority but Truth. Latin poetry celebrates the nakedness of Truth. The New Testament affirms it. The Graces are naked to betoken their candour. Even the medieval sculptor fashions a nude Temperance or Chastity, taking the undraped Venus as his

[1] The figures flanking the title, in Plate XL, represent Leicestershire and Antiquity (holding a book and torch). Below them is a foot-plan of Lindley. Naked Truth, at the top, holding in her hand her immemorial attribute, the sun, finds her complement and antithesis in winged Fame. For other and similar images of Truth, see Henry Peacham, *The Compleat Gentleman*, London, 1634, t.p.; Ch. II, Plate VII, and Ch. III, Plate XIII.

[2] T. N. Greenfield, 'The Clothing Motif in "King Lear",' *Shakespeare Quarterly*, V, 1954, 281–6.

model. In the art of the Renaissance and after, representations of *Nuda Veritas* become very nearly a convention. Botticelli paints a naked Truth. Bernini unveils her. To Titian, contrasting profane and sacred love, the nude Venus is the noble Venus. Beauty and Wisdom and Love of Virtue are drawn naked, in Ripa's *Iconologia.* God's Grace, as she is innocent, is naked. Beneficence is unclothed, and hence divested of vainglory and self-interest. Naked Truth holds the sun in her hand, to signify her pleasure in clearness. Her foot tramples on the globe, transcending mortality: she is, in her unambiguous purity, immortal. A sixteenth-century Italian printer takes the naked Truth as his emblem. A German printer, who is also a Protestant, discovers in it a pledge of reformation. Mary Tudor, to a Catholic like Cardinal Pole, epitomizes the Truth: in 1553, the year of her crowning, 'armed power prepared to destroye her, yet she being a virgin, helpless, naked, and unarmed, prevailed.' The Anabaptists, though as pious, were not so successful. On a wintry night in Amsterdam in 1535, a dozen of them stripped and ran naked through the streets, crying, 'Wo, wo, wo! The wrath of God, the wrath of God!' Nor would they put on their clothes when arrested. 'We are', they said, 'the naked truth.' Whether they went naked to the scaffold is unknown.

Thomas Middleton in the following century contrived to enter, in the Lord Mayor's Pageant, at least a naked-seeming Truth. John Davies of Hereford and Joseph Fletcher dwelt in their poems on Truth's nakedness. Shakespeare did also, in the first of his plays:

> The truth appears so naked on my side
> That any purblind eye may find it out.
> (*1 Henry VI*, 2.4.20f.)

Just as Cordelia is dismantled by the king of those many folds of favour (1.1.220f.) in which she was accustomed to go, so does she approximate more nearly to the person of Truth.[1] In time

[1] The debate of 'Nature and Reason' (Paris, Bibliothèque Nationale, MS. Fr. 379, fol. 33, *c.* 1500) is illustrated in *Stud. in Icon.*, fig. 111; as are similar representations of 'Nature and Grace' (on the Medal of Constantine, Vienna, Kunsthistorisches Museum, *c.* 1400), fig. 110; and 'St. Basilius between Worldly Happiness and Heavenly Life' (in a Byzantine miniature, Paris, Bib. Nat., MS. Grec. 923, fol. 272, ninth century), fig. 109. Mantegna's version of the *Geminae Veneres* is included in his painting, 'The Realm of Comus', in the Louvre. He reverses

Lear acknowledges that it is so. He grows to understand that those whose low sound reverbs no hollowness are not necessarily empty hearted (1.1.155f.); that those whose blood seems snow broth may be given to luxury and riot (4.6.120–5); that the gown of office, if it covers a king, will cover a dog as efficiently.[1] (4.6.161, 167) Then he can fall to railing against simulation, the disparity between substance and show. But then it is too late.[2]

If good words and good feature ran in tandem with good intent, Lear and Gloucester would not be put to so bitter a schooling. But the good and the wicked are alike disobliging. Truth's a dog must to kennel. (1.4.124) The good man, in his whimsy, takes the basest and the poorest shape that ever penury brought near to beast. (2.3.6–9) He presents himself to you in the garb of a servitor or bedlam. To prosecute his intent, he craves disguise. (1.4.2–4) As you value your life, you must

---

the Greek representation of Aphrodite Urania (Praxiteles, Knidos) as nude, and the terrestrial Aphrodite (Kos) as clothed. Horace writes of 'nuda Veritas' in *Carmina*, I. 24, 7; and Petronius of 'nuda virtus' in *Sat.* 88. For a New Testament reference, see Hebrews, IV. 13. Nude Truth enters the Middle Ages in the Quattrocento, by virtue of a mistaken reading of Lucian's description of the 'Calumny of Apelles'. The earliest known rendering, a miniature dating from 1350–1, is by Opicinus de Canistris (Cod. Pal. lat. 1993, fol. 26), fig. 114 in *Stud. in Icon.* Giovanni Pisano imitates the Venus Pudica in his pulpit (1302/1310) in the Cathedral at Pisa, fig. 113. Botticelli's 'Nude Truth' is a part of his 'Calumny of Apelles' in the Uffizi. Bernini's 'Naked Truth Unveiled', 1646–52, is in the Galleria Borghese, Rome; as is Titian's 'Sacred and Profane Love,' *c.* 1515. For nudity in Ripa, see under Amor di Virtu, Felicità Eterna, Amicizia, Anima, Bellezza, Chiarezza, Ingegno, Sapienza, Virtú heroica, Benificio, Conversione, Gratio di Dio, Gloria, Natura, Verità; and, in the Venice edn. of 1645, Idea. The Italian printer is Marcolino da Forlì; the German, John Knoblouch of Strasbourg (1521), whose mark is illustrated by Saxl, p. 203. Saxl, p. 207, quotes Cardinal Pole. Motley, I, 80, tells of the Anabaptists. Middleton's pageant dates from 1613. Davies wrote of naked Truth in *Humours Heav'n on Earth*, 1609; and Fletcher in *The History of the Perfect-Cursed-Blessed Man*, 1628, in which Truth holds a sun, as she does in Bernini's Tomb of Alexander VII, in St. Peter's, Rome. Gloucester puns on Truth's attribute in the opening lines of *RIII*. See also Berchorius, *Dictionarii*, Venice, 1583, under Nudus, Nuditas; and *Stud. in Icon.*, ch. V, 'The Neoplatonic Movement in Florence and North Italy', pp. 129–69, and in particular pp. 153–9.

[1] So the comely figure of False-Semblant or Hypocrisy in *The Romaunt of the Rose*: 'Whoso took a wethers skyn, And wrapped a gredy wolf theryn.' See Fragment C, ll. 6259f.

[2] See Spenser, *F.Q.*, Book II, Canto x, stanza 31, on Lear's belated discovery: 'The wretched man gan then avise too late, That love is not, where most it is profest.'

pierce the disguise. It is no good to plead myopia, to answer saying: When saw we thee an hungered, or athirst, or a stranger, or naked, or sick, or in prison, and did not minister unto thee? There is a sense in which the purblind man may be said to make love to his myopic employment.

The wicked also raze their likeness. They are not always vulpine, on their face. The heart of the fox is not figured by his coat, or not always.[1]

> Who cannot steal a shape that means deceit?
>
> (*2 Henry VI*, 3.1.79)

To know a man's mind, one must rip his heart. (4.6.262) For the evil are often beauteous, 'empty trunks, o'er-flourished by the Devil'. Only a child will wonder that a man's face can fold up murder in a smile. (*Titus*, 2.3.266f.) Nature connives at the practice of the hypocrite. Nature closes in pollution with a wall. (*Twelfth Night*, 3.4.403f.; 1.2.48f.) To choose another metaphor: *Cucullus non facit monachum:* But all hoods make not monks (*Henry VIII*, 3.1.23), a proverb which might serve as the epigraph, if one is fond of summary tags, at once for *Twelfth Night* and *Measure for Measure*. In those plays and, more notably, in *Lear*, Shakespeare picks up, but to dispute, not endorse, the pseudo-Platonic notion, widely received in the Renaissance, that

> the frame
> And composition of the mind doth follow
> The frame and composition of the body:
> So, where the body's furniture is beauty,
> The mind's must needs be virtue.
>
> (Ford, *'Tis Pity*, 2.5)

Marlowe, in *Hero and Leander*, approved the saying: those compounded of

> misshapen stuff
> Are of behaviour boisterous and rough.
>
> (I.203f.)

In the essay, 'Of Deformity', Bacon gave it his testimony: 'Deformed persons are commonly even with nature. For as

[1] To paraphrase Whitney (*Emblemes*, Sig Q2v, p. 124), who warns us to beware, not of open foes but those 'that doe in secret lurke'.

nature hath done ill by them, so do they by nature; being . . . *void of natural affection.*'

It is a pleasant and a popular fancy. To look is to know. The good man is good to look on; the evil man, by a stroke of luck, is evil favoured. When Ripa wants an emblem of a virtuous action, he finds it in the figure of a handsome young man,[1] whose superficial comeliness tells you what he is within. The ugly man, conversely, says the poet Eustache Deschamps, reveals in his face his ugliness of spirit:

> Que homs de membre contrefais
> Est en sa pensée meffais,
> Plains de pechiez et plains de vices.

The young Crookback is as crooked in his manners as his shape. (*2 Henry VI*, 5.1.157f.) His rivals and victims you would suppose to be sufficiently warned. But not so. After all he beguiles them, so smooth does he daub his vice with show of virtue. (*Richard III*, 3.5.29) It is Hastings, whose execution is already fixed, who is sure that you may know his heart by his face. (3.4.55) And so the lament:

> Oh, that deceit should steal such gentle shapes,
> And with a virtuous vizard hide foul guile!
> (*Richard III*, 2.2.27f.)

The forehead reveals the man, says the commonplace.[2] Shakespeare's understanding is less eupeptic. The painted outwall as often as not betokens dearth. (Sonnet 146) Outward show seldom jumps with the heart. (*Richard III*, 3.1.10f.) *Frontis nulla fides*. For

> man is made, of suche a seemlie shape,
> That frende, or foe, is not discern'd by face.[3]

There's no faith in the forehead.

> There's no art
> To find the mind's construction in the face.
> (*Macbeth*, 1.4.11f.)

[1] See *Iconologia*, under *Attione virtuosa*.

[2] *Frons Hominem Praefert.*

[3] Whitney, *Emblemes*, Sig. N2v, p. 100. See also Sambucus (from whom Whitney took the emblem), *Emblemata*, Sig. M1r, p. 177; and the figuring of the moral in *The History and Antiquities of Hawsted and Hardwick, in the County of Suffolk*, John Cullum, London, 1813, pp. 159–65, cited Green, p. 129.

The wolf has learned to mimic the lamb: in that way you are to gloss the fable of the pullet that laid the golden egg. *Ne regarder à l'apparence.*[1] Warm a snake in your breast, oblivious of its nature, and the snake will sting your heart. (*2 Henry VI*, 3.1.243f.) The reward of the goat who gives suck to the wolf, as the play is concerned to remind you, is that of the hedge sparrow: its head is bit off by its young.[2] (1.4.235f.) But the wolf also is gulled. Webster, in *The White Devil*, tells of Aesop's 'foolish dog that let go the flesh to catch the shadow'. (5.1) As the wolf is vicious, it is foolish: it worships shadows and adores false shapes. (*Two Gentlemen*, 4.2.131) It confuses a man with the bust of a man. (Plate XLI) It takes a mess of shadows for its meat.

Unwitting faith is foolish faith.[3] The fable of the elephant and the undermined tree dramatizes the saying. The improvident elephant, whose legs are for necessity, not for flexure (*Troilus and Cressida*, 2.3.114f.), sets his rest on a tree at which the hunters have been digging, 'And downe he falles, and so by them was slaine'.[4] The construction: simple strength, that declines to look about it, is disabled by a limping but a provident weakness, the case of Shakespeare's Caesar, a puissant man, and fatuous, who loved

> to hear
> That unicorns may be betrayed with trees
> And bears with glasses, elephants with holes.
> (*Julius Caesar*, 2.1.203–5)

So much for the ignorance that is bliss. The emblem of a heart and the seeing hand that holds it exemplifies the alternate way.[5] (Plate XLII) Works are more substantial than words. But Lear is covetous of words. And so like the elephant, he sets his rest on nothing, the avowals of Goneril and Regan. He trusts to summer days. He grows old, and forbears to grow wise. (1.5.48f.)

[1] Desprez, *Le Theatre*, p. 57.

[2] See Whitney, *Emblemes*, Sig. G1r, p. 49.

[3] *Nusquam tuta fides*, the legend Sambucus finds in the emblem of the elephant.

[4] Whitney's verses on his fate, Sig. T3v, p. 150. See also Sambucus, *Emblemata*, Sig. M4v, p. 184, in Green, p. 196.

[5] Rollenhagio's gloss, Sig. C4v, interprets the emblem: 'Fide, sed vide. Credule ne croy pas aux paroles trop belles, Mais iuge tes amis par les oeuvres fidelles; Et tousiours va portant un oeil dedans ta main, Croyant ce qu'elle tient pouvoir estre certain.'

How ill white hairs become a fool and jester!

He does not consult for winter in the spring. And winter overtakes him, as it overtakes the grasshopper, who believed he had white hairs in his beard before the black ones were there (4.6.98f.), and who, in consequence, is set to school to an ant, to learn there's no labouring in winter.[1] (2.4.68f.) (Plate XLIII) To plead a lack of prescience does not suffice. Time, which the grasshopper squanders in his ignorance, brings in its revenges upon him. He is wasted by time. Lear, as his ignorance is the more signal, is the more cruelly paid home. He scorns to learn the uses of time.[2] And so he tastes his folly: he mounts the wheel of fire. Ignorance is fatal: the old and reverend had better be wise. (1.4.261) It is, moreover, wilful. And

to wilful men
The injuries that they themselves procure
Must be their schoolmasters.
(2.4.305–7)

Goneril and Regan are more ensteeped in ignorance than Lear. Enamoured of power, they see between them and the gilded tombs they covet only those obstacles that are tangible, palpable: the appurtenances of physical power. That is why Goneril, requesting Lear 'A little to disquantity your train', describes herself as one who 'else will take the thing she begs'. (1.4.269f.) That is why Regan, to whom Lear has given all, announces baldly, with entire self-assurance, 'And in good time you gave it'. (2.4.253) The meaning is that Lear is stripped of real power.

For I lack soldiers.
(4.6.119)

[1] See also Whitney, *Emblemes*, Sig. V4r, p. 159; and Freitag, *Mythologia Ethica*, Antwerp, 1579, p. 29, who moralizes the fable of the grasshopper and the ant with the motto, 'Contraria industriae ac desidiae praemia,' and who appends to his emblem, as Desprez does (the one in Latin, the other in French), the Biblical saying 'The sluggard will not plow by reason of the cold; therefore shall he beg in harvest, and have nothing' (Proverbs, xx.4). Green, p. 129, quotes Freitag. The fable of the fly and the ant, as Camerarius treats it, is analogous: 'At ego aestate mediocri labore exerceor, vt hyeme quietam & securam vitam possim degere.' See T. W. Baldwin, *Shakespeare's Small Latine and Lesse Greeke*, I, 620f.; Muir, p. 86n.; and Proverbs, vi.6–8, xxx.25.

[2] Ford, *Perkin Warbeck*, 4.4: 'The use of time Is thriving safety, and a wise prevention Of ills expected.'

What is there, then, to balk his daughters in doing their will upon him?

> Who can arraign me for 't?
> (5.3.159)

Edmund, in his capacity as idolater of the outside, the extrinsic, in a word of all that is least consequential, offers, implicitly, an answer. Age has no rights because it has no power. (1.2.50–53) That is to say, there is no law but power. 'Our strong arms be our conscience, swords our law.' (*Richard III*, 5.3.311) It follows, for Edmund, that

> All with me's meet that I can fashion fit.
> (1.2.191)

Strength alone marshals the way. Those who are weak had best seem so. (2.4.203)

But appearances deceive. God is not, absolutely, on the side of the big battalions. The wicked sisters see too little. And lead is more precious than silver and gold, as Morocco, the unlucky suitor in *The Merchant of Venice*, whose apprehension is more collied than his skin, learns at considerable cost. The wicked sisters see too much. Like Stephano and Trinculo, the would-be villains of *The Tempest*, they dedicate themselves to the achievement of trash. Court persons, who ebb and flow by the moon, they find their emblem in Sisyphus, for ever rolling his stone.[1] Their ears are stopped to the sense of the melancholy question, a Kingmaker's question:

> Why, what is pomp, rule, reign, but earth and dust?
> (*3 Henry VI*, 5.2.27)

Sandblind as they are, they do not understand that the trumpery they covet is no more than stale to catch thieves, that the treasures they would lay up are open to corruption. In the event, the Scriptural saying is verified against them: sword, sceptre, and crown shrivel to ashes.[2] (Plate XLIV) Goneril and Regan,

[1] See Ripa, under *Vita inquieta*.

[2] Rollenhagio glosses emblem 86 (Plate XLIV), Sig. D2v: 'Sic transit gloria mundi. Il n'est rien icy las d'eternelle duree, La gloire du monde semblable a la fumee, Plus elle va brave, ses cornes eslevant, Plus elle s'esva novit, E devient à neant.' For a similar emblem (no. 73) of the globe with a city revealed in the centre, and smoke billowing up from it, Rollenhagio chooses as his legend the words,

who profess to be shrewd, are really most sanguine. Blithely they cast about for a tree in which to build. But God has sold the forest to Death.[1]

Pulvis et umbra. The gloss (Sig. C4v): 'Humana fumus. Les sceptres, les honneurs, E la gloire moidaine, Et tout ce qui depend de la grandeur humaine, N'est rien qu'une fumee, E pure vanité, Qui perit en naissant come un fleur d'esté.' Boissard, beneath the words, 'Homo Bulla', depicts the treasures of the earth heaped up beside a boy blowing bubbles, which are punctured as they ascend. *Emb. liber*, Metz, 1588, Sig. C4r, p. 23.

[1] In the words of Samuel Rutherford in a letter to Lady Kenmure, quoted Buchan, p. 20.

VIII

REDEMPTION

EVIL, which is yoke fellow to ignorance, stems from a failure rightly to distinguish the good. *Lear* documents amply the result of that failure. Its decisive manifestation is in the opening lines of the play. Thus one may speak of all that follows as a long denouement. The action wanes as it waxes. But the play describes a second curve, antithetical to the first. The action waxes as it wanes. The new moon is cradled in the arms of the old. This is to say that the delineating of the greatest evil is made that of the greatest good. Where you find Goneril, there do you find Cordelia. Edmund's cruelty is the occasion of Edgar's compassion, Lear's decline the condition of Lear's rejuvenescence.

> There is some soul of goodness in things evil,
> Would men observingly distil it out.
>
> (*Henry V*, 4.1.4f.)

The rising action of the play, the suspense it engenders, is, not in the adversity with which the characters are visited, but in their discovery of the uses of adversity. When Lear's daughters drive him out in the storm, there is in his banishment no discovery, or peripeteia. The wicked daughters confirm, it is true, their evil design. It is, however, a design that has been long maturing, long patent. Only Lear is oblivious of it.

> I know you what you are.

The exciting discovery he makes on the heath.

He had thought himself a king, in his lexicon a rare (an impossible) being, fenced off from the ills that flesh is heir to.

He discovers that the king and the outcast are one, that but for idle ceremony the slave has the forehand and vantage of the king. Ceremony, a king's prerogative, is not proof against the fever. (4.6.107) Divest a king of his robes, undeck the pompous body, and you find him a cipher (1.4.212, 251), just such a forked animal as any other. (3.4.110f.)

> But now a king, now thus.
> (*King John*, 5.7.66)

Who, from the skull of a king or a peasant, can distinguish the king or the peasant?[1] (Plate XLV) In this sense the garment determines the man. King Cophetua and the beggar maid are not so much different as the same.

> The king's a beggar, now the play is done.
> (*All's Well*, Epilogue)

One event happens to all. What is more: if man is kin to the angels, he is also, however you clothe him, kin to the worm. (4.1.33)

Discovering so much, Lear makes the unshunnable inference. Men are players merely, chimeras who pursue the chimerical. 'We are both on the stage,' writes the Parliamentary general Sir William Waller to the royalist friend whose defeat and wounding he brought about at the battle of Lansdown. 'We are both on the stage, and we must act the parts that are assigned to us in this tragedy.'[2] But the universal theatre presents more woeful pageants than the scene in which Waller and his adversary play. (*As You Like It*, 2.7.137–9) All the world's a stage to feed contention in a lingering act. (*2 Henry IV*, 1.1.155f.) You great men take the centre, says the Bastard in *King John*; lesser men stand around you

> As in a theatre, whence they gape and point
> At your industrious scenes and acts of death.
> (2.1.375f.)

[1] Rollenhagio, Sig. C1v, glosses the emblem of skull, sceptre, and farm tool: 'Mors sceptra ligonibus aequat. Le sceptre E le hoyau sont en leur fin semblables, Payants egal tribut aux Parques redoutables; Car qui pourra dire, que ce crane hideux, Ait esté d'un paisan, ou d'un Roy genereux?'

[2] Quoted in Patrick Cruttwell, *The Shakespearean Moment*, New York, 1960, p. 123.

The hurly, by definition, is only a simulacrum of the genuine drama. In that manner Nashe, in *Summer's Last Will and Testament*, describes it:

Heaven is our heritage,
Earth but a player's stage.

Totus mundus agit histrionem. All the world plays the actor.[1] All sweat without purpose, contend for a hollow applause. But you cannot feed capons so. It follows that man's life is a great stage of fools. (4.6.185) But the actor, as he plays his part there, is played upon also. And so the further inference: man's life, even at its zenith, is a theatre of all miseries. (Plate XLVI) His tormentors are fleshly lust, sin, and death.[2] His insistent business is sorrow, in all his entrances and exits. (4.6.180–5)

For sorrow holds man's life to be her own,
His thoughts her stage where tragedies she plays.[3]

If man is no more than this,[4] who should be mindful of him, or of the puerilities with which he wears out a life? True wisdom will hold the world but as the world.[5] To Herbert of Cherbury, delivering his 'Elegy Over a Tomb', the wise man is one who

did delight no more to stay
Upon this low and earthly stage
But rather chose an endless heritage.

Lear comes to concur in the wisdom of Antonio, the Merchant of Venice. He holds the world but as the world. He laughs at gilded butterflies (5.3.12f.) who attend on the flame that consumes them.[6] (Plate XLVII)

[1] Thomson, p. 113, drawing on T. W. Baldwin, traces the saying to Palingenius, whose astronomical text, *Zodiacus Vitae*, was the most popular treatise of its kind in the Renaissance. The idea is a commonplace. It occurs in Juan Vives and, ultimately, in the *Satyricon* of Petronius.

[2] *Lasciva caro, peccatum, morsque.*

[3] Fulke Greville, *Caelica*, sonnet 86. See also Wisdom, vii.3,5; Florio's Montaigne, i.107; Holland's Pliny, vii, Proem, edn. 1601, p. 152, cited Muir, p. 181n.

[4] With 3.4.105, cf. Hebrews, ii.6.

[5] *MV*, 1.1.77. Jaques' famous speech in *AYLI*, 2.7.139–65, is a parallel utterance.

[6] Rollenhagio, Sigs. B4r–v, glosses his emblem of the fly and the candle (Plate XLVII): 'Cosi vivo piacer conduce a morte. La douce volupté peste de nostre vie, Est de mille peinnes E mille maux suyvie, Car un poure amoureux semblable a un flambeau, Se consume soy mesme, E se mene au tombeau.' Heinsius, *Amatoria*, ?1613, Sig. F1r, p. 32, gives a similar emblem.

Thus hath the candle singed the moth.
Oh, these deliberate fools!
(*Merchant of Venice*, 2.9.79f.)

But he does not find out their folly with his eyes. He is able to see truly only when he can see feelingly. Like Timon, 'He will not hear, till feel'. (2.2.7) He who feels nothing knows nothing. (4.1.71f.) The eyes and ears are inadequate reporters. Gloucester stumbled when he saw. (4.1.21) Bereft of sight, he ceases to stumble. (3.7.91f.)

His overthrow heaped happiness upon him,
For then, and not till then, he felt himself.
(*Henry VIII*, 4.2.64f.)

Given, Edgar once more in his *touch*, he'd say he had *eyes* again. (4.1.25f.)

I see it feelingly.
(4.6.152)

Lear, humiliated and unheard before Cornwall's castle, and later, goaded from that castle, grows an adept in the art of feeling sorrows. (4.6.223)

I am not ague proof.
(4.6.107)

Wind and cold are councillors that feelingly persuade him what he is. (*As You Like It*, 2.1.10f.)

But to taste my own misery is common, is casual. Mere existence entails it.

We came crying hither.
(4.6.182)

To sorrow for my neighbour, to make his misery mine, is the uncommon case, and the harder. That is to shake the holy water from one's eyes. (4.3.31f.) Lear, like Cordelia, is vouchsafed that kind of pity. It is the chief leaven of his schooling.

In, boy, go first.
(3.4.26)

Charity solicits him; like Edgar, he gives it room. (5.3.166)

I'll forbear.[1]
(2.4.110)

[1] Prospero, in *The Tempest*, 5.1.25–27, is the comparable case.

None is without fleck. He declines, in consequence, to cast the first stone. But none is without merit. He learns to feel for the pariah, to assimilate him. The lash that falls on the prostitute is laid on his own back as well. (4.6.165–70) He learns, as Kent has learned, that self-love lacks in magnitude and savour, that a man knows no greater love than to hold his life but as a pawn for his friend.[1] (1.1.157)

But charity, if an attribute of Heaven, is not endemic in men but achieved. Charity is not gratuitous. One must be brought to thrust his fingers in the wounds, and not for ocular proof but, to change the sense of the story, to confirm on one's own pulses the misery of another. Lear, like Didymus called Thomas, is made to bear witness. Only then does he grow pregnant to good pity. (4.6.224) He feels necessity's pinch. (2.4.213)

> But what I am want teaches me to think on.
> (*Pericles*, 2.1.76)

It is at once his expiation and his schooling, a requital for wrong, a changing of vile things to precious, of precious things—the sign and flag of temporal power—to vile. (3.2.70f.) 'Like as Golde and Siluer is tried in the fire: euen so are acceptable men, in the fornace of aduersitie.'[2] The horror *Lear* treats of is causal in its origin, and thus one can endure the play. But the horror is also instrumental: it leads on to perceiving; and for that reason the play is not depressing but inspiriting.[3]

But suffering alone does not quit the king, nor make him wise. Antonio and Sebastian seek the lives of Prospero and Alonso; they suffer in consequence, but they are not schooled. They end as they began, confirmed in evil.

> But one fiend at a time,
> I'll fight their legions o'er.
> (*Tempest*, 3.3.102f.)

As well as suffering, one must know repentance.

[1] Camillo's office and understanding, in *WT*, 4.2.8f., parallel Kent's.

[2] Sig. F2 f7v in Palfreyman, *The Treatise of Heauenly Philosophie*, London, 1578.

[3] R. W. Chambers, *King Lear*, Glasgow, 1940, p. 48, in a fine phrase, sees Gloucester as climbing the Mountain of Purgatory, and—levying on Keats—the play itself as a Vale of Soul-Making.

Oh, my follies!
Kind gods, forgive me that.
(3.7.91f.)

Lear is elbowed by a sovereign shame: humanity renascent. (4.3.44, 47–49) It brings him to beg forgetting and forgiving. (4.7.84) But even more is incumbent on him. The good servant in *Pericles* advises his master

To bear with patience
Such griefs as you yourself do lay upon yourself.
(1.2.65f.)

Lear also must possess his soul in patience.[1] He must endure.[2] The progress he goes is the wonted progress of Shakespearean tragedy, which descends, through chaos, to harmony at the close. The way up and the way down are depicted in an unpublished commonplace book dating from about the year of the first quarto of the play (1608), and ascribed to one Thomas Trevelyon. The cycle of Peace and War, as Trevelyon represents it, turns downward on the entrance of Pride, whom you know by her peacock-feathered head-dress, and the fan of peacock feathers in her hand. In her wake come Self Indulgence or Pleasure, and Envy gnawing at her heart, and War brandishing the torch and sword. But as the lowest point is reached, a return to the highest is predicted: enter Poverty in rags; and after Poverty, Humility; and then Patience with clasped hands and eyes raised to Heaven. The final figure in the sequence, whose way these others have been preparing, is Peace.[3] So Lear, as he is patient, proceeds from misfortune to reconciliation.

And not only Lear. Edgar, made tame to Fortune's blows (4.6.222), enjoins patience. (4.6.80) Edgar endures. (5.3.211)

[1] In an emblem by Rollenhagio (no. 28: 'Victrix patientia duri'), a tree grows despite the board that blocks its progress. The gloss, Sig. B2r: 'De mesme que tu vois une palme umbrageuse, Contre le pesant faix se dresser genereuse: Ainsi par patience, on dompte le malheur, Et de luy triomphant, on en reste vainqueur.'

[2] *Vincit qui patitur.* So Whitney, *Emblemes*, Sig. e2v, p. 220, moralizes the fable of the oak and the weeds, bent before the storm. See also Desprez, p. 92: 'Endurer, quand on ne peut mieux'; and Rollenhagio, emblem 23, 'Patior, vt potiar'. The gloss, Sig. B1v: 'Qui veut donc recevoir quelque contentement, Il faut premier le mal porter patiemment.' Heinsius, *Amatoria*, Sig. C3r, p. 21, uses the same legend for an emblem of Cupid (who replaces the bear in Rollenhagio's emblem) taking honey from a tree.

[3] Chew, pp. 126–8.

Kent, at the worst, is equable still. (2.2.180) Cordelia is the pattern of all patience. (4.3.17f.) Gloucester, who would shake off his affliction (4.6.35–38), who, in a real sense, is tempted by the Fiend to throw himself down (4.6.219f.), resolves at last to bear affliction until affliction dies.[1] (4.6.75–77) But Lear himself is the great exemplar.

> Thou must be patient.[2]
>
> (4.6.180)

A man's office is to bear a cheek for blows,[3] to take the weight of the time (5.3.323), to abide it. (5.2.9f.) Ripeness is all. Charity, which saves because it instructs, rises from suffering and repentance and endurance. These, in Shelley's phrase, are the seals which bar the pit.

Now the humble, whom the world calls the foolish, are made to suffer most, in the nature of things. They ought in logic to enjoy a better chance, not to heap up the good things of Heaven —the crass promise of crude religions—but rather to live the good life, one founded in sophistication, in right reading. Poverty, says Primaudaye, 'is the mistress of manners . . . a schoole of vertue'. Philosophy finds her best scholars among the poor.[4] Not to be foolish, or wicked: if you beat a man enough, you make him insensible, no longer a man but a beast. But, in the ideal case (which is, I take it, the concern of the play, any play), the suffering man, who is likely to be one of the lowly, is more sensible to feeling than another, and so more acute in perceiving.

> Nothing almost sees miracles
> But misery. (2.2.172f.)

The world, alive only to his beggarly status, dismisses the fruit of that status. Thus the acuity of the humble man becomes, in popular estimation, the muddied vision of the fool. Kent, who has more man than wit about him, who takes one's part that's out of favour, had best put on the coxcomb. (2.4.42; 1.4.109–12) Kent is a fool; and Cordelia a greater, who pays contempt with kindness and ends in prison for her pains.

[1] Isabella's prayer, *MM*, 5.1.115f., anticipates Gloucester's: 'Then, O you blessed ministers above, Keep me in patience.'

[2] See also 3.2.37f.

[3] With 4.2.51, cf. Matthew, v.39.

[4] *The French academie*, p. 149.

And my poor fool is hang'd!
(5.3.305)

But Kent, for all that he is merely a retainer, is wiser than the king, in real fact the true blank of his eye. (1.1.159) The king is a fool. Lear's wicked daughters, who rejoice at the banishment laid on Cordelia, when all is said discriminate but poorly. It is they who are all-licensed fools. (1.4.220) Lear's Fool, who pines for Cordelia (1.4.79f.), is the better able to assay.

This is not altogether fool.
(1.4.165)

The Dutch patriots, who wore a coarse grey livery distinguished only by the cap and bells, were not so foolish as their well-attired oppressors, who had not the wit to understand that a Brutus might be found beneath the costume of a fool,

Covering discretion with a coat of folly.
(*Henry V*, 2.4.38)

The besotted are wise; they see whose eyes are dazzled.[1]

Much madness is divinest sense
To a discerning eye;
Much sense the starkest madness.

Gloucester, thrust out at gates to smell his way to Dover (3.7.93f.), is succoured by a bedlam beggar. Madmen lead the blind. (4.1.46) Gloucester's title does not exalt him a step above his fellows. Partly it is otherwise: as he ascends, he may be said to descend. But the words themselves are beguiling.

> If we consider how our common mother the earth, being prodigall in giuing vnto us all things necessary for the life of man, hath notwithstanding cast all of vs naked out of her bowels, and must receiue us so againe into her wombe, I see no great reason wee haue to call some rich, and others poore; seeing the beginning, being, and ende of the temporall life of all men are vnlike in nothing, but that some during this little moment of life haue that in abundance and superfluitie, which others haue only according to their necessitie.[2]

[1] The story of Egmont's retainers and their taunting of Cardinal Granvelle is given in Motley, I, 387. See also Florio's Montaigne, iii.284, 298, iv.19, quoted Muir, p. 252. Erasmus, in *The Praise of Folly*, plays on the ambiguity of the word, *fool*. Enid Welsford, *The Fool: His Social and Literary History*, London, 1935? New York, n.d., treats of it exhaustively.

[2] *The French academie*, p. 148.

Hierarchy, in first and last things, is a nonce word. To acknowledge the puissance of the lion—or king—is to be cognizant also of the claims of the hare:

> Those members . . . which we think to be less honourable, upon these we bestow more abundant honour . . . [for] God hath tempered the body together, having given more abundant honour to that part which lacked.[1]

The greater puissance is a fiction. The humble are exalted, and the mighty put down.

Lear, like Gloucester, must learn of the humble. His tutors are the Fool and Poor Tom. He calls them philosophers, learned justicers, sapient sirs. And the jest is not that he errs, but that he is right.

> The wise man's folly is anatomized
> Even by the squandering glances of the fool.
> (*As You Like It*, 2.7.56f.)

Foolishness is wisdom; and poverty, riches. Things hid from the wise and the prudent are revealed to the babe. The saying of the Evangelist (Matthew, xi.25) is tested and confirmed by the playwright, who

> in babes hath judgement shown
> When judges have been babes.
> (*All's Well*, 2.1.141f.)

As Lear's wits begin to leave him, he is lessoned, he grows wise. A fantastic, crowned with wild flowers, he figures as Christ, who is the king of fantastics.

> O thou side-piercing sight!
> (4.6.85)

But if the innocence of the infant is wisdom, the wisdom of the world is great folly. The knave turns fool that runs away. (2.4.85) Machiavelli is wrong. The shrewd choice is the stupid choice. Goneril and Regan, who think it shrewd to take a sister's portion, are not so well endowed as the sister who has lost it. Burgundy, shrewdly rejecting the dowerless Cordelia, is

[1] I Corinthians, xii.23–24. And see ch. I, p. 4, n. 3; and 'Tous peuvent servir au besoin' in Desprez, Sig. B2v, p. 12, for the fable of the lion and the hare, in which the passage from Corinthians is applied.

not a tithe so perceptive as France, who takes her up. To see nothing where everything is patent ought, you would think, to require a faith that reason without miracle could never implant. (1.1.221–3) It does not fall out so:

> Fathers that wear rags
> Do make their children blind,
> (2.4.48f.)

and so the gods discover when they walk among men. But the affluent, who bar their doors against a stranger, poorly led, are not so sophisticated as the humble, who take him in. *Pii sunt cura diis.*[1] Baucis and Philemon find their reward.

Peter, deserting Christ when the great wheel begins to run down hill, is not so sophisticated as Veronica, who tenders Christ her veil. One must be a fool for Christ's sake. He who would save his life must lose it. The last shall be first. Edgar, the son and heir of his father, is scanted.

> Edgar I nothing am.
> (2.3.21)

Become so little, he is fulfilled. A rich man shall hardly enter into the kingdom of Heaven. The bedlam and the pauper occupy his room.

> Willing misery
> Outlives incertain pomp, is crown'd before.
> (*Timon*, 4.3.244f.)

Justice, which weighs poverty in the scale against temporal power, gives you to see how light and how weak is that power.[2] (Plate XLVIII)

> The latter quick up flew, and kicked the beam.
> (*Paradise Lost*, IV.1004)

Nothing comes of nothing: power is nugatory: it displaces no air.[3] Edmund, who looks always to power, knows his mounted scale aloft: his eyes are bent, as he tells you, on nothing. (1.2.31)

[1] Ovid, *Metamorphoses*, Lib. viii, Fab. iv.97. And see Matthew, xxv.34–46.

[2] In Plate XLVIII the sub-title, 'The Triumph of Justice', is illustrated by the different positions of *forma Pauperis* and *Ira Potentis*.

[3] *Ex nihilo nihil fit.* See 1.1.90; and Muir, p. 9n.

Riches, power, sapience as the world describes it, do not denote real riches, power, sapience. The Beatitudes are apposite here. Motley may be the garb of the wise man, a material fool (*As You Like It*, 3.3.32), rich apparel the garb of the genuine fool, he who wears motley in his brain. For those honours laid upon him,

> He shall but bear them as the ass bears gold,
> To groan and sweat under the business.
>
> (*Julius Caesar*, 4.1.21f.)

His pride of accoutrement marks him the servitor, and gull.[1]

> If thou art rich, thou'rt poor,
> For, like an ass whose back with ingots bows,
> Thou bear'st thy heavy riches but a journey,
> And death unloads thee.
>
> (*Measure for Measure*, 3.1.25–28)

But the genuine fool is not simply a beast of burden but the servant of his servant: like Lear, he bears his ass on his back. (1.4.176f.) (Plate XLIX) It is the efficient cause of his destruction. It pulls him under. Thus the faithful steward to Timon of Athens:

> thy great fortunes
> Are made thy chief afflictions.
>
> (4.2.43f.)

The wretch—Edgar, at the worst, the lowest and most dejected thing of fortune (4.1.2f.)—as he is stripped naked by fortune, finds his burden lightened.[2] (Plate L) He is the better able to throw aside the torrent. His defects prove commodities. (4.1.22f.) Like Crates of Thebes, as Tom Nashe describes him, he gives what he has to the waters: his appetites are ungracious: it is better that they should drown than he himself.[3] In that sense, it is the naked who survive. Or, another metaphor: the wretch, who is blown to the worst, embraces the storm, yields and bends as it directs him (4.1.6f.) But the great man, who

[1] In Titian's 'Sacred and Profane Love' (*c.* 1515, Galleria Borghese), the nakedness of 'Felicità Eterna' (Ficino's *Venere Celeste* or eternal beauty) denotes her contempt for perishable earthly things. The handsome and costly dress of 'Felicità Breve' (Ficino's *Venere Volgare* or evanescent beauty) is emblematic of the ephemerality of mundane things. See *Stud. in Icon.*, fig. 108, and p. 150.

[2] *Levitas secura.* And see Rollenhagio, emblem 74, glossed Sig. D1r: 'Omnia mea mecum porto.'

[3] Nashe, *Anatomie of Absurditie*, *Works*, ed. McKerrow, I, 34; cited E. Taylor, 'Lear's Philosopher', *SQ*, VI, 1955, 364.

is given to command, little given to defer, seeks to outstare it. He is shattered.[1] (Plate LI) His means secure him.

> Merciful Heaven,
> Thou rather with thy sharp and sulphurous bolt
> Split'st the unwedgeable and gnarlèd oak
> Than the soft myrtle.
> (*Measure for Measure*, 2.2.114–17)

And so the injunction: 'Take no thought for your life, what ye shall eat, or what ye shall drink; nor yet for your body, what ye shall put on.'

The poor and the oppressed are the salt of the earth to the degree that they inherit, not its riches but its wisdom. Poverty, says the homilist, 'hath beene the onely and principall cause of enriching many with . . . [the treasures of wisedome and vertue]'.[2] If, unhappily, much of his eulogy is the conventional humbug: money is the root of all evil—still, the initial assertion may stand. The play is its surety. Prisoners, idiots, beggars, pedlars, slaves: all those whom the world, cozened by show, duped by appearance, calls nothing, those to whom the world denies substance, are invested with substance by Shakespeare. His mind beats on them constantly: they afford him the stuff of nearly half of the images he draws from classes and kinds of humanity.[3] Lear's redemption is signallized by the unwonted care he bestows on those poor naked wretches of whom, hitherto, he had taken little care. (3.4.28, 32f.) Like Gloucester, whose case exactly parallels his own, he would shake them the superflux:

> So distribution should undo excess,
> And each man have enough.
> (4.1.70f.)

Heaven collaborates in the charity of Gloucester and Lear. To the poor man, God holds out fullness; to the rich man, nothing

[1] See also William Strachey's sonnet, 'On Sejanus': 'How high a Poore man showes in low estate Whose Base is firme, and whole Frame competent, That sees this *Cedar*, made the Shrub of Fate, Th' on's little, lasting; Th' others confluence spent'; quoted Muir, p. xxiii. In Marlowe's *Edward II*, Mortimer, just before his fall, likens himself to '*Ioues* huge tree', to whom all others are shrubs, ll. 2579f. Praz, I, 201, cites Horace, *Odes*, II, x, 11, 12; and Ovid, *Rem. Am.*, 370.

[2] *The French academie*, p. 150.

[3] Spurgeon, p. 33.

at all.[1] Not to spy out the point of that final apportioning, to shut one's mind against it, to believe that the poor are intrinsically poor, that Cordelia, say, who utters nothing, means in fact nothing is to be reduced infallibly to nothing oneself. So Lear is reduced.

But not for ever. The play is a kind of *Commedia.* Life peers through the hollow eyes of death.[2] (Plate LII) The dry bones are made fruitful.[3] Lear, forgetting

> Aged contusions and all brush of time
> . . . like a gallant in the brow of youth,
> Repairs him with occasion.
> (*2 Henry VI*, 5.3.3–5)

As he ages, he grows young: the lost sheep is restored, the man who perishes is reborn.[4] (Plate LIII) But rebirth is founded on destruction. *Mors vitae initium.* The beginning of life is death.

> For nothing can be sole or whole
> That has not been rent.

Lear verifies the paradox. Like the phoenix, to be reborn he must consume his heart away.[5] Like the eagle, he must cast his

[1] The apposite illustration is in Furmer, *The Use and Abuse of Wealth,* first pub. in Latin, 1575, and trans. into Dutch by Coornhert, 1585, p. 6; given in Green, p. 489. *Timon of Athens,* in its constant exalting of the poor above the rich, is a long gloss on the sense of the emblem.

[2] *RII,* 2.1.270. Rollenhagio, Sig. B1v, glosses his emblem of grain growing from a skull (Plate LII): 'Mors vitae initium. Come un grain de froument, dans la terre mourant, En renaissant produict maint espi blondissant: Ainsi l'homme iuste par sa mort naturelle, Commence a vivre heureux une vie eternelle.'

[3] See Boissard, *Emblematum liber,* Metz, 1588, Sig. E4r, p. 39: 'In morte vita'; and *Spes Altera Vitae,* in Camerarius, edn. 1595, emblem 100, pt. 1, p. 102; given in Green, p. 184.

[4] See also Willard Farnham, *The Medieval Heritage of Elizabethan Tragedy,* Berkeley, 1936, p. 452: 'Lear loses the world only to save his soul'; and Matthew, xvi.25. Rollenhagio, Sig. C1r, glosses emblem 45 of a child and skull with the words: 'Ce qui perit renaist.' In Titian's 'Sacred and Profane Love', Cupid, who is placed near the figure of Venus Volgare, the generative goddess, stirs a fountain that is really an ancient sarcophagus. Once it held a corpse; now it is the spring of life. See *Stud. in Icon.,* p. 152, fig. 108. And so to T. S. Eliot.

[5] Freitag appends to his emblem of the phoenix the quotation from Ephesians, iv.22. See *Mythologica Ethica,* 1579; and Green, p. 381. The phoenix is reborn in Desprez, *Le Theatre,* p. 103; Boissard, *Emblematum liber,* Metz, 1588, Sig. F4r, p. 47; Whitney, *Emblemes,* Sig. Z1r, p. 177 (in Green, p. 387); and on the t.p. and again on the verso of the colophon, in each case with the motto 'Semper Eadem', in *La Pittura di Leonbattista Alberti Tradotta Per M. Lodovico Domenichi,* Venice, 1547. The

plumes before he can renew them.[1] *Lux ex tenebris*:[2] light treads on the limping heel of darkness. A captive, Lear is given his freedom; a sick man, he is given his health; a blind man, he is given his eyes again; a tatterdemalion, he is newly arrayed. The looped and windowed garments are forgotten, in which his worser hours were clothed.

> In the heaviness of his sleep
> We put fresh garments on him.
> (4.7.21f.)

He is made by the dramatist to remark his change of raiment (4.7.66f.): it is not simply a physical change. Neither is it adventitious, but rather a consequence of the discovery he makes on the heath. His new learning begets compassion: he grows pregnant to pity. That is to put off the old man, to put on the new. (Ephesians, iv.22–24) Age, because it is corrupted, is wasted. (Colossians, iii.8) 'Come, my old son,' says the Duchess of York to Aumerle, the repentant rebel of *Richard II*, 'I pray God make thee new.' (5.3.146) Age dies a felon's death: 'our old man is crucified'. (Romans, vi.6) Youth gapes to be his heir.

But youth, who is the scion, is also the parent of age. The working out of that riddle is the essential business of Shakespeare's last plays. Thus Pericles to his daughter Marina:

> Thou that beget'st him that did thee beget.
> (5.2.197)

In a curious and very tentative way, it is also the business of Shakespeare's earliest comedies.

> Would you create me new?
> (*Comedy of Errors*, 3.2.39)

But, whereas in a play like *The Comedy of Errors*, the recreating or renewal turns pretty much on sleight of hand, in the late romances and in a tragedy like *King Lear* it is made a matter of

---

t.p. moralizes the emblem with the phrase, 'De la mia morte Eterna Vita I Vivo'. Green, pp. 380–90, lists references to the phoenix as an emblem of redemption in Shakespeare, in his contemporaries, and in older writers.

[1] The eagle illustrates the legend, 'Renovata Iuventus', in Camerarius, emblem 34, 'ex Volatilibus', in Green, p. 369. And see Psalms, ciii.5.

[2] Bruck, *Emblemata Moralia & Bellica*, emblem 12.

Non est potestas Super Terram quæ Comparetur ei. Iob. 41. 24
LEVIATHAN
Or
THE MATTER, FORME and POWER of A COMMON WEALTH ECCLESIASTICALL and CIVIL
By THOMAS HOBBES of MALMESBURY
London
Printed for Andrew Crooke
1651

XXVI

XXVII

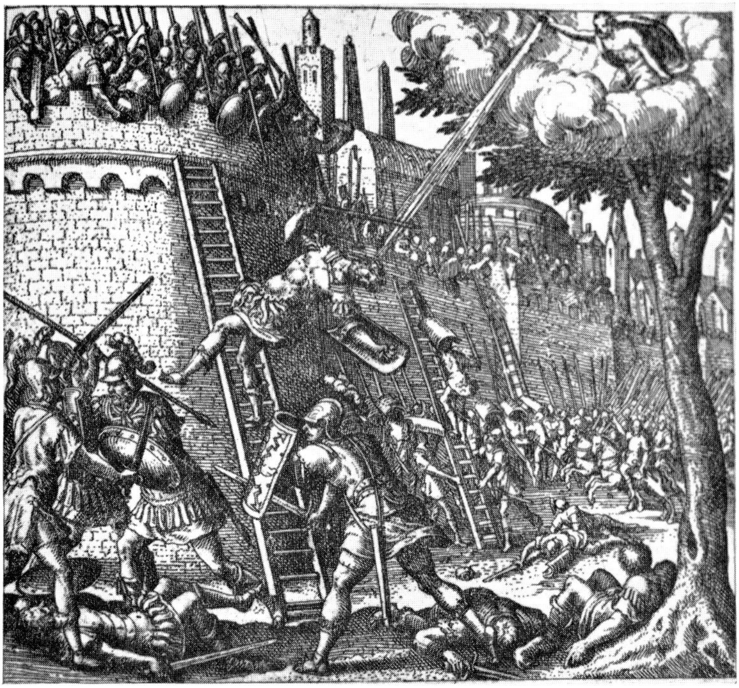

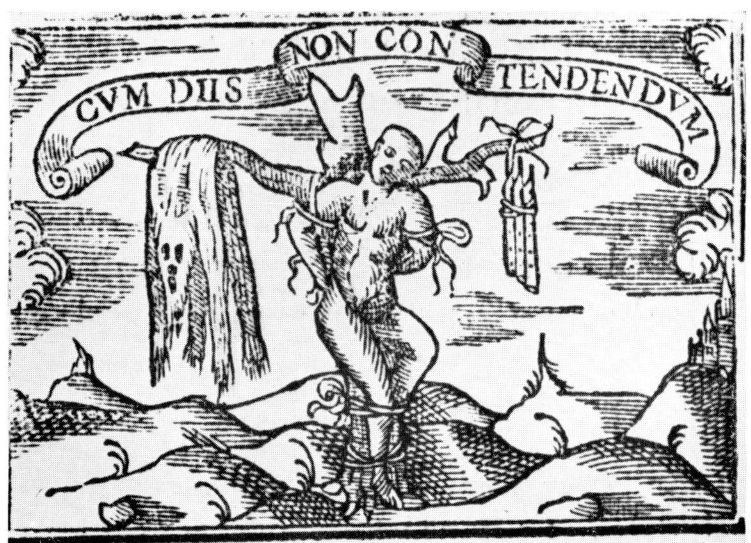
CVM DIIS
NON CON
TENDENDVM

XXVIII

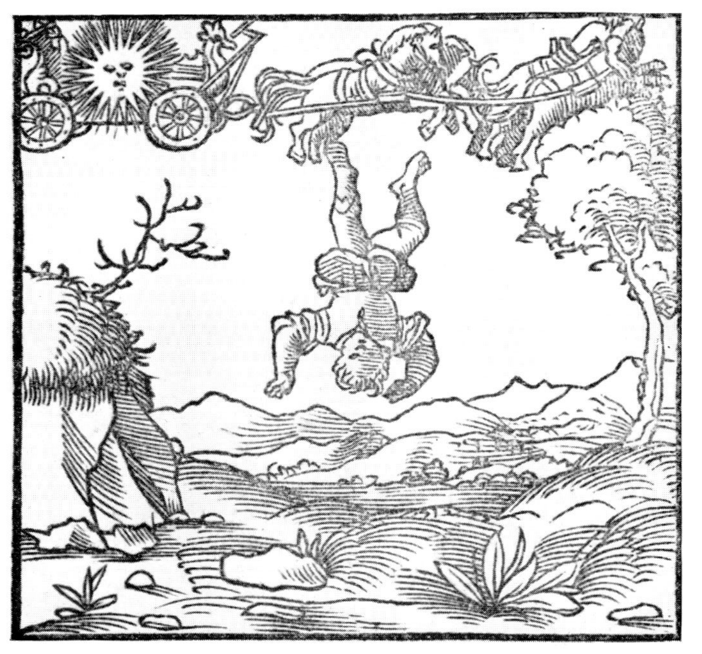

XXIX

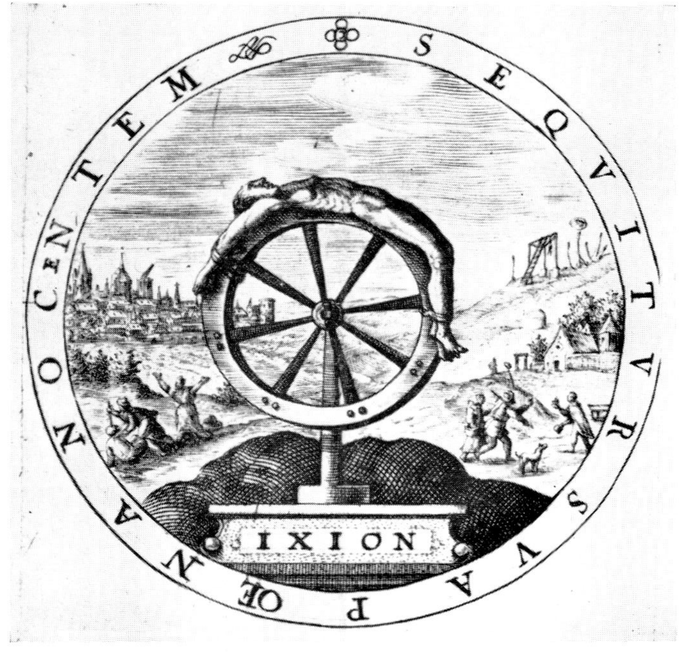
SEQVITVR SVA POENA NOCENTEM
IXION

XXX

XXXI

XXXII

LOVE KEPYTH THE LAWE, OBEYETH THE KYNGE, AND IS GOOD TO THE COMMEN WELTHE.
PRO LEGE REGE, ET GREGE
PRVDENCIA
IVSTICIA

XXXIII

XXXIV

XXXV

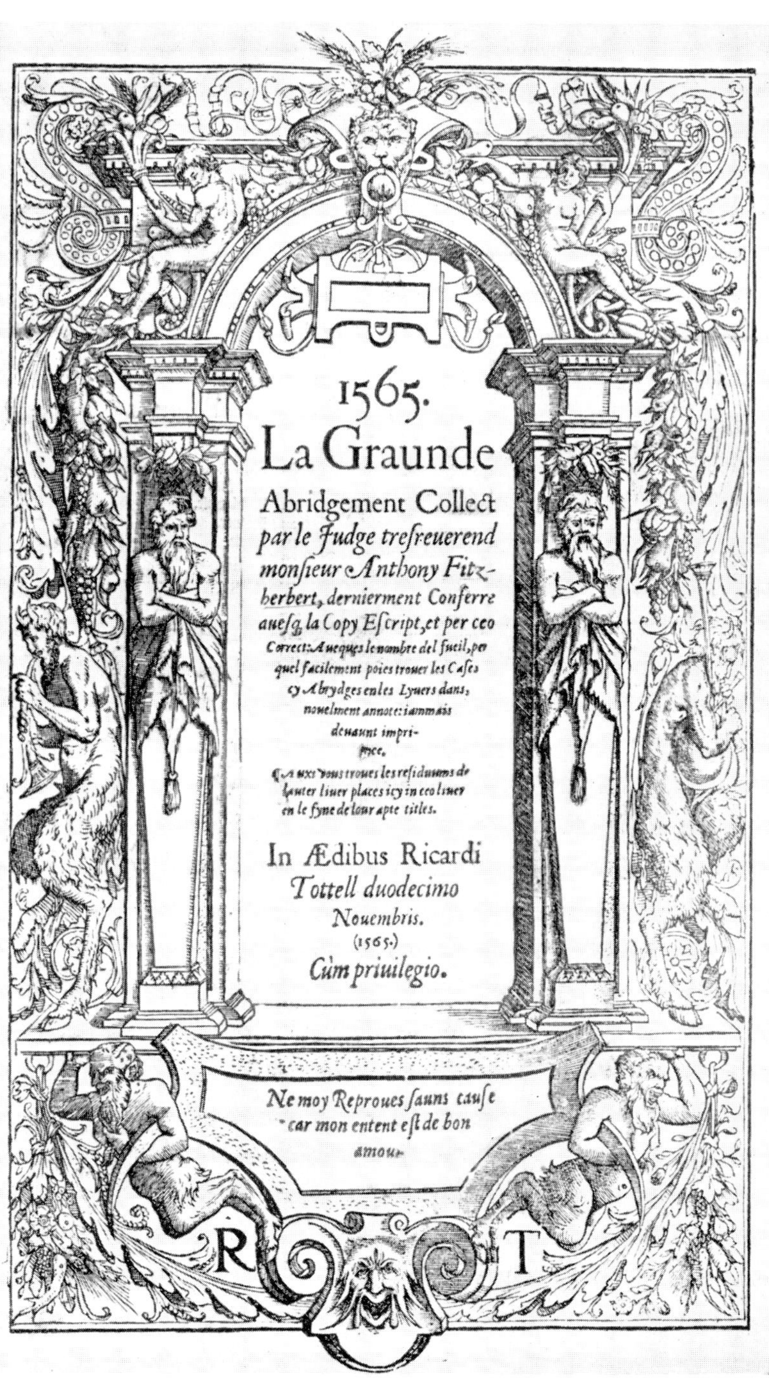

1565.

La Graunde

Abridgement Collect
*par le Judge tresreuerend
monsieur Anthony Fitz-
herbert, derniermment Conferre
auesq; la Copy Escript, et per ceo
Correct: Aueques le nombre del fueil, per
quel facilement poies trouer les Cases
cy Abrydges en les Lyuers dans,
nouelment annote: iammais
deuaunt impri-
mee.*

*¶ Auxi vous troues les residuums de
lauter liuer places icy in ceo liuer
en le fyne de lour apte titles.*

In Ædibus Ricardi
*Tottell duodecimo
Nouembris.*
(1565.)
Cum priuilegio.

*Ne moy Reproues sauns cause
car mon entent est de bon
amour.*

R T

XXXVII

XXXVIII

43

XXXIX

Fama
Truth.
The Description
OF
Leicester Shire
Containing
Matters of Antiquity, History,
Armorye, and Genealogy.
Written
by
William Burton Esqu:
London
Leicester Shire
Antiqvitye
Lindley

XL

XLI

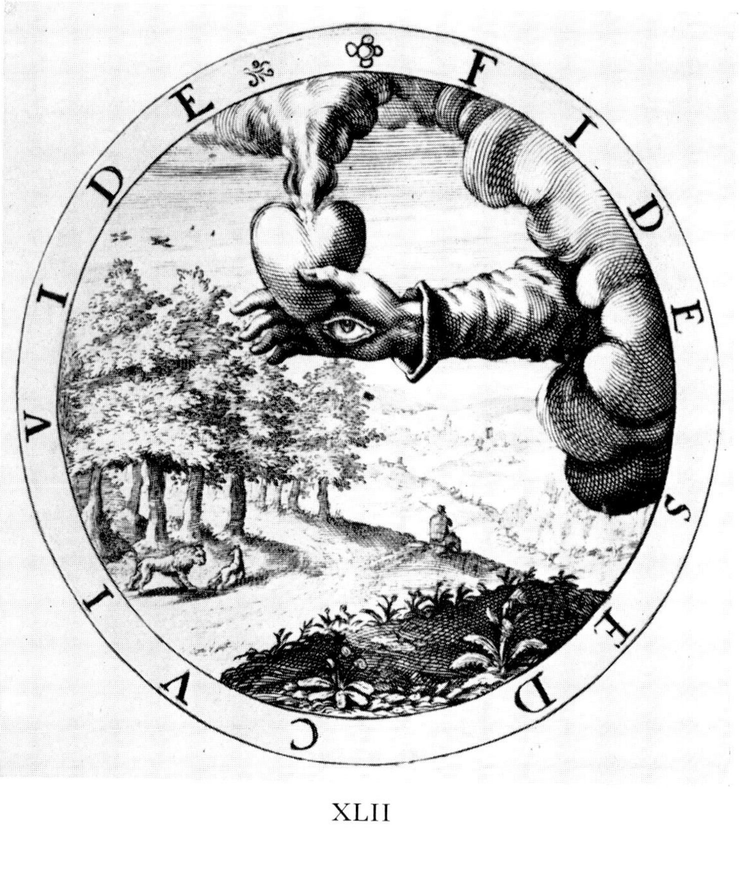

XLII

XLIII

SIC TRANSIT GLORIA MVNDI.

XLIV

MORS SCEPTRA LIGONIB9 ÆQVAT

XLV

XLVI

XLVII

XLVIII

XLIX

L

LI

LII

LIII

organic change in the protagonist. A prince is bereft of all his fortunes (*Pericles*, 2.1.9)—Lear, Pericles, or Prospero. In his adversity he makes himself over, puts on the whole armour (Ephesians, vi.11), the beaver, the brace, the coat of mail, that formerly he had neglected to wear. In comedy, even in the late comedies, though the protagonist suffers and changes, still the armour is given him by the god from the machine: in *Pericles*, it is washed up from the sea. In tragedy, in *Lear*, though—as in the romances—it is not his except he be born again, still he is seen and felt to deserve it, even to seize and fashion it himself. But the result of the metamorphosis in each case is the same. The old Adam is put off. The new man succeeds him, whose marks are forbearing and forgiving (4.7.84), and charity above all these others. (Colossians, iii.12–14)

Lear puts on the new man. It is right to insist that he earns his renewal. There is about Shakespearean tragedy, at least the appearance of logic and sequence. No suggestion of the miraculous intrudes in *King Lear*, as it does in *Pericles* and *Cymbeline*, *The Winter's Tale* and *The Tempest*. But if Lear earns or merits regeneration, it is also tendered him, not obviously, sensationally, as in comedy, but none the less gratuitously, if you like graciously. Really, it is independent of his willing. Shakespeare's comedies and tragedies, though superficially very different, are at bottom, in that particular, the same. The comedies emphasize intrinsic weakness, made good by the convolutions of the plot. Protagonists in comedy are felt to be moved.

> O Time, thou must untangle this, not I!
> It is too hard a knot for me to untie!
> (*Twelfth Night*, 2.2.41f.)

The tragedies have to do with strength. The tragic protagonist succumbs, it is true, but of his own volition: strength turning back on itself. He is, initially, one who moves.

> I dare do all that may become a man.
> Who dares do more is none.

The inference is clearly that Macbeth, a man sufficiently strong, unmans himself. It can hardly be otherwise in tragedy, which is fraught with suspense to the degree that it seems to admit of alternatives. Tragedy rests, formally, on conflict and choice.

Where everything is fated, nothing is dramatic. But when Macbeth, resisting all this while the importunities of his wife, declares suddenly, 'I am settled' (1.7.79), and commits himself to the murder of Duncan, it is hard, however closely you scrutinize it, to rationalize his choice. Why does he alter?

Macbeth, as he is innocent, is in the state of grace, to use the appropriate metaphor. But the perpetuating of his innocence seems a condition of the perpetual dispensing of grace.

> For every man with his affects is born,
> Not by might mastered, but by special grace.

The best of intentions, if you endorse Berowne's counsel in *Love's Labour's Lost* (1.1.152f.), cannot stand against wilful inclination. The plot of that play seems to offer corroboration. In *Henry V*, it is the cool and temperate wind of grace that overblows the clouds of evil behaviour. (3.3.30–32) Failing grace, they would rain down contagion. The king's passion is subjected to grace, as are the wretches fettered in his prisons. (1.2.242f.) But it is, at least a question, how much credit is owing to the king. For a man cannot enlist the aid of grace, as he can compel to his support the aid of reason. Grace is not within his giving; and yet it is indispensable. Withhold it, and the wretches burst their fetters. In the Fray of Cupid and Apollo, lust and reason, an engraving described by Vasari and dated 1545, it is necessary for the Mind, a beautiful woman poised on the clouds above the battle, to illuminate and so to succour reason by the flame of divine wisdom. Without that intervention, reason would falter.[1] 'Our dull workings', of themselves inadequate, function only as they are informed by 'the grace, the sanctities of Heaven'. (*2 Henry IV*, 4.2.21f.)

Innocence, then, as it turns on the accession of grace, is kindred to good fortune. It is as fragile as fortune and as dependent for its life on caprice. 'You are in the state of grace,' says an impudent servant to Pandarus, in *Troilus and Cressida*. (3.1.15) He means, You are fortunate, in favour. On the other hand, a frustrated lover, in *As You Like It*, is necessarily content

[1] The engraving, after Baccio Bandinelli, is reproduced in *Stud. in Icon.*, fig. 107. The Florentine neo-Platonism of Ficino is adduced as a gloss: 'For Reason can conquer the flames of man's lower nature only by turning to a higher authority for enlightenment.' See pp. 137, 149f.

with scraps of favour, because he is 'in such a poverty of grace' (3.5.100), because, that is to say, he is so little lucky. Helena, in *All's Well*, will cure the king of his sickness, 'The great'st Grace lending grace'. (2.1.163) The proviso is crucial. It is always crucial, though Shakespeare rarely adverts to it, and for the very good reason that its felt presence is inimical to real drama.

Grace is the condition of survival. Man does not have the bestowing of grace. But perhaps the indispensable gratuity, on the face of it antipathetic to the spirit of drama, may be assimilated and made dramatic, at least in part. For the offering of grace is not niggardly but magnanimous; grace is open to all men. But how does it happen that only some men receive it? What does it mean, to be 'past grace'? Imogen, in *Cymbeline* (1.1.137), offers an explanation: 'Past hope, and in despair; that way, past grace'[1]. Apemantus, in *Timon*, sneers at a page who 'outruns't grace'. (2.2.91) Richard III, affecting the philosopher, is sententious: 'All unavoided is the doom of destiny.' He is answered by Queen Elizabeth: 'True, when avoided grace makes destiny.' (4.4.217f.) Survival is the accepting, destruction the eschewing of grace. Man is weak, but grace buttresses his weakness. And grace is his if he will have it. Therefore man, potentially, is strong. He falls, not of necessity, but as he turns from the help that is offered him. To retrieve or to maintain his innocence, he has only to cry grace.

But after all the argument, the attempt to bring what is whimsical within the limits of the play, is not altogether successful. Richard falls—and after him, Edmund—because he avoids what he ought to receive. What occasions the avoiding? How account for the folly that runs away from grace? And if the receiving of grace is interdicted by despair, how account for the despair? Lear adjures the wicked to cry grace. (3.2.58f.) He is one of the wicked himself. And grace is bestowed on him. But his antagonists never taste it. You may say that they do not want to. But that is to argue in a circle: why are they indifferent, or hostile? Albany turns back, and Cornwall goes forward: grace is given to the former, or accepted by him; it is withheld

[1] J. M. Nosworthy, editing the New Arden *Cymbeline*, notes that commentators have detected in this passage an allusion to Calvin's doctrine of election. 'It is unlikely that these bear any relation to Shakespeare's own religious convictions.' (Pp. 10f.n.) But surely the attempt here is to get clear of Calvin's doctrine, and to make explicable the dispensing or withholding of grace.

from the latter, or repudiated by him. But the giving and withholding, the accepting and repudiating, are equally capricious. No man of himself can justify himself. The common measure is not strength but debility.

> None does offend, none, I say, none.[1]
> (4.6.172)

That is why, in the emblem, the halt conduct the blind (as, in the play, the bedlam beggar has the leading of old Gloucester); why, in the fable, the lowly rat must enfranchise the lion.[2] All are blind, all are crippled.

> Their malady convinces
> The great assay of art.
> (*Macbeth*, 4.3.142f.)

But 'the things which are impossible with men are possible with God' (Luke, xxviii.27) who, in His infinite whimsy, separates the elect from those who are devoted to death. It does not matter whether, disputing the current fashion, which makes Shakespeare a scholar of St. Thomas, you put away grace and choose another word in its room. The metaphor from theology has at least the merit of defining the random nature of those decisions on which the play turns. Who does not feel Angelo to be as guilty as Claudius? The attempt of each at repentance is essentially the same.

> Heaven hath my empty words,
> Whilst my invention, hearing not my tongue,
> Anchors on Isabel. Heaven in my mouth,
> As if I did but only chew His name,
> And in my heart the strong and swelling evil
> Of my conception.
> (*Measure for Measure*, 2.4.2–7)

Claudius is only more terse:

> My words fly up, my thoughts remain below.
> Words without thoughts never to Heaven go.
> (*Hamlet*, 3.3.97f.)

[1] See Romans, iii.23.

[2] See (for the halt and the blind) *Emblemes d'Alciat*, Sig. N2r, p. 195; Whitney, *Emblemes*, Sig. I1r, p. 65; and (for the fable of the rat and the lion) Desprez, Sig. A3v, p. 6.

But Claudius dies, presumably unregenerate. Angelo is redeemed. The decision, what to do with either, is the dramatist's alone, who plays Calvin's God. He looks down, as it were, and observes of the one:

> This my long sufferance and my day of grace
> They who neglect and scorn shall never taste;
> But hard be hardened, blind be blinded more,
> That they may stumble on, and deeper fall.

And, inscrutably, of the other:

> Once more I will renew
> His lapsèd powers, though forfeit and enthralled
> By sin to foul exorbitant desires.
>
> (*Paradise Lost*, III.198–201, 175–7)

Lear's powers are renewed. The renewal, it is true, does not save his life, as it saves the life of Angelo. But the difference, and it is the great observable difference between comedy and tragedy, is not so crucial as it looks. The clearest gods, who make them honours of men's impossibilities, are said to have preserved Gloucester in his supposed fall from the cliffs. (4.6.73f.) They do not care, as it happens, ultimately to preserve him, or his master the king, as they do—to choose at random—Prospero and his daughter, who put to sea in the rotten carcass of a butt, and who are, for a wonder, transported safe to land. But they do bring Lear and Gloucester out of the darkness, where Edmund and the wicked sisters remain, and that, *sub specie aeternitatis*, is intervention enough, an act as merciful, or whimsical, as the staying of a tempest, the saving of a life. There is in it more than nature was ever conduct of. (*Tempest*, 5.1.243f.) Arbitrariness remains at the heart of the play.

IX

SHAKESPEARE'S POETICS

It is, I suppose, the arbitrariness of *Lear* that disconcerted Nahum Tate, a good Augustan, and led him to revise and, as he thought, to clarify the play. More indulgent than Shakespeare and not so tentative, he was sure

> (Whatever Storms of Fortune are decreed)
> That Truth and Virtue shall at last succeed.

It is a pleasant and a good-natured conclusion to a harrowing tale. Unhappily, the antecedent action seems not to confirm it. But neither does that action, however harrowing, however wanting in ruth, lend support to Swinburne's judgement, two centuries later, that in the winding up of the business we are left darkling, that 'redemption . . . [and] explanation . . . are words without a meaning here.'[1] For though the play is fraught with agony, it is not, what Symonds called it, an 'inexplicable agony.'[2] *King Lear*, in this respect, does not differ from the first and the least of Shakespeare's plays, except in excellence, except in rigour: no less than the histories and the most benign of the comedies, it discovers and communicates an ascertainable design.

This is to say that Shakespeare is not so much protean as the same. In comedy as in tragedy a very similar poetics informs his work. The metaphors of Providence and Order, in the earliest plays as in the latest, infer the relation that is to obtain between man and the universe, and man and society. The war of Reason

[1] *A Study of Shakespeare* [1876], London, 1902, p. 171.
[2] *Shakespeare's Predecessors in the English Drama*, London, 1884, p. 370.

and Will, the fierce dispute, in Keats's phrase, betwixt damnation and impassioned clay, dramatizes the fragility of that relation and the tension to which it is subjected. Kind denotes the internal sanctions that enforce it. To treat of Anarchy or Fortune is to represent what happens when those sanctions are ignored and the relation disputed. To suggest that the ignorant man invokes his own destruction is to say that he repudiates Substance for Show. To explore the theme of Redemption is to illuminate the means by which his mistake may be recovered.

The words themselves are of course unimportant; each admits of alternatives. This metaphor, more exact and more expressive, may be substituted at will for that other. But the attitudes or principles the terminology embodies, the understanding of human conduct it implies, are not mutable but fixed. The underlying principles which sustain Shakespearean drama, and which may be described collectively as Shakespeare's poetics, remain constant throughout his career in the theatre. The opposite view—and it has been on the whole the more popular—is put succinctly by the Italian patriot, Mazzini: Shakespeare's 'drama is the drama of *individuality*'; Shakespeare 'shows neither the consciousness of a law nor of humanity'; 'enthusiasm for great principles [is in him] unknown'. This is the Shakespeare whose plays are familiar mostly as a congeries of elegant extracts. To read them in that manner is at least to know them a little. It is, however, to misapprehend and totally their nature and also their particular excellence. The same misapprehension is rank in Shaw's preface to *St. Joan*. *King Lear*, I should think, refutes it sufficiently.

But if great principles are manifest in *Lear*, they are ascertainable as well, in embryonic form, in so early a play as *Richard II*.

> Foul sin gathering head
> Shall break into corruption.
> (5.1.58f.)

The portents which prefigure and symbolize disaster in the tragedies appear first in Shakespeare's work in the opening lines of what is presumably his first play. Their function, and the attitude or state of mind which assigns that function to them, is the same in *King Lear* as in *1 Henry VI*. The self-torment which, in the second play of the trilogy, maddens Cardinal Beaufort on his deathbed is that which maddens Lady Macbeth. The bad dreams which haunt Richard on the eve of Bosworth Field anticipate, crudely but faithfully, the visitation which comes to Brutus on the eve of Philippi. The death of Richard, however melodramatic, is essentially the death of Edmund and Macbeth. Nor are the parallels fortuitous. Because Shakespeare's understanding of the relation between conduct and its consequences does not vary, although it deepens, the plays from first to last redact one another, and necessarily. To elicit and to describe that understanding, which is a legacy to the dramatist of a particular moment in time, is to attempt a definition of Shakespeare's poetics.

The early comedies, *The Two Gentlemen of Verona*, *Love's Labour's Lost*, *The Comedy of Errors*, *The Taming of the Shrew*, are all of them marked by a good deal of clowning, often tedious to read, moderately amusing, if performed with sufficient tact, to hear and to see. Generally the clowning has either to do with a kind of crude farce: the Induction to *The Taming of the Shrew* is an example; or with the exploiting of words, not as they further the business of the play, but simply for their own sake, for whatever pleasure is in them. There is, conventionally, a wretched servant, a Mr. Malaprop, for ever at odds with his master. His name is Grumio, in the *Shrew*, or Costard in *Love's Labour's Lost*, or Launce in *The Two Gentlemen*, or Dromio in *The Comedy of Errors*. When he walks he staggers, and when he uses words, they are susceptible of every connotation but the right one.

Doubtless, Shakespeare was amused. The savouring of verbal blunders is an amiable and conspicuous vice in him, and persistent. So is his propensity for fooling with the meanings of words, dilating with a kind of horrid insistence on the ambiguity of what looks to be plain. I suppose it a source of the great precision of his style. The young ladies and gentlemen of *Love's Labour's Lost* are, like Osric in *Hamlet*, absolute knaves who speak by the card. But the fashion in which they riddle and equivocate is apt to seem a tiresome business. Certainly it is rudimentary humour. It is, however, significant in that it depends on one device, however hoary; in that it confesses, and this in every case, but one burden, which tallies nicely with the business of the plays. The foolish servants, the termagant women, the lovers who protest too much, are 'senseless'[1]—not because they can stand against buffets and knocks, but just in this: each is surpassingly stupid, mistaken—incorrigibly stupid, one would say rather, were it not for the comic denouement.

The character of Sly, the drunken tinker of *The Taming of the Shrew*, is founded altogether on mistaking. The play commences as Sly, besotted and asleep in front of an alehouse, is carried off for a joke by a hunting party of noblemen, who wrap him in fine clothes, lay him in bed, set a banquet beside him, and then, as he wakes, pretend to pay him honour as their lord. Of course the aplomb with which Sly reacts is amusing. He accepts with an equanimity that only the man who is invincibly ignorant could muster the good fortune of a title, an estate, even a wife: 'Madam,' he says, 'undress you, and come now to bed.' (Ind., 2.119) His easy complaisance anticipates successfully the comic assurance of weaver Nick Bottom, in *A Midsummer Night's Dream*, not a whit more vulgar than Christopher Sly, nor more willing to let the world slip.

But the essence of this comedy is that Sly (like Bottom, in the later play) is deformed. A beggar who forgets himself, he is, for a little while, metamorphosed, to the delight of one of those feline contrivers in whom Shakespeare appears to have delighted. But if the anonymous Lord of the play finds in his rather puerile charade 'pastime passing excellent', as Portia does in her mummery—I think of the gulling of Shylock in the fourth act of *The Merchant of Venice*; or Henry V in his—I think of his disguise before Agincourt as a soldier, or of that earlier scene in which he toys with the conspirators who have plotted to take his life, toys with them as a cat caresses a mouse, knowing all the while that the mouse is to be eaten, as the conspirators are to be hanged; if—another example—the Duke of *Measure for Measure*, that connoisseur of the emotions of others, enjoys exploiting those emotions: 'Be absolute for death'—this, to the wretched Claudio in prison—it is always the butt, the person practised upon, who offers the occasion.

So Christopher Sly, to take him as the type of that recurrent figure in Shakespeare's plays, the man who mars his own features, and becomes a sport or puppet, by mistaking the role in which he is cast. Edmund, in a graver context, mistakes the

[1] *CE*, 4.4.25–29; *TS*, 1.2.37.

satisfying of the ego for the root and sole motive of conduct: the revenging gods bend their thunders against him. Goneril misreads her nature, its possibilities, its limitations: for her mistaking, she is slivered and disbranched. Fortune's fool, as he is ignorant of sequence, mounts the wheel: it throws him down as low as to the fiends. The slave of nature, misconceiving what is proper to a man, is turned for his error to something less: like Nebuchadnezzar, the archetype of the wild man, his hairs grow like eagles' feathers, his nails like the claws of birds. (Daniel, iv.33) Sly's kind—and that of Edmund and his father, or Lear and his unnatural daughters—is human kind. He abjures it, becomes a 'monstrous beast . . . like a swine . . . foul and loathsome'. (Ind., 1.34f.) If he were 'sensible', he would wonder with Cassio, Othello's drunken lieutenant, 'that men should put an enemy in their mouths to steal away their brains! That . . . [men] should, with joy, pleasance, revel, and applause, transform . . . [themselves to] beasts!' (*Othello*, 2.3.292–4)

But of course he is not sensible; he is 'bestraught,' infused with a foul spirit, an idle humour, possessed by strange lunacy, by abject lowly dreams. (Ind., sc.2) He has put off himself, and when he takes on the character of the nobleman who beguiles him, the disparity between what he is, and what in fact he ought to be, is made the more pronounced, and more risible. The drunkard is a masquer; so are those others whose comedy he is persuaded to witness. Thus a servant becomes the master he has served; the master essays the role of a scholar.

> Fathers commonly
> Do get their children, but in this case of wooing,
> A child shall get a sire. (2.1.411–13)

A wandering Pedant takes the name of a wealthy old gentleman; he, because what is incongruous has been changed to the matter of course, is called villain, knave, and cozener for going under his legitimate title. Propriety, in the extended series of mistakings which is the play, is separated from practice. The exploiting of the disparity is one way to humour.

But more than deformity goes to make laughter. A monster is most comical when he thinks himself comely, and seeks, moreover, to impose his erring perception on the superior wit of those who stand by.

Known unto these, and to myself disguised!
(*Comedy of Errors*, 2.2.216)

These, my knowers, are the auditors of the play. They see the masquer for what he is: the dramatist has given them to see. They understand, by convention, what he should be. What is more, they perceive and boggle at, the notion he entertains of himself and would make them swallow, too, if he could. Well, he cannot. And so they savour the grossness of the notion, so little conformable to fact; and the infatuation of the fellow, in thinking to make it go down; and their own acumen in finding him out.

I know you what you are.

Deformity and self-delusion, taken together, are the twin sources of humour in the plays. Because it is so fruitful and dependable a conjunction, Shakespeare had recourse to it constantly. Sir Andrew Aguecheek, in *Twelfth Night*, is a man, and so, by definition, forthputting in love. As it happens, he belies the definition; he is an eccentric. But he thinks himself a lover. And so the jest is readied. Confront him with Maria: he has not wit enough to bring his hand to the buttery bar. Malvolio is a steward, which is to say, an underling. Imagination blows him. He puts on, in fancy, a branched velvet gown. He is an absolute aberrant. His confounding is the absolute comedy. Dogberry and Verges are men of the watch. Their business, you would think, is with order. Not so: it is rather with confusion. They themselves mistake the one for the other, and that is a part of the jest. 'I am a wise fellow . . . and one that knows the law.' (*Much Ado*, 4.2.82, 85)

It is the same in Shakespearean tragedy. Shakespeare's villains are as foolish, as mistaken, as the least self-conscious of Shakespeare's clowns. The clue to their folly is in their avowal of self-sufficiency, a disputing of the sanctions of Providence and Kind. They venture to tell you, with King Edward the usurper in *3 Henry VI*, 'My will shall stand for law' (4.1.50); or with Crookback, intent on displacing his brother, 'I am myself alone' (5.6.83); or with Jack Cade, an early and a ruffianly Coriolanus, 'My mouth shall be the Parliament of England' (*2 Henry VI*, 4.7.16f.); or with Julius Caesar, 'The cause is in my will.' (2.2.71) Edmund in *Lear*, the most powerfully imagined and precisely drawn of the villains, is also the most deformed and deluded. 'I should have been that I am had the maidenliest star in the firmament twinkled on my bastardizing.' (1.2.143f.) This is security, in the Elizabethan sense. It is hubristic; it is Epicurean, a favourite word of Shakespeare's. It rests on the belief that man is the measure of all things, that the idea of kind is a fiction, but

An old bellows full of angry wind.

Folly so gross is always entertaining. The infatuated man is always a butt. Clarence, in the early tragedy of *Richard III*, entertains: he praises his brother Richard to the murderers whom Richard has sent against him. Hastings, in the same play, on his way to the Tower, entertains: he jests with Buckingham, who has connived in his impending death. Buckingham himself entertains most of all: he sneers at Queen Margaret's prediction that his death will follow after, and finds that prediction unerring. The audience in each case is aware; the unhappy protagonist is not. There is dramatic excitement, pleasure of a kind, in the fact.

It is easier, I suppose, to savour that pleasure when the audience has little sympathy with the speaker. Shylock exulting, 'A Daniel come to judgement!' (4.1.223) Caesar treading the purple: 'Hence, wilt thou lift up Olympus!' (3.1.74) this, just before he is stabbed, which is to say proved mortal; even Brutus crying, 'Peace, freedom, and liberty!' (3.1.110) as he bathes his hands in Caesar's blood—these speeches are right: the speaker is fooled: it is good that he should be. *Macbeth* excels in that kind of fooling. Its irony, like the irony of *Oedipus the King*, is, not prophetic merely, but reminiscent, retrospective. Lady Macbeth, careless of physiology, is sure that 'memory, the warder of the brain, Shall be a fume'. (1.7.65f.) She cannot sleep. She is sure that 'A little water clears us of this deed'. (2.2.67) She cannot wash. She is sure that 'What's done is done' (3.2.12); and must concede that 'What's done cannot be undone'. (5.1.75) One anticipates her concession, in a wry sense takes pleasure in it. After all, she has initiated murder.

In comedy, in tragedy, Shakespeare discovers entertainment in misapprehension. But the effect he is seeking, whether fear or hilarity or grief, depends on the perception in his audience of a norm that has been violated, a standard that has been misconstrued. That norm or standard the audience and the dramatist must carry with them as a kind of phylactery whose contents are at once deeply meaningful and so familiar, so much a matter of common experience, as not to need telling over. Order is such a norm, and chaos the confounding of it. Edmund Dudley in *The Tree of Commonwealth* (1509–10) describes the one:

> But let vs all consider that god hath set a due order by grace betwene himself and aungells, and betwen angle [*sic*] and angell, and by reason betwene Aungell and man, and betwene man and man, & man & beast, and by nature only betwene beaste and beaste, which order from the highest pointe to the lowest, god willeth vs firmly to kepe.[1]

But if the chaos which *Lear* describes is frightening to those who witness the play, it is because they share with the playwright a sense of the standard to which Dudley, in explicit ways, renders homage. You cannot treat, as Shakespeare does in *2 Henry IV*, of

> the strond whereon the imperious flood
> Hath left a witnessed usurpation,
>
> (1.1.62f.)

without inferring the conventional, the wonted limits of land and sea. There is no point, no fearful meaning in the vision of Ulysses, in *Troilus and Cressida*, of the waters lifting their bosoms higher than the shores (1.3.111f.), unless those waters, by definition, are bounded.

The convention, which the clown and the villain misconster, is the thing. Each image the dramatist fashions, every scene he contrives, appeals to it, of necessity. Man, by convention, balks when evil conduct is demanded of him. Signor Sooth, who never balks or demurs, who answers always in affirmatives, is, it follows, a knave or a fool. The man whom the common tongue stigmatizes as a fool is supposed, by convention, to utter inanities. If the dramatist represents him as telling home truths, he forces you to query what is possibly a superficial convention and, if you are perceptive, to put it aside for another, more nearly emblematic of reality, which discovers little wisdom in the wisdom of the world. Thus the sense of the grudging tribute paid to the jester in *Timon*:

[1] Manchester, 1859, p. 53.

Thou art not altogether a fool.
(2.2.119)

Honour and riches are understood to be ephemeral. You know the genuine fool in that he thirsts after tottering honour, and ties his treasure up in silken bags to pleasure death, to whom it descends. (*Pericles*, 3.2.40–42) The normal man is the provident man: he weighs time to the utmost grain. So Henry V, in whom you recognize the legitimate king. (2.4.137f.) The ignorant man who squanders time is abnormal: Richard II, in whom you recognize the pretender. Reflection, consideration are the tokens of conventional behaviour. To think them otherwise, and so, like Othello, to act on the gad, is, it follows, to act the part of a villain:

No, to be once in doubt
Is once to be resolved.
(3.3.179f.)

Amity in the family is normal; discord in the family transgresses the norm. And hence the shock explicit, in *3 Henry VI*, in the juxtaposing on stage of those patterns of ignorance, a son who has killed his father, a father who has killed his son. (2.5) A rational, a normal man acknowledges precedence; the comedian disregards it. That is the point of the similitude from *Titus Andronicus*:

The eagle suffers little birds to sing
And is not careful what they mean thereby,
Knowing that with the shadow of his wings
He can at pleasure stint their melody.
(4.4.83–86)

My freedom, by convention, is here, in this long-familiar place. To send me away is to inhibit my freedom. Banishment is there. But if, on receiving my sentence, I am able to cry, with Kent in *King Lear*, with Celia in *As You Like It*:

To liberty and not to banishment,
(1.3.140)

I give you to understand how radically my judge and ruler has misapprehended the convention, and how disordered, how little normal, and so how deserving of ridicule or censure is the state over which he presides.

The exploiting of misapprehension as a source of entertainment is not peculiar to Shakespeare. It is a part of the craft, then and now, of dramatists altogether unlike Shakespeare in their idiom and, in other respects, in their practice: of Ben Jonson, his contemporary; of Wycherley, to choose a Restoration playwright; of Gerhart Hauptmann, to come to the present. The great gull of *The Alchemist*, Sir Epicure Mammon, is, like Shakespeare's Sir Andrew, a knight; but the title is his that he may show you (unself-consciously) how little it suits him. Tribulation Wholesome, in name a man of God, embodies in proof the good sense of the saying: *Cucullus non facit monachum.* Wycherley, in *The Country Wife*, gives you ladies whose face between their forks presages snow. So much for appearance. Hauptmann's Von Wehrhahn ranks first, in status, among the persons of *The Beaver Coat.* He wears a monocle, and cutaway. He rules his court with the air of a Junker. He looks like a Junker. In fact he is a fool, not a tenth part so shrewd as the semi-literate washer woman to whom he condescends. The first shall be last, and the last shall be first.

This confounding, devoid of serious consequence, and understood by the audience to be a counterfeit presentment of what is normally current, of what is kind, is the first principle of Shakespearean comedy. Manifest in the earliest plays, one meets it again, in the ludicrous confusion of *A Midsummer Night's Dream*, and yet again, for the last time, in *The Tempest*, in that more parlous confusion, begotten of ignorant fumes that mantle the reason. It is a principle for ever the same. Given, Lysander, in love with Hermia. Let him be changed to the lover of Helena.

I am not what I am.

Given, Sebastian, the brother and the subject of Alonso, King of Naples, committed by nature to loyalty and love. Let him leap winking into destruction, collaborate, to his own undoing, in the murderous scheme of Antonio. Given, Prospero, the rightful Duke of Milan, or Frederick, the wrongful Duke in *As You Like It*, or Vincentio, in *Measure for Measure*, who rules over Vienna, the bubbling stew of corruption, itself an incongruity writ large. Take the one man from his throne, and set him down in an island with only Caliban for subject, who first was his own king. Corrupt the other from his obedience; let him usurp the sovereign power, let him banish his brother to the Forest of Arden. Metamorphose Vincentio from a prince to a friar; let Angelo, a deputy, put on the crown.

> Deformed beyond deformity, unformed,
> Insipid as the dough before it is baked,
> They change their bodies at a word.
> And then?

The question is from Yeats. The answer is that then the sport begins. Put forward as your protagonist a paragon of women, a Cordelia, and treat her as a scullion. In lieu of Cordelia—if comedy is your business—put forward Bianca, the good daughter in *The Taming of the Shrew*. The disparity between what she is and what she is forced to become is so great, so little credible, so little just, that it is, necessarily, greatly comic. She is called a Minerva in wisdom (1.1.84), one who humbly subscribes to the pleasure of her parent (81), who renders to her elders obedience in all things, so well does she understand her duty. (2.1.6f.) Her reward is to bear the penance of her shrewish sister's tongue (1.1.89), to be made that sister's bondmaid and slave. (2.1.2) So much for use and wont, and the customary sequence of things.

A reversal even more preposterous, and so even more comic, is Katharina's, the Shrew's. Owning a body 'soft and weak and smooth, Unapt to toil and trouble in the world' (4.2.165f.), bound to give attendance on her lord, she figures nonetheless as 'an irksome brawling scold' (2.2.188), a wench 'stark mad or wonderful froward', indeed a fiend of Hell. (1.1.69, 88) She is

> Katharine the Curst!
> A title for a maid of all titles the worst.
> (1.2.129f.)

As Bianca takes delight in music and poetry (1.1.93), so she, like the dullard of whom Lorenzo warns you, in *The Merchant of Venice*, unmoved with concord of sweet sounds, wields her lute like a club against the head of her sister's lover. Bianca is pleased best with true rules and old fashions. (3.1.80f.) Kate is an innovator, to whom the precepts of husband and parent are as light and as little commendable as chaff.

To you your father should be as a god,
One that composed your beauties—yea, and one
To whom you are but as a form in wax.
(*Midsummer Night's Dream*, 1.1.47–49)

This is good orthodox doctrine. The heretic who is the shrew will have none of it. So she rounds on her father: 'What hast thou to do? Father, be quiet.' (3.2.218f.)

What makes for humour in this ranting discourse, this cantankerous and untoward behaviour, is that it is unnatural behaviour, restrained of course by the dramatist from logical issue. Compare Goneril, in *Lear*:

Be then desired
By her that else will take the thing she begs.
(1.4.268f.)

It is unnatural, and hence comic, because violence has been done to the nature of woman, and the relation of woman to man, as that nature and relation are understood or given in the play. By definition a suppliant, the shrew has never prayed in her life (4.1.81f.), never learned to entreat. (4.3.7f.) The saying of her husband, 'She is my goods, my chattels; she is my house' (3.2.232), seems to her the saying of a jolly surly groom. But prayer, entreaty, and the subordination of a wife to her husband, these, at least for the few hours' traffic of this play, are things belonging to woman.

The beasts, the fishes, and the wingèd fowls
Are their males' subjects and at their controls.
Men more divine, the masters of all these,
Lords of the wide world and wild watery seas,
Indued with intellectual sense and souls,
Of more pre-eminence than fish and fowls,
Are masters to their females, and their lords.
(*Comedy of Errors*, 2.1.18–24)

You can, if you like, in despite of St. Paul, stand the old notion on its head. The normality, which is for a while to be confounded, you can make to consist in the empery of woman over man. This of course is what Chaucer does, in *The Wife of Bath's Tale*, and Shaw, in *Candida*, redacting *A Doll's House*, and Fletcher, redacting Shakespeare, in *The Tamer Tamed*, and Shakespeare himself, in *The Merry Wives of Windsor*. So Ford at last submits, in the climax of that play:

> Pardon me, Wife. Henceforth do what thou wilt.
> (4.4.6)

All that one needs, in any case, is a standard, so that when Albany says, of Goneril,

> Proper deformity seems not in the fiend
> So horrid as in woman,
> (4.2.60f.)

and when Kate says, of her sex,

> To wound thy lord, thy king, thy governor
> . . . blots thy beauty . . .
> Confounds thy fame . . .
> And in no sense is meet or amiable,
> (4.2.138–41)

the audience is able to concur, and to know why it concurs.

Often in comedy, and sometimes in what aspires to be tragedy, the ordinance which is slighted was enacted only yesterday and is apt to be rescinded tomorrow. You can find the standard or norm of the typical Elizabethan farce in the courtesy books, in Peacham, in Hoby. Thus the short life of most farcical drama, which depends for its vitality on the idiom or dress or manners of the moment, and which fails of its point as the merely fashionable goes out of fashion. Shakespeare's farce is generally more substantial. The canons whose disputing evokes laughter owe their origin to something deeper and more permanent than the mode. It is true, in the early farces, as in the later and more serious comedies, Shakespeare's persons are given more than they might be to the less interesting kind of mistaking, as of the meaning of words, the identity of twins. But in almost all the plays—I should say in all but *The Merry Wives of Windsor*, which seems to me a mechanical *réchauffé*—the vital mistaking, for which the others stand as symbols, is that of human nature or kind.

The process by which the gull, the ignorant protagonist is brought to confess his error, or treason really, his role hitherto as 'foul contending rebel' (*Taming of the Shrew*, 5.2.159), would be a painful process, no question, except for this: in comedy, the gull is not a legitimate person at all. The shrew, however vivid, is not real. Neither is her husband nor, certainly, those lesser protagonists, whose business in the play is to be beaten or fooled. The banishing of real flesh and blood: flesh, which may be tormented, blood, which may actually flow, this, I suggest, is the second principle of Shakespearean comedy. The auditors of such comedy may be likened to men who look down from great heights—on crows and choughs not half so gross as beetles, on anchoring barks diminished to their cocks, on other men, less happy, whose altercations appear like those of mice.

This trick of transporting the audience aloft makes perforce in that audience for a certain detachment. Or if, as sometimes happens, one is brought close to those who act out the play, he is never made witness to any turmoil of spirit that is carefully explored and capable of rationalization, to the real thing, that is to say. He sees arms flailing, faces contorted; he hears imprecations. All this is formal.

I have *tremor cordis* on me.

The first three acts of *The Winter's Tale* dramatize with tremendous power the jealousy of Leontes. But, unlike the first act of *Macbeth*, they do not investigate in detail the soul of the wrongdoer, who is felt therefore neither to sin greatly nor to sin wilfully. This is to say (with Dr. Johnson) that comic writers are concerned with the face of the clock: Henry Fielding, rather than with its inner workings: Samuel Richardson.

A further consequence of that concern is the drawing of a charmed circle about the protagonists. Demetrius and Lysander, the interchangeable lovers of *A Midsummer Night's Dream*, walk together to the edge of catastrophe. He who fears for them, however, as they bristle and gesticulate, who anticipates their mingling in a tragic affray, even as Romeo and Paris, is not alive to their invulnerability. Nor is it strength which protects them; it is rather an essential supineness, as of the Raggedy Ann, or Aunt Sally. Comic characters in Shakespeare are, in curious ways, like the hero-villains of Shakespearean tragedy after they have made the tragic and irreversible choice, which means: when choice has been taken from them, when they have become heteronomous. But Shakespeare, in the comedies, is meddlesome and benign. He looks after the slaves and ministers who are incapable of looking after themselves. If by chance they should collide, ill met by moonlight, neither will fall before the sword of the other. The dramatist has made them of straw. It is his way of hedging the bet.

The technique is familiar, and generally efficacious. When, in Synge's *The Tinker's Wedding*, an avaricious priest is gagged and tied and stuffed in a sack, you do not recoil at the hard handling of a fellow human being. It is only another scarecrow trussed up to be pummelled, after all only another Malvolio. So long as the characters are impervious to hurt, or kept at a remove, or approximate to stock figures, so long as they smack of the pedant or braggart, or the rustic servant or parasite or old pantaloon, you do not suffer for them or sympathize with them, whatever the indignities they are made to endure. But if, as sometimes happens, a mere figure of fun is conceded real speech, if real lineaments reflect, however briefly, real emotion, then the dramatist is in trouble, and the audience, for a moment, at sea. It is as if the butt or cipher who, as I suggest, shares with the tragic character an incapacity to fend for himself, were all at once to share with him also the genuine pain that follows that loss of autonomy. Edmund you observe abdicating to Fortune, and Lear turning anarch, and Cornwall giving rein to the will, and Goneril and Regan preferring the shadow to substance. Each is disfranchised and made, in consequence, to suffer. But the comic character is too circumscribed, really to choose, and so your sense of justice is offended if, like the others, who are or who seem to be observably culpable, he is permitted to agonize at every pore. So long as Holofernes, the pompous schoolmaster of *Love's Labour's Lost*, keeps true to his antecedents, he offers legitimate sport. But when the Pedant of the *Commedia dell' Arte* becomes the injured party—or person, rather—of the last act of the play, when, beaten and sore, he exclaims to his tormentors,

> This is not generous, not gentle, not humble,
> (5.2.632)

when Holofernes, so to speak, discovers a heart, one wishes uneasily that he had not.

The baffled Shylock, the cuckolded Pinchwife, in Wycherley, I think indecorous, inconsiderate, in much the same way:

better, in any case clearer, had the one continued to whet his knife, with splendid and undivided malevolence, thus sparing his auditors the notion that he also was a man; better, in any case more consistently amusing, had the other, on apprehending his defeat, forborne to stand doggedly, with his hat before his eyes. The auditor is indifferent to the humanity of the gull. He does not want to advert to it.

Shakespeare, in the comedies, contrives by and large that he need not. The shrew whose taming he watches, he abides: she is not a woman as Cordelia is, or Desdemona. Like in every point to other creatures, she is unlike them in one: she has not the capacity to suffer. She is a puppet, made to work for your delectation and mine.

> My falcon now is sharp and passing empty,
> And till she stoop, she must not be full-gorged.
>
> (4.1.193f.)

The pleasure is in watching a creature not altogether human compelled, by various sleights, to look upon her lure. It is an intellectual, not an emotional, pleasure.

That is why Shakespeare's comedies are so full of riddling, of arbitrary conundrums, whose solution is a mathematical exercise. The close of *Twelfth Night*, of *As You Like It* and *Measure for Measure*, of *All's Well* and *Cymbeline* coincides with, in fact depends on, the working out of the riddle. *The Winter's Tale* puts the riddle at the heart of the play: 'the King shall live without an heir if that which is lost be not found'. (3.2.135–7) In *Pericles* it figures at the very beginning, and is not resolved really until the hero finds the daughter whose office it is to beget him anew:

> He's father, son, and husband mild;
> I mother, wife, and yet his child.
>
> (1.1.68f.)

And the point of the parallel is that Pericles and Leontes, chief actors in a sort of comedy, are, like Posthumus and Bertram, Orlando and Viola and Mariana of the moated grange, neither human nor free, as Shakespeare's tragic actors seem to be human and free. In what they do, they are determined; and also, at least ostensibly, in what they are. The conversion to good conduct of the usurping Duke of *As You Like It* is, like the evil conduct that goes before it, simply prodigious. Shakespeare, with his customary cheerfulness, attempts (without success) to fob it off by introducing as agent that infallible sign of the playwright's embarrassment or fatigue, 'an old religious man'. He is less cursory in reporting the conversion of Oliver, the wicked subject, but no more convincing. Nor does the repentance of Proteus convince, in *The Two Gentlemen of Verona*. It is hard to see how it could. For these are involuntary persons who love and hate as if in fact they were star-crossed, predestined, or (in the Galenic sense) the prey to an overmastering humour. The comedies seem almost to dramatize the theology of Calvin. The comic character is the slave of nature: Duke Frederick, who falls to hating Rosalind, absolutely on the gad. He does not deliberate; he is. But why he is as you see him is a question neither you nor he can answer. Oliver hates his brother Orlando, 'yet I know not why.' (1.1.171) Cymbeline, with as little cause, is attracted to Fidele: 'I know not why nor wherefore.' (5.5.95) The question that is asked of Parolles in *All's Well* might be asked of Malvolio or Cloten or Caliban: 'Is it possible he should know what he is, and be that he is?' (4.1.48f.) The villainy of Leontes, unlike the villainy of Othello, whom he most nearly resembles, does not emerge from within: reason pandering will. It is affixed from without; it is given. Nor does reason assist him in understanding his error. The situations which characters in comedy confront may be described in terms of those Elizabethan pictures, intelligible only from a particular point of vantage,

> perspectives which rightly gazed upon,
> Show nothing but confusion, eyed awry
> Distinguish form.
>
> (*Richard II*, 2.2.18–20)

The normal intelligence, the conventional apprehension, do not suffice.

But comic characters, if insufficient like fools and children, are generally protected, as fools and children should be. *Pericles* treats of disasters at sea. So do *Twelfth Night* and *The Tempest*. But no one with his wits about him really supposes that any of the characters in those comedies are going to drown. Comic characters are denied the dignity of drowning. They are denied the right to suffer. If they die, as happens rarely, they are minor characters who are fashioned of wax, like Mamillius, the little boy of *The Winter's Tale*, and so beget no lamentation. Even Antigonus, the luckless courtier of that play, who carries out his king's command to abandon the infant Perdita on some desolate sea coast, and who is eaten in consequence:

Exit, pursued by a bear,

even Antigonus must, one feels, have been swallowed up entire, as the foolish duck is swallowed in Prokofiev's *Peter and the Wolf*. You can still hear him, quacking inside. The end of Antigonus is essentially comic, and very probably by intention: an attempt on Shakespeare's part to palliate the unhappy business.

By the same token, no comic character may really be said to be free. Leontes, of course, in *The Winter's Tale*, is capable—waiving his initial folly—of good conduct or bad. The happy ending seems to hang on his choice of the good.

> Sir, you . . . have performed
> A saintlike sorrow. No fault could you make
> Which you have not redeemed, indeed paid down
> More penitence than done trespass.
>
> (5.1.1–4)

But the happy ending, if made acceptable, made suitable, to those who look on by, say, the long travail of the King of Sicilia, is ultimately a piece of contriving. The dramatist elects to bring the riddle to good resolution. The dramatist plays God. Without his benign intervention, his more or less arbitrary decision, the sufferings of Leontes would be as bootless as the sufferings of Gloucester and Lear.

I suppose that decision, to rescue a character unable to rescue himself, to be the hallmark of the comedies. It is signallized by the riddle: the play is a kind of mathematics: the characters are so many ciphers: the dramatist, by virtue of superior wit, conducts them at last to good fortune. The protagonist can do nothing to extricate himself.

In tragedy it appears to be otherwise. The look of all of Shakespeare's later tragedies is volitional. The insistence in all of them is on the free will of the hero, or villain. The watchword is causality. The dramatist does not admit of the interposition of chance, or caprice. 'The poet's function is to describe'—I quote from Aristotle's *Poetics*—'not the thing that has happened, but a kind of thing that might happen, i.e. what is possible as being probable or necessary.' (Ch. 9) It is probable that Othello will swallow the insinuations of Iago, and so strangle Desdemona in her bed, because Othello plumes the will. It is necessary that Antony decline to a sworder, that he find himself beguiled to the very heart of loss: he has made rude will the lord of his reason. To Shakespeare as a tragic dramatist, what's past is always prologue. Things do not happen *post hoc*; they happen *propter hoc*. (Ch. 10)

> To wilful men
> The injuries that they themselves procure
> Must be their schoolmasters.

Man, by his own actions, determines his destiny. This, the conventional reading of man's fate, is the view explicit in the tragedies. Pico della Mirandola dramatizes it in a treatise devoted, appropriately, to the dignity of man. God is the speaker:

> To thee, O Adam, we have given no certain habitation nor countenance of thine owne neither anie peculiar office, so that what habitation or countenance or office soeuer thou dost choose for thyselfe, the same thou shalt enioye and posses at thine owne proper will and election—We have made thee neither a thing celestial nor a thing terrestrial, neither mortal nor immortal, so that being thine owne fashioner and artificer of thyselfe, thou maist make thyselfe after what likenes thou dost most affecte.
> (*De Dignitate Hominis*, para. 3)

The parallel utterance in Shakespeare is Helena's, in *All's Well*. It is perhaps the clearest statement of man's freedom, and hence of his responsibility, in any of the plays:

> Our remedies oft in ourselves do lie,
> Which we ascribe to Heaven. The fated sky
> Gives us free scope. Only doth backward pull
> Our slow designs when we ourselves are dull.
> (1.1.231–4)

We are prone to that enervating dullness. It is a legacy to us of the offending Adam. But it is not felt to be overmastering.

The good man, repudiating what is base in his inheritance, may display as much alacrity as he will:

> Consideration like an angel came
> And whipped the offending Adam out of him.
> (*Henry V*, 1.1.28f.)

Always in the conclusion of the comedies, the latent remedy emerges. The hero manifests a kindness nobler than revenge. Valentine in *The Two Gentlemen*, Orlando in *As You Like It*, Isabella in *Measure for Measure*, Posthumus in *Cymbeline*, Prospero in *The Tempest*, though they are put upon, choose to be merciful.

> Pardon's the word to all.
> (*Cymbeline*, 5.5.423)

And so the villain may look up and be happy: Iachimo, Angelo, Oliver, and Proteus. But their happiness is nothing to that of the man who is able to tender the reprieve. His nature is made stronger than his just occasion. (*As You Like It*, 4.3.129f.)

The possibility of that victory is always there in tragedy, if not so often achieved. Without the possibility, tragedy is insupportable. It is dangerous, if excessively common, to say that the tragic hero is fated, dangerous because subversive of tragic drama. There are no heroes or villains, no virtue or vice, there is no victory or damnation in the close of the play, and hence no suspense, no entertainment, unless you are able to assume that heroism and virtue and victory were open at one time to the protagonist. The goodness of Banquo, of Albany, of Cordelia is useful dramatically and honourable ethically, only if the badness of Macbeth and Cornwall and the sisters is felt in some sense to be a voluntary badness. The appearance of free choice is the indispensable condition of Shakespearean tragedy. In the event, the worser element is always predominant: the tragic hero is always destroyed. But there is always about the conflict the look of freedom, of election. Macbeth need not have murdered Duncan, nor Brutus collaborated in the assassination of Caesar.

And yet, if it is good and necessary, ethically and dramatically, to make that assertion, one need not be altogether satisfied with it. 'For the good that I would I do not: but the evil which I would not, that I do.' The quotation from Romans (vii.19) is so poignant because it is, recognizably, so true of every man's experience. The hero, Antony or Lear, does not wish to lose his way; his way is lost, even so. And thus the question Alcibiades raises in *Timon* is uneasy with implication:

> To be in anger is impiety;
> But who is man that is not angry?
>
> (3.5.57f.)

Lear's anger destroys him. Is it accurate and convincing to suggest that he need not have given it room? *Troilus and Cressida*, I think more than any other of Shakespeare's plays, is concerned to answer that question. My election, says the hero, my commitment to anger or lust,

> Is led on in the conduct of my will,
> My will enkindled by mine eyes and ears,
> Two traded pilots 'twixt the dangerous shores
> Of will and judgement.
>
> (2.2.61–65)

The pilots, the senses, are traded: experienced. May one, therefore, rely on them wholly? Clearly one may not. As we are nature's, says the Countess in *All's Well*, passions, which darken judgement, are ours.

> This thorn
> Doth to our rose of youth rightly belong.
> Our blood to us, this to our blood is born.
>
> (1.3.135–7)

Sometimes the blood is

> So madly hot that no discourse of reason,
> Nor fear of bad success in a bad cause,
> Can qualify the same.
>
> (*Troilus and Cressida*, 2.2.115–18)

The pilots, our eyes and ears, are no friends to us then. They are a sort of traitors. It is

> As if those organs had deceptious functions,
> Created only to calumniate.
>
> (*Troilus and Cressida*, 5.2.123f.)

That Hamlet declines to sweep to his revenge, or Coriolanus or Lear to bridle his pride, or Othello his jealousy, or Macbeth his ambition, or Antony his lust, is perhaps at bottom no more surprising than that Kate, in the *Shrew*, declines for so long to know her keeper's call. Her mistaking and theirs is conventional enough, the nub of many stories older than Shakespeare's. A man is repelled by an ancient crone. If he succeeds in disputing the verdict of his senses, the crone at once is seen to be beautiful. Not many men are so shrewd, or so lucky. The moral, as Imogen applies it, in *Cymbeline*, is that 'Our very eyes Are sometimes like our judgements, blind.' (4.2.301f.) It is this unhappy truth that accounts for the fatuity of Malvolio, and Leontes, and Bertram, in *All's Well*, whose essentially stupid rejection of Helena turns on naïve faith in what he sees, or thinks he sees:

> In such a business give me leave to use
> The help of mine own eyes.
>
> (2.3.114f.)

A credulous trust in appearance beguiles the tinker, Sly. It beguiles Gloucester, and costs him his life. It is the undoing of Othello, whose eyes, he would swear to you, are witness of Desdemona's lightness. It is the reason why Kent is mistaken by Cornwall, who confuses the manners with the man. Lear also is mistaken: his eyes are bleared by counterfeit supposes. He sees when he is ready to forswear all belief in appearance. When at last his eyes are opened, he will trust in them no longer, for the eyes, which owe a friendly office to the reason, are prone, to man's confusion, to pander for the will.

In tragedy as in comedy, the protagonists are mistaken, are gulled. To paraphrase a line in *The Two Noble Kinsmen*, perhaps the last play in which Shakespeare had any part, the intemperate surfeit of their eyes distempers their other senses. (4.3.76f.) This is to say that man is host to and in part the victim of a

> Bifold authority! Where reason can revolt
> Without perdition, and loss assume all reason
> Without revolt.
>
> (*Troilus and Cressida*, 5.2.144–6)

The abrupt and absolute change which overtakes characters in comedy begins to seem not so very remote from the preposterous change which alters the tragic hero, making him swerve from good conduct to bad. How different are Antony, and Macbeth, and Hector, in a perfect non sequitur intermitting his resolve to send Helen out of Troy, from Burgundy the turncoat in 1 *Henry VI*:

> Either she hath bewitched me with her words,
> Or nature makes me suddenly relent.
>
> (3.3.58f.)

You cannot rationalize his conduct; neither can you the conduct of the others. It is as if all men are named Proteus, and all action is random action, and self-conscious decision no more than a feather in the scale when weighed against contingency. In the crisis of *The Comedy of Errors*, to cite one of the very earliest of the plays, Antipholus of Syracuse runs for his life—into the priory where his long-lost mother is abbess. And so he is brought to harbour, but blindfolded, in ways that have nothing to do with his own deliberation or contriving. Our deep plots pall; our indiscretion serves us well. In the latest of the plays, the shaping divinity of which Hamlet is conscious is everything. In *Cymbeline*,

> Fortune brings in some boats that are not steer'd.
>
> (4.3.46)

The passive voice governs. Virtue, in the conclusion of *Pericles*, is

> preserved from fell destruction's blast,
> Led on by Heaven and crowned with joy at last.
>
> (5.3.89f.)

The animus against the rich, a remarkable fact in the late comedies, suggests the inconsequence of material power, and thus complements the sense of those plays. The good and the bad alike enjoy, only the illusion of power:

> Whereby I see that Time's the King of men:
> He's both their parent and he is their grave,
> And gives them what he will, not what they crave.
>
> (*Pericles*, 2.3.45–47)

Shakespeare's comedies, and especially the final comedies, are a gloss on and a corrective of the optimism of the tragedies.

Man's freedom of action, it would appear, is very largely a fiction. In the last analysis, good fortune or bad is absolutely beyond his control. That much is certain, and will not come as a revelation except to the eupeptic man who believes in poetic justice. It is the discovery which Sophocles dramatizes in *Oedipus the King*. But, what is far more important, and daunting, good conduct or bad seems also to be determined, independent of volition. How, then—to restate the basic question—can the mistreadings of the tragic hero or villain be held against him? how can the good that he does redound to his credit?

> The error of our eye directs our mind.
> What error leads must err.
> (*Troilus and Cressida*, 5.2.110f.)

But the speaker is Cressida, in whom, perhaps, the wish is father to the thought. The evil that she does, like all evil, like Lear's initial mistaking, is committed in the name of the good. The will, says St. Thomas, and Aristotle before him, never moves except under the show of goodness. And 'if the passions of the minde be strong,' writes Hooker in *The Ecclesiastical Polity*, 'they easily sophisticate the vnderstanding, they make it apt to beleeue vpon very slender warrant, and to imagine infallible truth, where scarce any probable shew appeareth.'[1] How else may one explain Lear's rejection of Cordelia? But Hooker prefaces his equation of stupidity and sin with the qualification, 'if the passions be strong'. The inference is that day by day one may whip and attenuate those passions; or, and this is what happens in tragedy, let them slip, until at last the understanding is in fact powerless against them. Given, a long indulgence of the passions, and the tragic hero is determined in evil.

> How use doth breed a habit in a man!
> (*Two Gentlemen*, 5.4.1)

You can predict, from what you know of their characters, that Morocco and Aragon, in *The Merchant of Venice*, like Goneril and Regan in *Lear*, will have the wisdom by their wit to lose, when the caskets are put before them.

> There is a history in men's lives,
> Figuring the nature of the times deceased.
> (*2 Henry IV*, 3.1.80f.)

[1] London, 1622, Book 5, Epistle Dedicatory, Sig. V3v.

In this sense, 'Hanging and wiving goes by destiny.' (*Merchant of Venice*, 2.9.83) But, given the long coercing of the passions, and the hero need not be trapped by seeming truth:

> That monster, custom, who all sense doth eat,
> Of habits devil, is angel yet in this,
> That to the use of actions fair and good
> He likewise gives a frock or livery
> That aptly is put on.
>
> (*Hamlet*, 3.4.161–5)

The intellectualist view of evil, the view of Aristotle, Aquinas, and Hooker, the view that Shakespeare, at least formally, dramatizes in the tragedies, rests ultimately on choice. If 'use can almost change the stamp of nature', reason need not pander will. The slave of nature is, potentially, the servant of good.

Cymbeline, who is blind for so long to the wickedness of his queen, cannot blame his senses: she was beautiful and full of flattery.

> It had been vicious
> To have mistrusted her.

Still, his ignorance is felt as culpable; he need not have surrendered manhood with his trust:

> yet, O my daughter,
> That it was folly in me, thou mayst say,
> And prove it in thy feeling.
>
> (5.5.62–68)

Troilus concedes that 'something may be done that we will not', but adds,

> When we will tempt the frailty of our powers,
> Presuming on their changeful potency.
>
> (4.4.96–99)

It is only when the passions are nourished that pleasure and revenge grow

> more deaf than adders to the voice
> Of any true decision.
>
> (2.2.171–3)

That is how Lear's daughters explain the pleasure and revenge which darken the understanding of the king. He is indeed determined, unself-conscious, incapable any longer of meditated choice. But if his unruly waywardness oversways him, it is because that waywardness is long-engrafted. And it is the man himself who has permitted it to grow. 'The best and soundest of his time hath been but rash.' (1.1.298f.) After all the tragic hero is responsible. There are no situations which are not human situations. If conduct seems involuntary, it is because you have come too late to the play. Permissiveness goes before the loss of freedom.

But that fatal permissiveness remains a mystery which only God can fathom. If man is free and responsible, man at whatever moment you meet him is also determined. '*Liberty*, and *Necessity*,' declares Hobbes, in *Leviathan*, 'are consistent.' He goes on to attempt a resolution of that paradox:

> As in the water, that hath not only *liberty*, but a *necessity* of descending by the Channel; so likewise in the Actions which men voluntarily doe: which, because they proceed from their will, proceed from *liberty*; and yet, because every act of mans will, and every desire, and inclination proceedeth from some cause, and that from another cause, in a continuall chaine, (whose first link is in the hand of God the first of all causes,) [they] proceed from *necessity*. So that to him that could see the connexion of those causes, the *necessity* of all mens voluntary actions, would appeare manifest.[1]

The same perception, conspicuous in Shakespeare's comedies, is I think implicit in the tragedies. To emphasize it would be to enter a plea of no contest. And so it is tentative, and couched always in a metaphor or symbol. But it is there. Why does Macbeth murder Duncan? It is as if he proceeds to his crime under some fatal hallucination, embodied dramatically in the Witches, the extra-human. Why, really, does Othello murder Desdemona? Is there not something patently absurd in asserting that he does so because he wants to?

> For nature so preposterously to err,
> Being not deficient, blind, or lame of sense,
> Sans witchcraft could not.
>
> (1.3.62–64)

And in fact there is about the play the taint of witchcraft and

[1] London, 1651, Sig. P1v, p. 108 (ch. XXI).

the arcane, repeated mention of foul charms, of drugs, of arts inhibited and out of warrant, chains of magic, spells and medicines bought of mountebanks. It is all, to quote Iago, 'as if some planet had unwitted men'. (2.3.183) It may be true, what Othello says of the handkerchief: 'There's magic in the web.' (3.4.69) His rationalization, his explanation of the killing of Roderigo suggests a reading of the play that has little to do with the strife of wit and will:

> It is the very error of the moon.
> She comes more nearer earth than she was wont
> And makes men mad.
>
> (5.2.109–11)

Enchantment, in a similar manner, hovers about, serves to rationalize, the decline of Mark Antony. It is fair and pertinent to say that he knew what he was doing and chose, deliberately, the worser course:

> These strong Egyptian fetters I must break,
> Or lose myself in dotage.
>
> (1.2.120f.)

And yet the images which characterize Cleopatra suggest that the fetters are not merely to be willed away. For Cleopatra is this great faery, and grave charm, this spell, this witch. Antony, one feels, is not so much a culprit, as a man in the toils.

What is said of the rebels who follow Jack Cade (and the Jews who decline to follow Christ) may be said of the hero-villains of tragedy:

> Oh, graceless men! They know not what they do.
>
> (*2 Henry VI*, 4.4.38)

Only by receiving the gift of grace are they able to know. But this supernatural and essentially anarchic intervention on their behalf, because it is whimsical, gratuitous, makes against human dignity and human endeavour. And thus no playwright is permitted to believe in the principle of grace, except metaphorically, as a Marxist believes in the Dialectic but works to precipitate the revolution, or as a Calvinist believes in predestination but lives the good life in testimony of his election. Shakespeare as a tragic dramatist endorses the Englishman's heresy, Pelagianism. Really he has very little option. Milton, when he comes to write his great dramatic poem, does the same. His good angels stand by their own strength and not by the compulsive grace of God. The treatise *On the Christian Doctrine* reiterates the heresy. In the plays of Shakespeare, the interposition of grace is never observable. The vicious protagonist in his viciousness grows hard, and thus is impervious to it. Prodigal men, says Cicero, in Ben Jonson's *Catiline,* 'Feel not their own stock wasting'. The virtuous protagonist does not grow hard altogether (you must take the dramatist's word for that), and so can accept of redemption. It is the necessity of taking the dramatist's word that makes for the arbitrariness of the plays. But if the play purports to be dramatic, you must believe that the protagonist, however evil or bemused, has been given a chance to save himself. This means, theologically, that grace has been tendered him, and rejected. It means, dramatically, that the hero, rejecting the voice of reason, has commended the poisoned chalice to his lips.

Shakespeare seems to dramatize that mysterious moment, in Lear's banishing of Kent and Cordelia, or in Macbeth's abdication in favour of his wife. The play, by its nature, demands such a representation. But in fact the rejection, making for the seeling of the eyes and the look of inevitability in the doom of the hero, is always anterior to the beginning of the play—if you will pardon, for the sake of the point, a suggestion of Mrs. Jameson and Mrs. Cowden-Clarke. Hamlet's malaise, Lear's imperiousness, Antony's self-indulgence, Othello's credulity, Macbeth's unholy ambition, Timon's fatuous refusal to count the cost—all these are given from the first. But one assumes even so that the hero was at one time unspotted and so autonomous, which is to say metaphorically, receptive to grace and thus capable of achieving a final victory. That is the reason why Ophelia is made to praise the Hamlet that was, and Octavius his rival Antony, and Othello, at the end of his story, himself. It is not true, that Lear has ever but slenderly known himself.

When, however, you encounter him first, in the opening scene of the play, he is as blind to what he is as the drunken tinker or the shrew or the weaver who puts on the ears of an ass. Now since man, by definition, is a rational or knowledgeable being, to be mistaken, to be purblind, is *ipso facto* to be deformed.

The greater the deformity, the greater the disparity or gulf between what one is and what, by convention, one ought to be, the more amusing or more terrible is the character or the play. Consider Caliban. The greatest disparity, as it is the prelude to suicide, is evil. In tragedy the chains are struck from evil: Edmund is enfranchised; the result is catastrophe. In comedy evil is girt round, kept from doing any ultimate harm; the result is laughter. That is why Lucifer is a comic figure in the medieval drama. Consider Ancient Pistol. But here, two provisos. You need, one, a fixed standard or norm or—Coventry Patmore's phrase—a *punctum indifferens* or point of rest, so that the audience will know when to laugh or cry, to hiss or applaud. You do not shudder at the crimes of Richard III, or rejoice at the follies of Malvolio, unless you understand that a king is not to murder his subjects, or a steward to aspire to the hand of his mistress. You do not—to offer an analogy—applaud variation in a poet's verses unless you are conscious of the norm from which he is departing. Sometimes the norm or standard is embodied in character. Edgar in *Lear* is such a character. He is the *punctum indifferens* of the play. He gives you to see just how evil Edmund is: how aberrant. Horatio, the man who is not passion's slave, is supposed to fulfil a similar office in *Hamlet*. As it happens, he is a kind of failure.

The second proviso: you need a dramatist—himself the *deus ex machina* of the play—ready at any moment to nip a desperate situation before it can proceed to disaster: this, if you are dealing with comedy. The presence of the puppet master is decisive. In comedy,

> The fingers of the powers above do tune
> The harmony of this peace.
>
> (*Cymbeline*, 5.5.467f.)

If, conversely, the play is tragic, you need a dramatist just as ready to step aside, forbear to meddle, and let the action run on to its logical close. The entertainment in each case derives from the exploiting of incongruity, which takes its rise from ignorance. In comedy the incongruity may be very great. It is, however, divested by the dramatist of serious consequence. No sword is ever thrust all the way home. No character is endowed with the capacity to suffer. The auditor is involved only intellectually. He watches a game. Comedy is a-logical. It is not felt as sinister, only because the dramatist is pregnant to pity.

In tragedy the ignorance of the protagonist is understood to be incorrigible, at least until the crisis is past. The decision that it should be so lies, once again, with the dramatist. It is a wholly arbitrary decision. But, once taken, it cannot be rescinded. Tragedy is logical. That is why it is supportable. The dramatist does no more than set things going. Like the God of the eighteenth century, he winds up the watch and departs. His protagonists, denied his protection, his intercession, are destroyed. But he does not intercede, even so. It is not that he is indifferent to them, but that he has relinquished control. No longer the prime mover, estranged from his creations, unable to mitigate their suffering, he can do no more than utter valedictions.

WORKS CONSULTED

Ad serenissimum . . . Iacobum Quintum . . . strena, Edinburgh, *c.* 1530?

Aesop, *Fables D'Esope, avec les Figures de Sadeler*, Paris, 1689.

Aesticampianus, *see* Rhagius.

Agrippa, Henry Cornelius, *Of the Vanitie and Vncertaintie of Artes and Sciences*, tr. Ia. San[ford]. Gent., London, 1569.

Alciati, *Andreae Alciati Emblematum Libellus*, Paris, 1536.

—, *Emblemes d'Alciat . . . A Lyon*, 1564 (bound with Sambucus); Paris, 1561.

[Amman, Iost], *Icones Novi Testamenti: Arte et Industria Singulari Exprimentes*, Frankfurt, 1571.

Angermundt, *see* Bruck.

Arber, Edward, *A Transcript of the Registers of the Company of Stationers, 1554–1640*, 5 vols., London, 1875–94.

Arias Montanus, *Humanae Salutis Monumenta*, Antwerp, 1571.

Armstrong, Edward A., *Shakespeare's Imagination, A Study of the Psychology of Association and Inspiration*, London, 1946.

Auerbach, Erna, *Tudor Artists . . . from the Accession of Henry VIII to the Death of Elizabeth I*, London, 1954.

Bacon, Francis, *The Advancement of Learning*, London, 1954, Everyman edn.

Baldwin, William, *A treatise of Morall Phylosophie, contaynyng the sayinges of the wyse*, London, 1547 and ?1550; and, with Thomas Palfreyman, 1564.

Beham, Hans Sebald, *Biblia Insignium Historiarum simulachris*, Gryphius, 1541.

Berjeau, J. Ph., *Early Dutch, German, & English Printers' Marks*, London, 1869.

Bernheimer, Richard, *Wildmen in the Middle Ages*, Cambridge, Mass., 1952.

Bethell, S. L., *Shakespeare and the Popular Dramatic Tradition*, London, 1944.

Bible, The Holy, by Robert Barker, London, 1611.

Bing, Gertrud, 'Nugae circa Veritatem: Notes on Anton Francesco Doni', pp. 304–12 in *Journal of the Warburg Institute*, London, 1937, vol. I.

Blenerhasset, Thomas, *The seconde part of the Mirrour for Magistrates*, London, 1578.
Bloomfield, Morton W., *The Seven Deadly Sins: An Introduction to the History of a Religious Concept, with Special Reference to Medieval English Literature*, East Lansing, Mich., 1952 (Appendix I: 'The Association of Animals and Sins').
Bocksperger, Johan, *Neuwe Biblische Figuren*, Frankfurt, 1564.
Bodius, H., *Vnio Dissidentium*, Coloniae, 1531.
Boissard, J. J., *Emblemata*, Frankfurt, 1593, 1596.
—, *Emblematum liber*, Frankfurt, 1593; Metz, 1588.
—, *Theatrum vitae humanae*, Metz, 1596.
Bradbrook, M. C., *Themes and Conventions of Elizabethan Tragedy*, Cambridge, 1935.
Bradley, A. C., *Shakespearean Tragedy*, London, 1904.
Brant, Sebastian, *La nef des folz du monde*, tr. Pierre Rivière, Paris, 1497.
Brathwaite, Richard, *Natures Embassie*, London, 1621.
Brief Discours de la Tempeste et Fouldre Advenue en la Cite de Londres . . . sur . . . sainct Paul, Paris [1561].
Bruck, Jacob de [Angermundt], *Emblemata Moralia & Bellica . . . Argentorati*, 1615.
—, *Les Emblemes Moraulx et Militaires*, Strasbourg, 1616.
Buchan, John, *Montrose*, London, 1949.
Buell, Llewellyn M., 'Elizabethan Portents: Superstition or Doctrine?' pp. 27–41 in *Essays Critical and Historical Dedicated to Lily B. Campbell*, Berkeley and Los Angeles, 1950.
Burton, Robert, *The Anatomy of Melancholy*, Oxford, 1621.
Burton, William, *The Description of Leicester Shire*, London, 1622.
Caius, Dr. John, *A boke, or counseill against the . . . sweatyng sicknesse*, London, 1552.
Calvin, John, *An Admonicion against Astrology Iudiciall and other curiosities, that raigne now in the world*, tr. G. G[ylby], London [1561]
—, *Sermons on the Epistles to Timothie and Titus*, London, 1579.
Campbell, Lily B., *Shakespeare's Tragic Heroes: Slaves of Passion*, Cambridge, 1930.
Canter, Howard Vernon, *Rhetorical Elements in the Tragedies of Seneca*, Univ. of Illinois Studies in Language and Literature, vol. X, Urbana, Illinois, 1925.
Carroll, William Meredith, *Animal Conventions in English Renaissance Non-Religious Prose (1550–1600)*, New York, 1954.
Carter, Thomas, *Shakespeare and Holy Scripture*, London, 1905.
Caxton, William, *The Mirror of the World*, London, 1480.
Chambers, R. W., *King Lear*, Glasgow, 1940.
—, *Thomas More*, Ann Arbor, Mich., 1958.

Chappell, William, *Popular Music of the Olden Time*, 2 vols., London [1855–9].

Chew, Samuel C., *The Virtues Reconciled: An Iconographic Study*, Toronto, 1947.

Clemen, Wolfgang H., *Shakespeares Bilder*, 1936, tr. as *The Development of Shakespeare's Imagery*, London, 1951.

Colding, Torben Holck, *Aspects of Miniature Painting*, London, 1953.

Coleridge, Samuel Taylor, *Lectures and Notes on Shakspere and Other English Poets*, London, 1883, Bohn edn.

Collection of Seventy-Nine Black-Letter Ballads and Broadsides, Printed in the Reign of Queen Elizabeth, Between the Years 1559 and 1597 [from the library of Henry Huth], London, 1867.

Collins-Baker, C. H., and W. G. Constable, *English Painting of the Sixteenth and Seventeenth Centuries*, Florence and Paris, 1930.

Court of Venus, The, ed. R. A. Fraser, Durham, N.C., 1955.

Cranmer, Thomas, *Cathechismvs . . . [or] shorte Instruction into Christian Religion*, London, 1548.

Crowley, Robert, *One and Thyrtye Epigrammes*, London, 1550.

Cruttwell, Patrick, *The Shakespearean Moment and Its Place in the Poetry of the Seventeenth Century*, New York, 1960.

Cunningham, William, *The Cosmographical Glass*, London, 1559.

Curry, W. C., *Shakespeare's Philosophical Patterns*, Baton Rouge, La., 1937.

Danby, John F., *Shakespeare's Doctrine of Nature: A Study of 'King Lear'*, London, 1958.

Daniel, Samuel, *The Worthy tract of Paulus Iouius*, London, 1585.

Day, Richard, *A Booke of Christian Prayers*, London, 1578.

Desprez, Philippe, *Le Theatre des Animaux*, Paris, 1620.

Dudley, Edmund, *The Tree of Common Wealth*, 1509–10, first printed Manchester, 1859.

Elyot, Sir Thomas, *The boke named the Gouernour*, London, 1531.

Erasmus, *see* Taverner.

Farnham, Willard, *The Medieval Heritage of Elizabethan Tragedy*, Berkeley, 1936.

Fitzherbert, Sir Anthony, *La Graunde Abridgement*, London, 1565.

Fluchère, Henri, *Shakespeare and the Elizabethans*, New York, 1956.

Foxe, John, *The first [and second] volume of the ecclesiasticall history contaynyng the actes and monumentes*, London, 1570.

Fraser, R. A., 'Political Prophecy in "The Pilgrim's Tale" ', *South Atlantic Quarterly*, LVI, no. 1, Jan., 1957, 67–78.

Godfrey, F. M., *Christ and the Apostles: The Changing Forms of Religious Imagery*, London and New York, 1957.

Green, Henry, *Shakespeare and the Emblem Writers*, London, 1870.

Green, John Richard, *A Short History of the English People*, New York, 1900, 2 vols.

Greenfield, Thelma N., 'The Clothing Motif in "King Lear" ', *Shakespeare Quarterly*, V, 1954, 281–6.

Gresham, Edward, *Strange fearful & true newes, which hapned at Carlstadt in the kingdome of Croatia*, London [1606].

Guigue, Georges, *L'Entrée de François Premier Roy de France en La Cité de Lyon le 12 juillet 1515*, Lyons, 1899.

Hall, Edward, *The Triumphant Reigne of Kyng Henry the VIII*, ed. Charles Whibley, 2 vols., London, 1904.

—, *The union of . . . Lancastre & Yorke*, London, 1550.

Hall, John, *The Court of Virtue*, London, 1565 [ed. R. A. Fraser, London, 1961].

Harsnet, Samuel, *A Declaration of egregious Popish Impostures*, London, 1603.

Heilman, Robert B., *This Great Stage: Image and Structure in 'King Lear'*, Baton Rouge, La., 1948.

Heinsius, Daniel, *Emblemata Aliquot Amatoria*, n.p., n.d. ?1610.

Hobbes, Thomas, *Leviathan*, London, 1651.

Holbein, Hans, *Icones Historiarum Veteris Testamenti*, Lyons, 1547; English version, Lyons, 1549; ed. Henry Green, London, 1869.

Holmes, Elizabeth, *Aspects of Elizabethan Imagery*, Oxford, 1929.

Hooker, Richard, *Of the Lawes of Ecclesiastical Politie*, London, 1622.

Horozco, *Libro Segundo De Las Emblemas Morales. Hecho por Don Iuan de Horozco Couarruuias*, Segovia (bound with his *Emblemas* of 1589).

Johnson, Alfred Forbes, *A Catalogue of Engraved and Etched English Title-Pages . . . to . . . 1691*, Oxford, 1934.

Kellett, E. E., *Suggestions: Literary Essays*, Cambridge, 1923.

Kernodle, George R., *From Art to Theatre: Form and Convention in the Renaissance*, Chicago, 1944.

King Lear, ed. Kenneth Muir, New Arden Shakespeare, London, 1955.

King Leir, The True Chronicle History of, London, 1605.

Kreider, Paul V., *Repetition in Shakespeare's Plays*, Princeton, 1941.

La Primaudaye, Peter de, *The French academie*, London, 1618.

Lavater, Ludwig, *De spectris*, Zurich, 1570; tr. R. H.: *Of Ghostes and Spirites Walking by Nyght*, London, 1572; ed. J. Dover Wilson and May Yardley, Oxford, 1929.

Lobel, Matthias de, and P. Pena, *Stirpium Adversaria Nova*, London, 1570.

Lyly, John, *Euphues. The Anatomy of Wit, 1579. Euphues and His England, 1580*, ed. Edward Arber, London, 1868.

McKerrow, R. B., *Printers' & Publishers' Devices in England & Scotland 1485–1640*, London, 1913.

McKerrow, R. B. and F. S. Ferguson, *Title-page Borders Used in England and Scotland 1485–1640*, London, 1932.
Marston, John, *The History of Antonio and Mellida*, pt. I, London, 1602.
Maynard, Theodore, *The Cross and the Crown*, New York, 1950.
Merchant, W. Moelwyn, *Shakespeare and the Artist*, London, 1959.
Modius, Francis, *Gynaeceum, Siue Theatrum Mulierum . . . expressos à* [designed by] *Iodoco Amano* [Iost Amman], Frankfurt, 1586. Reprinted as: *Gynaeceum; or, The Theatre of Women*, ed. Alfred Aspland, London, 1872.
Montaigne, *The Essayes or Morall, Politike and Millitarie Discourses of Lo: Michaell de Montaigne . . . done into English By . . . Iohn Florio*, London, 1603.
Morton, Thomas, *Apologia Catholica*, London, 1605.
Motley, John Lothrop, *The Rise of the Dutch Republic*, London, 3 vols., n.d.
Mourey, Gabriel, *Le Livre des Fêtes Françaises*, Paris, 1930.
Nashe, Thomas, *Christs Teares Ouer Ierusalem*, London, 1593.
New Testament, The, by R. Jugge, London [1552].
Noble, Richard, *Shakespeare's Biblical Knowledge and Use of the Book of Common Prayer*, London, 1935.
Pack of Autolycus, The, ed. H. E. Rollins, Cambridge, Mass., 1927.
Palfreyman, Thomas, *The Treatise of Heauenly Philosophie*, London, 1578.
Panofsky, Erwin, *Meaning in the Visual Arts*, New York, 1955.
—, *Studies in Iconology: Humanistic Themes in the Art of the Renaissance*, New York, 1939.
Patch, Howard R., *The Goddess Fortuna in Mediaeval Literature*, Cambridge, Mass., 1927.
—, 'The Tradition of the Goddess Fortuna', *Smith College Studies in Modern Languages*, Northampton, Mass., 1922, III, 131–235.
Peacham, Henry, *The Compleat Gentleman*, London, 1634.
Peyton, Thomas, *The Glasse of Time*, London, 1620.
Praz, Mario, *Studies in Seventeenth-Century Imagery*, 2 vols. (Vol. II a Bibliography of Emblem Books), London, 1939.
Prior, Moody E., *The Language of Tragedy*, New York, 1947.
Rabelais, François [attributed to], *Les Songes Drolatiques de Pantagruel*, Paris, 1565.
Ralegh, Sir Walter, *The History of the World*, London, 1614.
Recorde, Robert, *The Castle of Knowledge*, London, 1556.
Reynolds, Arthur Graham, *English Portrait Miniatures*, London, 1952.
Ripa, Cesare, *Iconologia*, Padua, 1611; and *Iconologia: or, Moral Emblems*, London, 1709.

Roberts, Lewis, *The Marchants Mapp of Commerce*, London, 1638.

Robertson, D. W., Jr., 'Five Poems by Marcabru', *Studies in Philology*, LI, 4, Oct., 1954, 539–60.

Robinson, James Howard, *The Great Comet of 1680: A Study in the History of Rationalism*, Northfield, Minn., 1916.

Rollenhagio, Gabriele, *Nucleus Emblematum Selectissimorum*, Cologne, 1611.

Roper, William, *The Lyfe of Sir Thomas Moore, knighte*, ed. Elsie Vaughan Hitchcock, London, 1935.

Sambucus, *Emblemata, cum aliquot nummis antiqui operis, Ioannis Sambuci Tirnaviensis Pannonii*, Antwerp, 1564.

Saxl, Fritz, 'Veritas Filia Temporis', *Philosophy & History: Essays Presented to Ernst Cassirer*, ed. Raymond Klibansky and H. J. Paton, Oxford, 1936, pp. 197–222.

Seager, H. W., *Natural History in Shakespeare's Time*, London, 1896.

Seznec, Jean, *The Survival of the Pagan Gods: The Mythological Tradition and Its Place in Renaissance Humanism and Art*, tr. B. F. Sessions, New York, 1953.

Shakespeare Apocrypha, The, ed. C. F. Tucker Brooke, Oxford, 1908.

Shakespeare's England [planned by Sir W. Raleigh and ed. by Sir S. Lee and C. T. Onions], 2 vols., Oxford, 1916.

Sidney, Sir Philip, *The Countesse of Pembrokes Arcadia*, vol. I of *The Complete Works*, ed. Albert Feuillerat, 3 vols., Cambridge, 1912.

Silesio, Mariano, *The Arcadian Princesse*, London, 1635.

Sousa, Antonio de Sousa de Macedo, *Lusitania Liberata* (J. Droeshout), London, 1645.

Spurgeon, Caroline F. E., *Shakespeare's Imagery and What It Tells Us*, New York, 1935.

Starnes, DeWitt T., and Ernest William Talbert, *Classical Myth and Legend in Renaissance Dictionaries*, Chapel Hill, N.C., 1955.

Stow, John, *Survey of London*, London, n.d., Everyman edn.

—, *The Annales of England*, London, 1592.

—, *The Annales, or Generall Chronicle of England . . . continued and augmented . . . by Edmond Howes*, London, 1615.

Strachan, James, *Early Bible Illustrations*, Cambridge, 1957.

Strachey, Lytton, *Elizabeth and Essex*, London, 1928.

Swinburne, A. C., *A Study of Shakespeare* [1876], London, 1902.

Symonds, J. A., *Shakspere's Predecessors in the English Drama*, London, 1884.

Taillepied, Noel, *A Treatise of Ghosts*, Paris, 1588; tr. Montague Summers, London [1933].

Taverner, Richard, *Flores aliquot sententiarum . . . The flowres of sencies gathered . . . by Erasmus*, London, 1550.

Taverner, Richard, *Prouerbes or Adagies, gathered oute of the Chiliades of Erasmus*, London, 1552.

Taylor, E. M. M., 'Lear's Philosopher', *Shakespeare Quarterly*, VI, 1955, 364–5.

Taylor, Rupert, *The Political Prophecy in England*, New York, 1911.

Tervarent, Guy de, *Attributs et Symboles dans L'Art Profane 1450–1600. Dictionnaire d'un Langage Perdu*, Geneva, 1958 (Tome I), 1959 (II: completed).

Thompson, Elbert N. S., *Literary Bypaths of the Renaissance*, New Haven, Conn., 1924.

Thomson, J. A. K., *Shakespeare and the Classics*, London, 1952.

Tillyard, E. M. W., *The Elizabethan World Picture*, London, 1943.

Topsell, Edward, *The History of Four-footed Beasts and Serpents*, London, 1658.

Traversi, D. A., *An Approach to Shakespeare*, New York, 1956.

True Report of the burnyng of the Steple and Churche of Poules in London, The, London, 1561.

Truth Brought to light and discovered by Time, London, 1651.

Waterhouse, Ellis K., *Painting in Britain 1530 to 1790*, Melbourne, London, Baltimore, 1953.

Watson, Arthur, *The Early Iconography of the Tree of Jesse*, Oxford, 1934.

—, 'The Imagery of the Tree of Jesse on the West Front of Orvieto Cathedral', pp. 149–64 in *Fritz Saxl 1890–1948 A Volume of Memorial Essays*, ed. D. J. Gordon, London, 1957.

Welsford, Enid, *The Fool: His Social and Literary History*, London, 1935? New York, n.d.

Whitney, Geoffrey, *A Choice of Emblemes, and other Devises*, Leyden, 1586; and, in MS. (the author's dedication copy to Robert Dudley, Earl of Leicester, *c.* 1585), Harvard, no. 138, MS Typ 14.

Whittington, Robert, *De sillabarum quantitate congeries*, London, 1519.

Withington, Robert, *English Pageantry: An Historical Outline*, 2 vols., Cambridge, Mass., and London, 1918.

Wittkower, Rudolf, 'Chance, Time, and Virtue', *Journal of the Warburg Institute*, London, 1937, I, 313–21.

—, *Gian Lorenzo Bernini*, London, 1955.

Woodward, John, *Tudor and Stuart Drawings*, London, 1951.

INDEX

INDEX

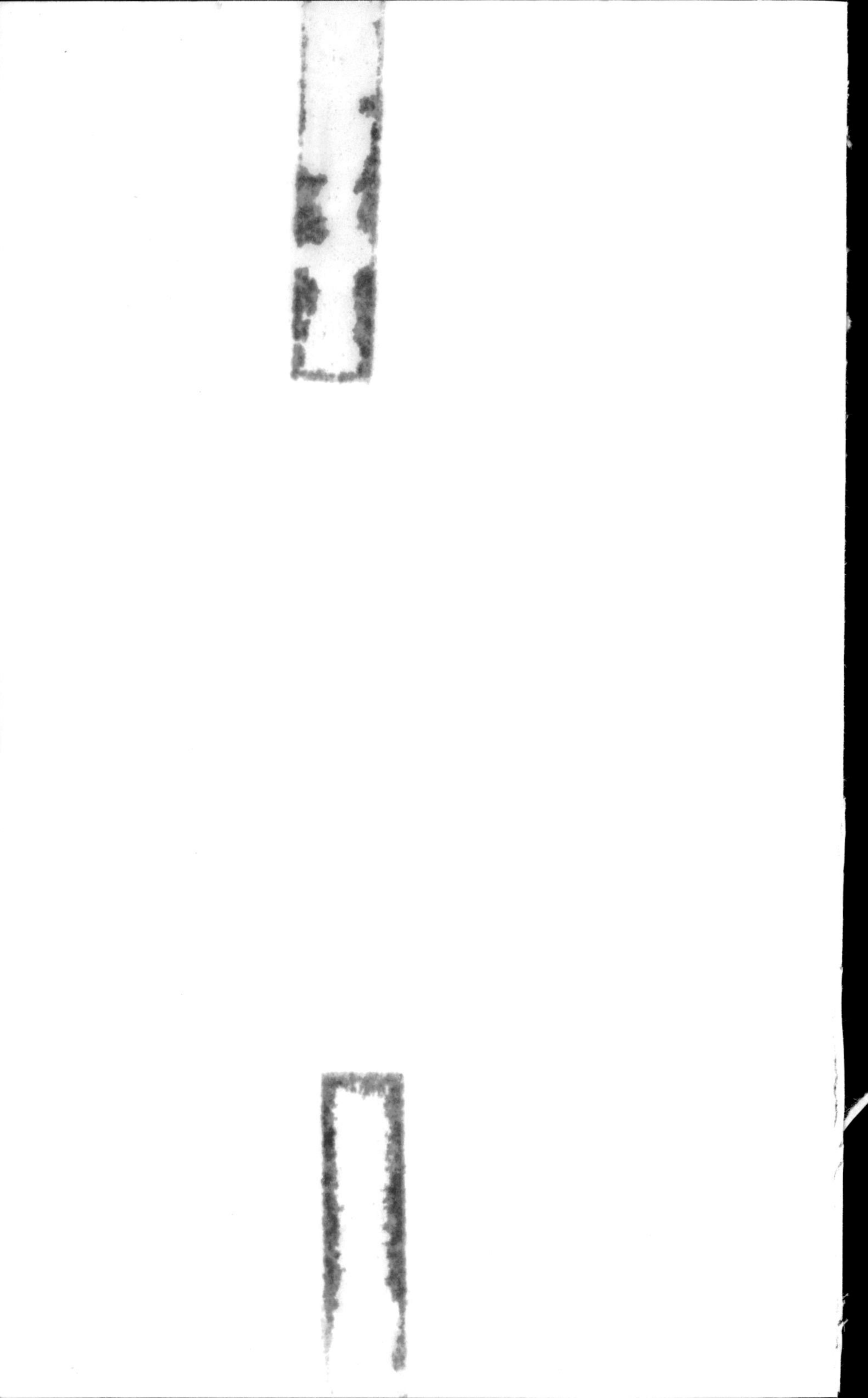